Automotive Upholstery
HANDBOOK

by Don Taylor

FISHER
er
BOOKS™

Foreword

Well friends, here it is. I'm giving you a thorough overview of the trade. As a skill, it is neither a science nor an art, yet, together, both. If you read the directions laid out here for you, and follow them, you'll be dealing with the science part.

Only when you begin to work the materials, sew a smooth seam, and pull out wrinkles, will you begin to practice the art.

And practice there must be. No "art" was ever learned without practice be it music, medicine or auto trim. Practice on friends' used cars. Let them pay for the materials. You do the work and offer no guarantees.

When you begin to get a handle on it, then you can begin to charge them a few dollars for your labor.

If you're going to get serious about the trim trade, save those few dollars toward a good sewing machine and some of the other tools which speed your work and increase quality.

If you only do it as a hobby I know you'll have a world of fun. Each job is a new challenge and brings reward in satisfaction of a job well done and a serviceable product.

I hope you enjoy the work as much as I have for lo these many, many years.

The outstandingly handsome upholstery on our cover car was created by Eddie Salcido of Master Craft Auto Interiors in Tucson, Arizona. The beautiful 1937 Ford two-door sedan is owned by Gare Perry of Farmington, New Mexico. The car was featured in the December 1991 *American Rodder* magazine.

Publishers:	Bill Fisher
	Helen Fisher
	Howard Fisher
	J. McCrary
Editors:	Bill Fisher
	Tom Monroe
	Sheryl Clapp
	Sean Stewart
Photography:	Don Taylor
Cover photo:	Paul Martinez
Back cover photos:	Bill Fisher

Published by Fisher Books
4239 W. Ina Rd. Suite 101
Tucson, AZ 85741
(520) 744-6110

©1993 Fisher Books
Printed in U.S.A.
Printing 10 9 8

Library of Congress Cataloging-in-Publication Data

Taylor, Don (Donald D.)
    Automotive upholstery handbook / by Don Taylor.
        p.   cm.
    Includes index.
    ISBN 1-55561-171-0
    1. Automobiles--Upholstery.
    I. Title.
TL256. T38 1993   93-7376
629.26--dc20   CIP

Table of Contents

Acknowledgments

This book turned out to be a bit more of a project than I originally anticipated. It was started in Escondido, California (Avocado Capital of the World) where I had a thriving auto-trim business, and finished in Framingham, Massachusetts, where I didn't. Therefore, as the book was written on both coasts, I must thank friends on each.

Escondido, Avocado capital though it may be, is also home to one of the foremost Thunderbird restoration facilities on the west coast. Jerry Olmsted, "The Birdman of Escondido," minds the store there and sent tons of work over to my shop. The first two trim projects in the book are Jerry's truck seat and a Packard seat cushion he sent over for some help. The Packard seat belonged to Roscoe "R.C." Ivy.

R.C. is a friend of the shop who many years ago took the pencil and yellow pad out of my hands and introduced me to the world of electronic word processing. Now my extra-bedroom office looks like the bridge on the Starship Enterprise! Thanks, R.C. What a difference!

There's a young man left to thank—I don't know whether he belongs to the west coast or east coast folks—Danny Wiener, who has helped from both locations (and on three books). He just sort of turns up. We met in California when he came out to live with his dad. About a year after I moved east Danny showed up there, returning to his roots. Whenever I needed leg work to be done and when I needed a slick red Comet to do a headliner chapter—Danny was there.

This book was completed in Massachusetts using the extensive help of some of the nicest folks I've met, the staff and management of Just-Rite Auto Upholstering & Restyling Center. This is a 40-year-old, family-run business in Chelsea. Owners Sidney and Janice Levine and front office staff gave me full run of the shop for weeks on end. I met some very able craftspeople there: Charlie Colanna, Jeff Priest, Marvin Carr, Joe Encalada, Camille Gallagher (one of several outstanding young women coming up in the trade). Thank you, friends. I hope you had as much fun as I did.

Just down the road from Chelsea about 10 miles is Saugus, home of Van-Go. This outstanding van conversion, sales and repair firm is owned by the Lampert family. Dad Mel and his son David keep this business running smoothly, creating some of the most exciting vans in New England.

Helping up front in the sales room, Larry Levine seems to always find what the customer needs. He certainly helped me find the information I needed. In the back, Barry Vytal, shop foreman, converts customers' ideas into reality. He's ably assisted by Bill McCarthy. Both helped me get the van photos you see in Chapter 16. They quickly learned what "hold it!" meant. Thanks, guys.

At Fisher Books I want to thank Bill Fisher for the excellent editing he did on the manuscript. Sheryl Clapp came in at the last minute and made the the pieces into a real book. And Sean Stewart, through the magic of electronics, made my photos look far better than they ever did before.

To all of these friends, old and new, I extend a most heartfelt thanks for your help. It made writing this book possible and a heck of a lot of fun!

1

Tools of the Trade

As with every new endeavor, the first thing you need to know as a *trimmer* is what tools you'll need to do the job. And yes, an automotive upholsterer is called a *trimmer* in the trade. He may also be known as a *mechanic*. In this chapter I first discuss those power and hand tools you'll need to know about as you begin your work. In the second half I discuss the materials you'll need, both covering and inside (filling) materials.

SEWING MACHINES & OTHER POWER TOOLS

Of all the power tools used in the trim shop, sewing machines create the most interest. I'll divide sewing machines into two categories: industrial and commercial. Industrial machines are those biggies that sew anything including thin aluminum and plywood! Commercial machines are those used in the home or in a shop for very light duty.

Single-needle Machines

The *single-needle, dual-foot* machine with forward- and reverse-sewing capabilities is the industry standard. Get this type of machine if you purchase or rent one. A single-needle machine, with its 1/3- to 1/2-horsepower motor, uses a

German-made Pfaff industrial sewing machine is a workhorse of the trim industry. If you can afford an industrial machine, buy it! It will be an excellent investment. Although 20-years old, this machine costs the same today as when it was new. If you bought it now and kept it another 20 years, you could probably expect the same.

full spool for the top thread and a bobbin for the bottom thread. It has two presser feet, one beside the needle called the *needle foot* or *sewing foot,* and one behind the needle, usually referred to as the *presser foot* or *dual-feed foot.*

Material being sewn is pulled through in a number of ways. Every machine has a serrated bar under the needle called a *feed dog.* The feed dog, in time with the needle, moves up under the bottom fabric, catches it with its serrations and pulls it one stitch

forward. In the earliest machines this is all there was. Today's machines incorporate additional means to move the material.

In addition to the feed dog, some machines have a *walking needle.* This needle moves forward one stitch, passes through the material and, along with the feed dog, pulls the material one stitch forward. In addition to the needle, other machines have either of the feet do the walking. The machine you get should have either a walking needle or walking

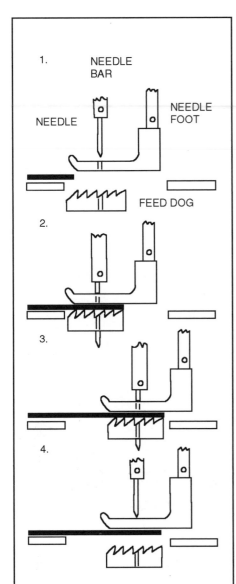

Older-model Singer® sewing machine: Note that mechanical parts look like they're from a new machine. There is no reverse. This model 111W155 was introduced in the late '40s or early '50s. Although paint is worn and machine has been rebuilt once or twice, it is still an excellent machine and worth more now than what it cost new.

These illustrations show how a feed dog operates. The presser foot is omitted for clarity. Step 1: needle is in the up position and material is ready to be fed in. Feed dog is at its lowest, front position. Step 2: needle lowers into the material. This causes the feed dog to rise, clamping the material between it and the needle foot. Step 3: all three items, needle, needle foot and feed dog moved a distance of one stitch forward. Finally, step 4: needle has risen to the up position, releasing feed dog. Needle is now ready to return to its original position to repeat the cycle.

foot in addition to the feed dog. Avoid the old 1930s-model Singer® sewing machines. While they are readily available for under $100, they have none of these features. Early model Singer machines still have their place, but not as a machine for the novice trimmer.

Another consideration is the ability of a machine to sew in reverse—a highly desired feature for the trimmer. By being able to sew in reverse, you can lock the beginning and ending of a seam. This prevents it from opening, making a much sturdier seam.

Materials to be sewn are placed into the machine and four or five stitches are made. By pressing a lever, the machine sews backward over those same stitches, locking everything in place. This action is repeated at the end of the seam, locking it also.

Sewing backward is convenient, not mandatory. The same effect can be created by lifting the foot of the machine, moving the material forward or backward, then sewing over the top of the seam. This method is not without its problems. It's slower and tends

to bunch the material at either end of the seam. However, if you come across a great buy in a machine that doesn't have reverse, grab it. You can learn to live without it. In a production shop, however, the time saved warrants the additional expense for the reverse feature.

Double-needle Machine
One of the specialized machines found in some trim shops is the *double-needle* machine. It works the same way as the single-needle machine—usually without the reverse feature—but sews a double seam. These machines are used where a lot of zippers are installed. Material on both sides of the zipper can be sewn at one time. They are also used where the strength or decoration of two seams is needed.

Double-needle machines are generally found in production shops where miles of double seams are sewn. However, if you need to sew a double seam, it can be accomplished with your single-needle machine.

Serging Machines
These are found in shops that do a lot of carpet work. A serging

Nifty machine called a *serger* binds edges of carpets and heavy material to keep them from fraying. Three large spools of thread on the spool tree are monofilament, just like fishing line—a clear, plastic, single strand. There is no bobbin. One spool is the top thread, the other two interlock with the top thread to form a complete wraparound at the edge of the material.

Above: A double-needle machine such as this will be found in most shops. It is used for sewing French seams (see Chapter 2) and decorative seams. It has two needles, two threads and two bobbins.

Right: Big Pfaff's baby sister. This used commercial machine can't be considered an investment—it's only worth half its original purchase price. But that's okay; it was cheap.

machine is used to bind carpet edges with a matching thread. (Don't confuse a serged carpet edge with one bound in vinyl or cloth.) These interesting machines whipstitch a bound edge about 1/2-inch wide around the carpet, keeping it from fraying.

While the serging machine does the stitching, it also has a little knife that trims the carpet edge first. This prevents lumpy edges. All sewing machines should be oiled once a day or, if used heavily, twice a day. A serging machine works so hard that hand oiling is not enough: it has a small crank-

case in which you deposit a quart of oil at a filling. It then oils itself continuously much like an auto engine.

Chain-stitch Machines

The most frustrating part of sewing is running out of bobbin thread in the middle of a seam. The bobbin is a tiny spool of thread inserted into the machine under the needle. This allows the machine to make what is called a *lock-stitch*. Such a stitch cannot unravel because the top and bottom stitches are physically hooked around one another. (This is different than "locking a stitch" at the

beginning and end of a seam as described on page 2.) Changing the bobbin takes a lot of time. In big production shops, a chain-stitch machine is used to eliminate the need for a bobbin.

Pet-food, charcoal, chemical and fertilizer sacks are usually stitched closed with a chain-stitch machine. You've probably learned that you can grab one of the threads and pull, unraveling the whole seam.

Chain-stitching allows the machine operator to use two spools of thread, each of equal size. By using huge 2- to 5-pound

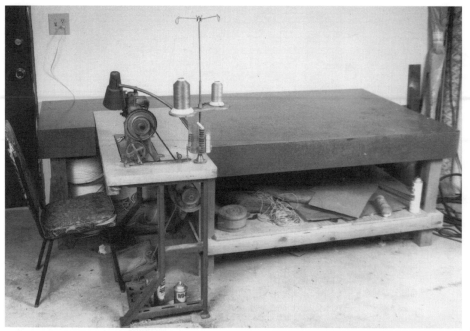

You don't need a huge bench to do trim work. Top of this one measures 4 X 8 feet. Cutout for machine allows material being sewn to lie flat and level to the left.

For home trim work, a Sears® compressor will give years of satisfactory performance. Used compressors are readily available.

Trimmers have found a use for inexpensive spray guns from the Orient—to spray glue! Notice gun has its own pressure gauge. This allows you to read and set the pressure accurately at the gun. If pressure is too high, cement will come out in cobwebs rather than a fine mist.

A trimmer's staple gun will speed the job. These are inexpensive but require an air compressor. Unfortunately, they cannot be rented.

spools of thread, the operator can sew for hours without stopping. Sounds good, but this is not a machine for you unless you've inherited one. Then, it's fine!

Commercial (Home) Machines vs. Industrial Machines

Any top-of-the-line commercial machine under 20-years old should serve you well as an upholstery machine. I say this with the following reservations:

Most commercial machines cannot handle more than two layers of *expanded vinyl* (see page 9). If you wish to sew a seam with a welt, you are faced with sewing through four layers of material. The typical commercial machine can't handle this. It won't feed material through and the needle tends to bend. Now for the second shortcoming.

Because of its physical size, the commercial sewing machine is limited to the size of the needle it can handle. This prevents you from using a heavy thread, thereby limiting the strength of the seam. Now, what does this mean to you as a trimmer? Just this: it means the thread size you are limited to will be more susceptible to weakening from ultraviolet (UV) decay from the sun's rays. I haven't been able to find a full selection of thread colors in nylon or dacron, or of heavy enough weight to use in my commercial machine for auto-trim work. Black and white, however, are usually available. Cotton and rayon materials comprising most of the threads available on the commercial market, will not last as long as nylon when exposed to the sun. So forget it for saltwater-boat work! These threads won't last the season.

Perhaps you can't afford to rent an industrial machine for your project. If the limitations listed do not apply to you, then you should have no problems with a commercial machine. Buy the largest needle available, nylon thread where possible, and go to work!

In Chapter 2, I explain the operation of industrial and commercial machines.

Air Compressors

This is a piece of equipment that you don't absolutely have to have. Of course, your job will be harder, but not impossible. An air compressor is primarily used for powering two trim tools: a staple gun and a sprayer for paints and cements. Beyond this, it can also be used for any other pneumatic tools you have in your tool box: drills, impact wrenches, sheet-metal nibbler, etc. For the trimmer, however, the staple gun and glue pot are of the greatest concern.

The minimum compressor that will serve your needs is a one-cylinder compressor capable of delivering 4.5 cubic feet of air per minute (cfm) at 40 pounds per square inch (psi). A 12-gallon tank and a 1-hp electric motor complete the machine. Don't even consider a diaphragm-type (as opposed to piston) compressor unless it can deliver an air supply at the suggested volume and pressure minimums. A *diaphragm compressor* uses a rubber diaphragm to compress the air and is used only for light-duty painting.

Operating a pneumatic staple gun requires a minimum pressure of about 60 psi at the gun, but not more than 80 psi. Any more than 80 psi will damage the standard trimmer's staple gun. Air volume is irrelevant because the gun uses so little with each staple. This, of course, only applies to a one-man operation. If you are going into business and will be operating a number of guns, cfm capacity becomes a consideration.

For operating a glue gun, which is merely a paint gun with a #80 tip, 80 psi is about the maximum-allowable pressure. If you have a quality gun, you can increase pressure to about 100 psi. Minimum pressure depends on the viscosity of the glue you'll be spraying. Generally, 40 psi will be minimum. If the cement is thinned

to spray with less pressure, it will tend to dry before contacting the surface.

Spraying Equipment

Glue guns are very handy. If you intend to do any vinyl tops, these are a must. Glue guns are used when laminating vinyl to Polyfoam® (see page 12) or for other laminating processes. For the home craftsman, an old paint spray gun is just the ticket. If you don't mind spending a bit more, one of the spray guns made in the Orient for shooting primer works just fine for applying contact cement.

Commercial shops generally use one of the 2- to 5-gallon commercial paint pots with long hoses. If you're going to spray gallons of contact cement, this is the way to go. Usually, though, you'll be satisfied with a 1-quart spray gun. If you don't have a compressor, don't worry. You can still do the job.

Every supply house has a line of aerosol contact cements with nozzles that don't clog. These work fine for small jobs. The cement is strong and dries quickly. So, if you'll only be doing a little cement work, choose the aerosol.

A 1-quart paint gun is nice to have around the shop. You can use it to paint metal parts, especially when texturing,

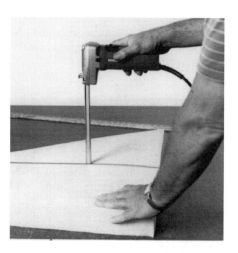

Before there was such a thing as a foam saw (pictured in top three photos), the trimmer used whatever worked to cut foam. You can use a butcher knife as shown above, or you can use an electric knife, straight razor, single-edge razor blade, hacksaw blade, cross-cut or rip saw, or a band saw.

Yes, it looks like a hair dryer. I've used this heat gun on my long-haired dog, but I must hold it way, way back. Heat gun has two settings, one for air only and one for hot air.

Trimmer's shears are available in right- and left-hand models. If you're a lefty, don't try to use right-handed shears. Get one for your left hand and your right-handed neighbor will never borrow it!

Tools for marking and measuring: Be very careful when using a marking pen. Its marks stay on forever. If you should accidentally get it on vinyl, soak a piece of cotton cloth in liquid bleach and apply it to the mark. Let this sit, wetting affected area with more bleach, until the mark has disappeared as much as possible.

spraying vinyl dye and applying rust inhibitors to seat frames.

If paint work will show, buy or rent a *quality* paint gun. A gun that spits or fails during the color coat can ruin a job. Be careful here; use good equipment.

Staple Guns

As with any tool, there's a staple gun for every purpose. The trim trade generally uses two types: a regular trimmer's gun and a narrower version called a *pin gun.*

Trimmer's staple guns, manufactured by several companies, shoot an aluminum staple 3/8-inch wide and 1/8- to 1/2-inch long. Staple-wire size varies from manufacturer to manufacturer. Some manufacturers, such as Senco, Bostich and others, manufacture staples of different materials. These include stainless steel and bronze for applications where saltwater exposure is a factor. These non-rusting staples are necessary for boat furniture and such applications as convertible tops for cars used in coastal areas with salt-laden air.

Pin guns have all the features of the trimmer's staple gun. The difference is staple width. Instead of the usual 3/8-inch wide, pin-gun staples are a mere 1/8-inch wide. This allows the staple to be placed where a standard staple won't fit or would otherwise be seen when it should be hidden.

An electric staple gun is another option. The two staple guns described above are pneumatically (air) powered. If you don't have a compressor, but still want the convenience of a staple gun, Bostich makes an excellent 110-volt electric gun. It utilizes an electromagnet. Electric staple guns are heavier and more expensive than equivalent pneumatic guns.

Foam Saws

Another convenient tool is the foam saw. This Bosch-manufactured tool cuts Polyfoam and Nimbus® quickly and neatly. It looks a bit like a sabre saw with a foot on it. On close inspection, however, you'll see that it has two blades instead of one. The two blades reciprocate in opposite directions side-by-side. This allows the blades to cut through the foam. A sabre saw has only one blade which grabs the foam and moves it up and down. Use a sabre saw only for cutting wood.

Another feature of the foam saw is its removable base plate.

When fastened to the blade guide, it serves as a *rolling* platform. Four brass wheels are in the base plate. This plate can be removed for shaping foam (page 43). You will do this when it's necessary to repair foam on a seat cushion or back. The old foam is cut away, a new block of foam is cemented in place, then it's shaped to the desired contour.

As with all other power tools but a sewing machine, a foam saw is not a necessity. In its place a sharp butcher knife may be used. It's not as efficient, of course, but a butcher knife is not as expensive either!

Heat Guns

The last trim-related power tool I will discuss is the heat gun. This looks much like a family hair dryer, but, unless you want to be bald, never use it as such. A heat gun puts out enough heat to melt paint. That's what it was originally designed for. Chances are you can buy a heat gun at a commercial paint-supply house or home-supply store for less than you'd have to pay at a trimmer's supply.

Heat guns are used wherever high heat is needed. For example, cold vinyl can be warmed to make it more pliable. With care and practice, small wrinkles in vinyl can be removed with a heat gun. Convertible-top *curtains* (rear windows), which are always wrinkled when first installed, tighten right up with judicious application of heat. And old contact cement will release easier when heat is applied. Best of all, if you get your socks wet on a cold day, you can dry them in three minutes flat.

HAND TOOLS

Let's look at the hand tools you will need. These I divide into three categories: tools you *must* have, tools you *should* have, and tools too expensive to buy! These I list in addition to a basic set of mechanic's tools, which I assume you already have. If not, you should purchase them.

Tools You Must Have

Scissors

Buy a good pair of trimmer's scissors. These are usually referred to as *shears.* Don't be tempted to try and use the family's sewing scissors. Some of the materials you'll be working with will only cut well if you're using a heavy pair of shears.

Scissors can be purchased in three sizes: small, medium and large. The little ones are called *machine scissors,* the medium sizes are referred to as *hand shears* or *trimmer's shears* and the big guys are *bench shears.* The best to start with are trimmer's shears. Bench shears are used for cutting fabrics quickly at the bench. As for machine scissors, they are very small and usually reserved for clipping threads. So start with a good pair of trimmer's shears. Use them for all of your trimming needs.

Tape Measure

Get the standard 16-foot mechanical tape. You'll find one at a hardware store. Carpenters' 20-foot tapes are too heavy and the smaller 10-foot tapes are too light. Above all, don't try to use a tailor's cloth tape. These gradually stretch over a period of time and lose all accuracy on the long side.

Yardsticks

Buy two "yardsticks," one 36 inches long and the other 60 inches long. All of the fabrics you use will range from 36 to 60 inches wide, with most of them in the 54 to 56-inch range. For wider fabrics, a simple yardstick will be too short. You'll soon come to wonder how trimmers managed before the days of the "big stick."

A framing square also comes in handy when cutting and measuring.

Chalk & Marking Pens

Three kinds of chalk are available to the trimmer: blackboard chalk, trimmer's chalk and tailor's chalk. Blackboard chalk, though readily available, is too soft. Tailor's chalk has a wax base that won't come off most fabrics and even fewer vinyls. This leaves trimmer's chalk, which comes in white and yellow. Yellow chalk seems to stay on the material forever. I prefer white because it is easier to remove. Even when working with white material you can easily see white marks.

Marking pens are those big black pens with washable ink. These are used to mark *Polyfoam*®, carpet back and *Fiber-Fill*®. Never use a marking pen on vinyl. It won't come off. Likewise, never mark the *back* of vinyl with one of these pens. The ink will bleed through to the front. This is also true for ballpoint pen. Use only chalk or soft-lead pencil on vinyl.

Trim Pins

Trim pins are to the trimmer what dressmaker pins are to the tailor. Trim pins come in two lengths, 3-1/2 and 4 inches. Determine the size you prefer; one works as well as the other. Trim pins are used for such things as holding material to a seat while you mark it, as temporary fasteners, finding blind holes and any number of things. Buy them by the gross because they disappear.

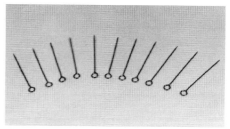

The loop in these trim pins protects your fingers as you place them. They are convenient—to remove a stubborn pin, pass another pin through the loop and use it as a T-handle to pull it out.

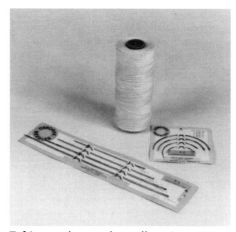

Tufting and curved needles: At center is a spool of nylon tufting twine. With a tufting needle and some twine, you can install a button in a cushion or seat back. Twine is passed through loop in the button and through eye of the needle. Then needle is inserted in the cushion and the twine drawn through. It is then tied off, securing the button. Twine is available in cotton as well as nylon.

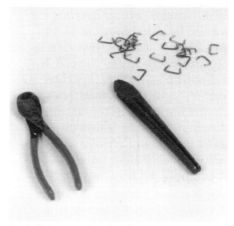

At left is a pair of side cutters, at right a straight pair of hog-ring pliers and rings. Side cutters work much better than pliers for removing hog rings.

You'll use a hand stapler when you be-gin to set together two pieces of fab-ric.

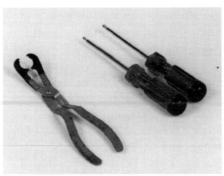

Inexpensive window-crank and door-handle-clip remover, left, pays for it-self the first time you use it. Torx wrenches, right, are the only thing that will remove a Torx-head bolt. You'll need Torx drivers for screws with recessed Torx pattern.

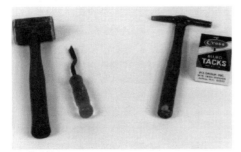

If you don't have a staple gun, these tools will become very familiar. At right is a trimmer's hammer and a box of tacks. Small end of hammer is magnetized to pick up tacks. At left are two tools used to remove tacks.

Needles

Needles come in all sizes, both straight and curved. Get a good se-lection. You'll need 2-, 3- and 4-inch-long curved needles as measured across from point to eye. Straight needles, more com-monly called *tufting needles,* should be purchased in 6-, 10- and 12-inch lengths. If your sup-ply house has any of the old 16-inch tufting needles, buy three or four and put them away. These are almost impossible to find, but are very handy. In the following chap-ters I demonstrate the use of curved and straight needles.

Hog Rings & Hog-ring Pliers

No, you don't have to go into farming to subsidize your trim work! The term *hog ring* origi-nated from the rings clipped through the snouts of pigs to pre-vent them from rooting around in yards and gardens. The rings also give the farmer something to hook

onto to lead the pig about. Imag-ine a ring through your nose! You'd go wherever the ring went!

Hog rings for trim work are smaller and are used to secure fabric to seat frames. The fabric is wrapped around the seat frame and, with a ring inserted in the pliers, the hog ring is clamped around the fabric and frame to hold the two together.

Hog-ring pliers come in sev-eral configurations. They are bent to one side, bent forward or just straight. These bends allow you to get into tight places a little easier. I find, however, that it takes too much time to switch back and forth, so I use the straight pliers for most of my work.

Side Cutters

You may call them *diagonal cut-ters, dikes, side cutters, wire cut-ters* or *nippers,* but they're all the same. Next to shears, side cutters are the tool you'll use the most. They're about the only tool that will remove a well-secured hog ring. In trim work, they are used to pull tacks, staples and nails. I wouldn't know how to straighten a cotter key without one.

Buy the very best pair you can find. Be sure you can open and close them with one hand. Some "brand-X" models are too stiff to open with only one hand. Also, buy a pair with vinyl-cushioned handles.

Tools You Should Have
Hand Stapler

This can be the office type or heavy-duty stapler used in packaging. The hand stapler is very handy for temporarily joining two pieces of fabric. This is often done before sewing, especially while you're learning.

Window/Door-handle-clip Remover

Many domestic cars, especially early and mid-'60s models, se-cured window cranks and inside door handles with little horseshoe clips. These are conveniently re-moved with a tool for just this pur-pose, see photo at left. If you don't want to buy one, you can use a trim pin, it only takes longer.

Tack Hammer & Tacks

Remember the example about what trimmers used before power tools were available? Well, before power staplers, trimmers used tacks installed with tack hammers. If you want to try this, go ahead. It works well and it's kind of fun.

A tack hammer has a magnet on one end of its head. A few tacks are placed in the mouth and held between the cheek and lower right or left gum as you would a wad of chewing tobacco. An indi-vidual tack is fished out with your tongue and held between your front teeth, head facing out. Place the magnetic end of the ham-mer against the head of the tack and draw it out of your mouth. Turn the hammer and gently drive the tack in place as you hold the material tightly in place. Turn the hammer to the nonmagnetic end and drive home the tack.

Tacks come sterilized to pre-vent health problems. However, to-day you can never tell. If you're worried, instead of putting them in your mouth, spill a few onto the bench and pick them out one at a time with the magnetic end of the hammer.

Like staples, tacks come in a va-riety of sizes. Number 1-1/2 is the smallest, going up by even num-bers to 20. If you decide to use tacks instead of staples, good. You're following a long and noble tradition. It is such a tradition that some auto-restoration buffs will only permit trimmers to use tacks in cases where they were originally used.

Mallet & Tack Puller

Whether or not you use tacks, if the work you're doing includes autos of the '50s and earlier, you should invest in a tack-puller and a mallet to drive it. A tack puller looks like a chisel with an S-curve in it and a plastic handle on the end, which is exactly what it is. The business end of the chisel is placed against the tack head, the handle is whopped with the mallet and the tack flies out. Simple.

If you only have a few tacks to remove, dig them out with a flat-blade screwdriver.

Staple Puller

You'll run into a lot of staples in your project. If you don't want to buy a staple puller, find a small worn-out Phillips-head screwdriver and grind the end to a point. It will work quite well.

Spring Clamps

An assortment of spring clamps similar to those shown on this page will give you a "third hand." As with most trimmer tools, they're a big help, but you can do the job without them. If you plan to do a number of jobs, the investment may repay itself in time saved.

Mechanic's Tools

Earlier I said I assume you have a minimum set of mechanic's tools. These should include screwdrivers, wrenches, pliers, socket sets . . . the works. You may want, in addition to standard tools, some of the specialized tools used in today's auto trim. This includes things like Torx wrenches (drivers), Torx sockets, metric Allen wrenches, trim-bezel removers and any number of specialized tools car manufacturers come up with for specific jobs.

These tools are not usually available at local trim-supply houses. Instead, they may be pur-

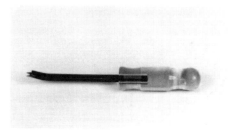

Fancy little tool removes staples. Save your money; buy an ice pick. Or make one by sharpening a small, worn-out, Phillips-head screwdriver; both work well.

chased at the parts department of your local auto dealer or auto-parts stores. Explain to the parts man what you're trying to disassemble and he'll tell you what tool you'll need.

Tools Too Expensive to Buy

There are tools of the trade that are simply too expensive to buy for the few times you may need them. These include such things as a button-making machine, scissor-sharpening jig, foam shredder, spring cutters and benders, and other esoteric pieces of equipment. When you find a need for one of these tools, visit your local trim shop and ask them to do the job for you. Even if they charge you the proverbial arm and leg, it will still be much less expensive than paying for the special tool. Fifty cents a button seems awfully expensive until you consider that a button machine with dies costs about $300.

MATERIALS

Let's look at some of the materials you'll be using in your project. Many you'll use constantly, others only seldom. Gain a working knowledge of all of them so you can discuss these materials intelligently. They are in two basic categories: *outside materials* (those you see) and *inside materials* (those you don't see).

Outside Materials

Vinyl

This is the most popular covering in the trim trade. Naugahyde®, the

You'll think of dozens of applications for assorted spring clamps.

brand name for vinyl made by Uniroyal, is the best-known. Other manufacturers also make vinyl. Naugahyde, then, is not a type of material, but a brand name. By the way, the correct pronunciation is NAW-GUH-HIDE.

Vinyl comes in three weights (thicknesses): *service weight, standard weight* and *expanded.* Service-weight material is very light. It has a thin layer of vinyl over a cloth backing. The cloth may be jersey or cotton. Service-weight vinyls are used in areas of little wear such as headliners, outside seat-backs and other areas that receive little or no flexing.

Standard-weight vinyls are similar to service-weight vinyls. The difference is in the thickness of the vinyl itself. It is much thicker than service-weight vinyls.

Expanded vinyl is the king of vinyls. With this material, a layer of foam rubber is backed on one side with cloth and faced on the other with vinyl. This gives a very soft, supple material suitable for seating, door panels and any heavy-wear application.

One vinyl I didn't include above is *clear vinyl.* It is used for the rear *curtains* (windows) of convertibles. Learn to call this *clear vinyl* rather than plastic. It shows you have a command of the trimmer's jargon.

Cloth/Fabric

When trying to categorize cloth, we run into all sorts of potential confusion. Literally hundreds of different types of cloth are used in auto trim. Most of them are not

Greg Graaves, owner of Escondido Fabrics, uses a mechanical counter to measure body cloth. A rubber wheel on the counter measures yardage as material is pulled through it.

SERVICE-WEIGHT VINYL

STANDARD-WEIGHT VINYL

EXPANDED-WEIGHT VINYL

Three weights of vinyl are illustrated. Service-weight vinyl has a thin layer of vinyl backed by fabric, usually jersey or drill. Standard-weight vinyl is similar, but it uses a thicker layer of vinyl. Expanded-weight vinyl has a thin layer of vinyl foam bonded between the vinyl face and the cloth backing.

even *cloth* in the old sense of the word—meaning cotton, wool or linen. Now all but the most exotic are petrochemical products.

Body cloth is the generic term for fabrics used in auto trim. These include rayons, cottons, nylons and blends, of which fabrics are made. Although the threads are all spun from the above materials, they can be woven to feel smooth, textured, coarse, soft or any way the manufacturer wishes. So when you drop by the trimmer's supply looking for something with which to replace your cloth seat covers, go to the *body-cloth* section.

Velvet or velveteen make up many of today's luxury interiors. Velvet is made in the same way as carpet. It begins with a backing material, usually cotton or rayon, but some-times nylon. Millions of tiny loops are then woven into this backing. The best velvets use nylon thread for these loops; cotton runs a close second. After the *pile* (loops) has been woven, the top of the pile is sheared off, leaving the individual threads standing up. This gives velvet its unique feel and look.

Velveteen is velvet with a less-dense pile cut shorter than velvet. Usually, velveteen is all-nylon.

Mohair is what car interiors of yesteryear were almost all done in. Mohair is 100 percent wool. It is woven two ways; *flat* and *napped*. Napped is woven just as velvet is. It looks similar to velvet, only coarser. If moths are kept from mohair, it will look better and for longer than any other material.

Flat mohair is like any other piece of cloth—woven. But the very soft wool from which it is made gives it a beautiful, luxurious feel. Today, it is far too expensive to use in production auto trim. But it does have an excellent market in custom work.

Leather
What can be said of this material that is not already known by everyone? The very best leathers come from Scotland where at one time cattle for leather were kept in walled rather than fenced areas. This protected their hides from getting scratched. These hides were used by Rolls-Royce, Bentley and many of the marques that are now history. Today, Scotland still produces the finest leathers, but cost prohibits isolating cattle that are raised solely for the leather works.

If you elect to use leather in one of your projects, consider that U.S. leather costs about two-thirds of what most imported leathers cost. Mexican leather is a different matter. It is less expensive than domestic leather, but doesn't have the same quality. Typically it is very thick and stiff. However, if you have access to a large selection of Mexican leather, you might be able to find some satisfactory hides. Generally, though, the quality is not comparable to domestic leather.

Convertible-top Material
Convertible-top material comes in

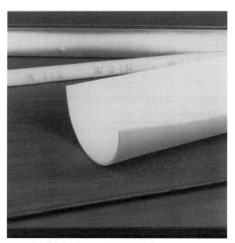

Piece of vinyl-top material with piece of closed-cell foam (on top) used as an underpad.

For the plushest carpet, select a cut-pile nylon.

If tight budget is a problem, loop-pile rayon gives satisfactory results.

two styles: *vinyl sport top* and *Haartz Cambria*®. Vinyl sport top is made in the same way as expanded vinyl. A layer of rubber is bonded to a heavy cloth back and a heavy vinyl face. This material is then treated to give it UV (ultraviolet) light protection. Don't ever make the mistake of using standard-weight vinyl for sport topping. It won't last because it doesn't have the needed UV protection.

Cambria is also a three-layer product. However, instead of vinyl, it uses a cloth blend—also treated against ultraviolet. This material is often referred to as *canvas top* or *rag top*. A few decades back it was the standard of the industry. Today it is found only on European luxury cars and in domestic custom work.

Vinyl-top Material
This is another vinyl treated to resist UV light. It's used on all vinyl-topped cars in the industry. The thing to know about this material is to use it exclusively on vinyl tops. *Never use an interior vinyl to replace a vinyl top.* The cement used to hold it will bleed through. And "sunburn" will peel off what's left after it shrinks! Take a look at vinyl-top material when you visit a trim-supply store.

Carpeting
Carpet in an automobile is a relatively new item. In the early days,

rubber floor mats were the rule. It wasn't until a few years after World War II—the early '50s—that carpet became popular and rubber floor mats were relegated to trunks and pickup trucks. This, of course, has now changed as well.

Carpet is available in three materials and two styles. Materials include nylon, rayon and wool. Styles are *cut pile* and *loop pile.*

Remember velvet? Carpet is made using the same basic process. If the top of the loops are cut, it's called *cut pile;* if they're left as is, it's called *loop pile.*

Nylon carpet wears better than rayon carpet and, subsequently, is more expensive. Wool is still the king and is found in European luxury cars.

Summary, Outside Materials
The preceding was a general list of outside materials used in auto trim. There have been many others milled once or twice and never used again. New materials and styles will probably be manufactured while this book is being written, however you now have enough information to talk a little about outside materials. Now let's look *inside* and see what supports the outside materials.

Inside Materials

Cotton
Cotton has been the most popular

of all inside padding materials. Today, molded Polyfoam, a *polyurethane foam,* is used exclusively in

LOOP-PILE CARPET

CUT-PILE CARPET

Loop-pile carpet is constructed of a series of single filaments woven into a backing material. Cut-pile carpet is woven the same way, but tops of loops are sheared off in a second step. When possible, avoid drilling through loop-pile carpet. The drill bit can catch a filament, wrapping it around the drill-bit, causing a long, obvious "run" across your new carpet. Instead, make holes in the carpet with an awl or punch to avoid the problem.

85/15 cotton: even though it is 85 percent linters, it is one of the best paddings available, regardless of price.

Trimmer's supply house can give you Polyfoam or Nimbus in any size or density. Thicknesses range from 1/2 to 4 inches, up to 12 inches at some shops.

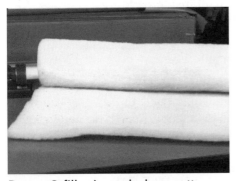

Dacron® filler is used where cotton might tear in use. Dacron's "skin" prevents it from being torn while the trimmer works it.

Jute felt, although used mainly as carpet padding, is also used as a padding over seat springs, as a sound deadener between the headliner and roof, and for insulation between the firewall and passenger compartment. You'll discover other uses as well.

the manufacture of new seats. But when such seats are recovered, a layer of cotton gives new and added padding.

Cotton is purchased in rolls that are sold by the pound. These rolls generally weigh from 17 to 20 pounds. This cotton *batting* is 1 to 1-1/2 inches thick and 26 to 28 inches wide. When you order a roll of cotton, ask for it by its volume of linters to pure cotton fiber. This is expressed as a ratio, linters/cotton: 85/15, 75/25 or 50/50. The first ratio means that 85 percent of the material is *linters*—seeds, pods, stems and other bits and pieces. The other 15 percent of the material is

pure-cotton fiber. Again, the first number is linters, the second fiber.

Polyfoam®/Nimbus®

At the end of World War II a new product was introduced to the trim industry. This was foam rubber, given the name *Airfoam*. This excellent, natural-rubber product was manufactured by B.F. Goodrich. It was used extensively throughout the trim and upholstery trades. B.F. Goodrich held exclusive patents to the product. To compete with it, polyurethane was catalyzed to produce an *open-cell*, foam-type substance simply called *Polyfoam*. In 1963 the B.F. Goodrich factory that manufactured Airfoam burned to the ground and the product was

never produced again.

Polyfoam, which took over the market, can be molded into any size or shape, and in a number of densities, to produce a complete range of auto-trim paddings. Polyfoam is found in seats, instrument panels, door panels, headliners, sunvisors and even carpet padding.

For the trimmer, Polyfoam comes in an equally large array of sizes and densities. Your local trim-supply house sells it cut to any number of standard widths and thicknesses which you may buy one piece at a time.

Although B.F. Goodrich held the foam-rubber patents, a clever inventor was able to mix natural rubber with polyurethane foam, giving us the product called *Nimbus*. This half-rubber, half-polyester material has all the advantages of each. It costs more, but for custom work it's the material of choice.

Closed-Cell Polyfoam

Polyfoam used for cushioning has an open-cell configuration to make it soft. Another type of Polyfoam is *closed-cell* foam. It is used where some cushioning is desired, but strength is needed. An example is the Polyfoam padding under vinyl tops, which is of the closed-cell variety. It's like a bunch of little balloons bonded together. If you used open-cell foam, it would compress under load as the vinyl is stretched over the steel top, essentially eliminating the desired padding effect.

Fiber-Fill

Dacron® spun into threads and bonded into padding is called *Fiber-Fill*®. This product has become very popular in the last two decades. It looks a little like pure-white cotton and is used in place of cotton where weight and density must be considered. It comes in rolls and is sold by the pound. The material is about 2 inches thick and comes in 36- and 60-inch widths.

Carpet Padding

Carpet padding is more important

Good old chipboard has many uses. I even make shipping boxes with it.

Don't know what materials you want to use on your new project? The supply house has all of its materials available on sample cards. For a small refundable deposit, you can usually take them home to study at your leisure.

than most trimmers realize. For one thing, carpet-padding density determines, in part, the amount of heat and noise that gets transmitted from the engine and road to the passenger compartment.

Carpet padding is available in three different materials.

Jute felt is the most expensive and the best noise and heat insulator. Real jute felt from Indonesia is getting harder and harder to find. Fortunately, a good petrochemical substitute that has some natural jute fibers in it is available. This is still referred to as *jute felt,* but is not 100- percent natural fiber.

The next best padding is *rebond Polyfoam.* Here Polyfoam trimmings from the factory are ground up and bonded back together. The material is then sliced into 1/2-inch-thick pads. Although this is a satisfactory product, it crushes flat over time. And if a solvent is spilled on it, such as a cleaning solvent, it decays into a gummy mess. So, if you use this product, avoid letting any carpet-cleaning solvent go through the carpet.

Rebonded fabric selvages, the least-effective material for carpet pad, is similar to rebonded Polyfoam. Carpet pads made from rebonded

fabric selvages are inexpensive. As you may expect, to get a good feel of padding under your feet, two layers must be used. This, of course, affects material costs.

Springs

Let's move from soft materials to hard materials. The first such material is seat springs. Early autos used coil springs, just like those used in some furniture. Today, these springs have given way to what we call *No-Sag*® or *zig-zag* springs. They are as effective, but much lighter. No-Sag springs may be bought in rolls of two weights, one for seat cushions and one for seat backs. Back springs use lighter material. For many cars and light trucks, complete spring units are available from the manufacturer or from the large aftermarket trim-products company, AuVeCo.

Even older are *seat-a-lators*— a universal seat-cushion-spring replacement. These were discontinued in the '50s. They are basically a wire grid with tension-type coil springs around the periphery attaching to the seat-cushion frame. A number of manufacturers make seat-spring units for hot rods which are similar to the old seat-a-lators.

Panel Board

If you wish to do a door-panel project, you can buy panel board in both regular and water-resistant types. These boards comes in 1/8 X 39 X 62-inch sheets. Black is the standard, but it is also available in many complimentary colors.

Chipboard

This is old-fashioned cardboard, only it's about twice as thick as cereal-box cardboard. Actually, it's 1/16 inch thick, 28 inches wide and 38 inches long. Cut it to the desired shape and cover it with vinyl or cloth to make panels.

Chipboard can also be used to make patterns. Sew it, staple it or glue it together. There are a hundred uses for this material.

Summary, Inside Materials

We've just looked at the basic inside materials. As you move further into this book, you'll learn more about specialty materials such as windlace, webbings, Velcro®, zippers and hundreds of other products of the trimmer's trade.

In the next chapter you'll become familiar with the sewing machine and how it works, how to use it to sew and all of the interesting things you can do with it.

A few of the products available to the trimmer—some in aerosol cans, some in bulk material for use in a spray gun.

The very best contact cement available: Always use 3M® Super Weatherstrip Adhesive to be assured of getting the right product. Accept no substitutes even though they may be yellow! When the product gets stiff and gummy, throw it out and buy a new tube.

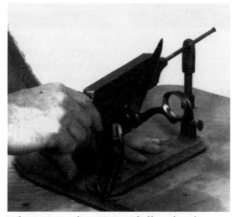

When your shears get dull, take them to your local trim shop and have them sharpened on this type of fixture. This sets a perfect edge. They'll charge a small fee, but it's worth it to have good, sharp shears. Sharpen them by hand and you'll lose the set, causing the material you're trying to cut to bunch-up between the blades.

MAKING TUFTING BUTTONS

The process of making buttons begins by cutting a strip of material about 1/2 inch wider than the cutter and as long as needed for the number of buttons you will make.

Material is folded accordion-style until you have a few more folds than buttons needed. The extra material is for mistakes. Two pieces of chipboard are placed under the material and over a wood cutting block to protect cutting block from the cutter.

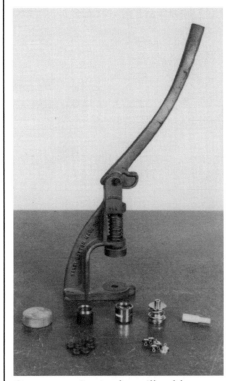

One expensive tool you'll seldom need—a button press. With these tools, you can cut fabric and make buttons. Every shop has one. Let them make your buttons. It will cost less in the long run.

Result is a number of round discs that will become button covers.

Button cover is placed facedown in die. A female button mold is placed over the button cover and together they are pushed into the die.

Male mold, or eyelet, is placed into other side of die.

Two dies are brought together and the machine handle pulled down. This forces the female mold with the cover over male eyelet and clamps the two parts together.

Result is a perfectly formed button.

2 *Learning to Sew*

Sewing is not difficult. It is easily learned providing you apply yourself, take it step-by-step, then practice. Practice is the most important of the three. That's what makes a professional out of an amateur. Once you learn the technique, it is similar to driving a car or riding a bike. Sit down at the machine after years away from it and you'll sew just as you did before.

I hope sewing becomes fun for you. I also want you to try your hand at sewing other things. Many trimmers enjoy upholstering furniture, making drapes and curtains, or doing many of the arts and crafts associated with sewing. Once you can use a sewing machine, all sewing is basically the same. You just use different materials.

This is the chapter in which I discuss sewing skills. Begin by learning the names of sewing-machine parts so we "sing from the same sheet of music." Then learn how to thread the machine, both the top stitch and bobbin (bottom) stitch.

The first step in sewing is learning how to sew a straight seam. Next, learn to sew a curved seam to the right, then to the left. After practicing the operations explained in this chapter, you should be able to do all of the above plus sew a *welt* to a *panel* and add a *boxing*.

Once you've mastered these techniques, you can go on to sew most any piece of auto trim. Let's take a look at the sewing machine and learn the names of the parts you'll be using.

SEWING-MACHINE PARTS

As you sit in front of your machine, you see an assembly of three major parts the largest of which is the *bench* or *stand*. Sitting on top of the stand is the *machine head*, generally called the *head*. On the far right side of the head a drive belt passes through the stand to the motor-and-clutch assembly.

Sitting just under the belt and mounted to the stand you may find a *bobbin winder*. I say "may" because a bobbin winder is not always built in.

Letting the machine do the work.

Now look under the stand at the motor-and-clutch assembly. The rod from the motor and clutch extends to the floor to the *foot-control* pedal, usually called the *treadle*.

While you're looking around, notice the bar extending below the bench at knee level. This is called the *presser-bar activator*, or more commonly, the *knee lift*. When you push this lever to the right, the presser feet raise, allowing you to move the material around

17

Machine head mounted to stand: Note bobbin winder against drive belt which is attached to handwheel and spool tree behind head. This machine is equipped with reversing feature.

Treadle, or foot control. Learn to tap it gently when starting to stitch.

Knee lift is a handy feature. With it you can raise feet without using your hands. This increases both your speed and dexterity at the machine.

Handwheel allows you to move needle by hand. Always rotate it *toward* you.

Left: To operate machine in reverse—sew backwards—lift reversing bar.
Above: Compare to reversing bar on Nakajima (arrow) which is pressed down to reverse machine.

under the feet. These are the main components of the sewing machine. Let's look carefully now at the head and learn its parts.

Head Nomenclature

Working from the far right as you face the machine, part of the pulley assembly is the *balance wheel*. I refer to it by its more common name of *handwheel*. With your right hand on the handwheel and pulling it toward you, you can slowly move the needle and other connecting parts. This is a convenient feature for which you'll discover dozens of uses. Slightly to the left and down is the *reverse bar*.

If your machine is equipped with this feature, it will always be in this location. Compare the Pfaff with the Nakajima. To reverse a stitch with the Pfaff, you lift the bar; on the Nakajima you push down on it. To change stitch size on the Pfaff, rotate the reverse bar clockwise or counterclockwise; the Nakajima changes stitch size with a dial just above the bar.

Above the reverse bar a small rod sits upright on the top center of the machine, the *spool pin*. But it is seldom used for mounting a spool of thread. Usually the thread spool is mounted on a *spool tree* behind the machine. Sometimes a small commercial thread spool is mounted on the spool pin. When using large industrial spools of thread, the spool pin acts as a thread guide to the *upper-thread tensioner.*

Here is where tension of the top thread is regulated. This is the part with the large coil spring and knurled nut with which you adjust tension. Tightening the nut increases top-thread tension, pulling the bobbin thread closer to the top material. Turning the knob counterclockwise and loosening it reduces top-thread tension.

Now the bobbin thread will pull the top thread closer to the bottom of the material. This allows the machine to sew from one to eight layers of material while keeping both top and bottom threads under equal tension.

The *take-up lever* is the next important part along the thread route. This takes up slack in the thread as the needle moves up and down. Without it, thread at the tip of the needle would not stay tight. Soon, thread would be wrapped around everything and no sewing would get done.

The next functional piece is the *needle bar.* This carries the needle and propels it up and down, making the stitch. Next to the needle, supported by the *needle-foot bar* and attached to it is the *needle foot.* This foot is interchangeable so you can use different types of feet for different jobs. These include specific feet for sewing a zipper, welt, binding or just sewing two pieces of fabric together.

The foot behind the needle bar is called the *presser foot.* It, too, is interchangeable and is changed in conjunction with the needle foot. Generally, these feet come in pairs and are used as such. Remember the knee lift? It lifts both of these feet when actuated. These can also be lifted with the *presser-bar lifter,* on the back side of the machine. Finally, there's the needle itself.

Learn names of head parts so you can talk intelligently with other trimmers and machine repairmen.

Thread Size Related to Needle Size		
Thread Size	Needle Size	
	mm	in
#69 Nylon	1.25	.049
#18 Nylon	0.70	.027
#16 Polyester	0.70	.027
16/4 Cotton	1.30	.051
24/4 Cotton	1.25	.049

Needles are available in several different widths (eye diameters) and points. For any one given machine, they have the same lengths. The length may be different from one brand of machine to another. Generally you cannot use a Pfaff needle in a Consew machine and vice versa.

The other needle variable is the point. The point of a needle can be very sharp or it can be a *ball point.* A ball point is used when you're sewing very light cloth. A *chisel-point* (sharp) needle tends to grab a thread in the fabric and pull it. This is eliminated with the ball-point needle which slips between the fabric threads.

Directly beneath the needle is

Two-spool tree is the most common thread carrier, but you may see a four-spool one.

the *feed dog.* As discussed in the first chapter, the feed dog pulls fabric through the machine along with the walking needle or walking foot.

Depending on the brand of machine you have, to the right or left of the feed dog is a sliding plate called the *shuttle-cover plate.* If you slide the cover plate

I've removed presser feet to expose needle bar and feed dog. Feed dog is serrated piece with hole in it. It moves with needle, pulling bottom layer of material along with the top.

Needle foot and presser foot are replaced. Presser foot shown is a universal foot used for all sewing operations. This works, but if possible, use separate feet for particular jobs: one for welts, one for zippers, one for seams, etc. See photo below.

Feet are removed by taking out or loosening setscrew.

Lever sticking out from back of machine (arrow) is presser-bar lever. Like the knee lift, lever raises presser feet. On an industrial machine this lever is very tight and hard to use. Try to find a machine with a knee lift. One advantage of the lever, however, is that it locks feet in the lift position when raised to maximum height.

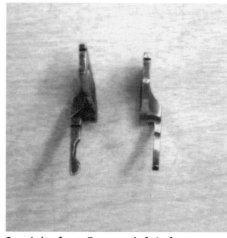

Specialty feet: Foot on left is for sewing welt and travels to left of needle foot. At right is a zipper foot which travels to right of needle foot.

back, you can get to the *shuttle* and *bobbin case*. Lift the *bobbin-case latch* and you can remove the bobbin case and bobbin.

With all of these names in mind, you should be able to talk about the machine and not become confused. Certainly there are names for all of the other parts I haven't discussed. These, however, are generally reserved for the repairman and need not concern you just now.

THREADING THE MACHINE

Before you jump in and start sewing, you must learn to thread your machine. Reach around behind the machine and raise the presser-bar lifter until it locks into place. This raises the presser foot and needle foot. It also opens the upper tensioner.

Select the color thread you will use and a corresponding bobbin. Place the spool of thread in the spool tree, reel off about 30 inches and pass the end of the

thread through the spool pin on the top of the machine. Next, feed the thread through the eye behind the upper-tensioner guide, then over the top of the guide. Pass the thread between the two tension plates in the upper tensioner and pull it snug.

In front of the upper tensioner is another thread guide that leads to the take-up lever. Run the thread through this guide. On the inside of the guide is a plate with a small lip. Pass the thread behind and over this lip, then down and under the guide spring. The thread can now feed through the take-up lever. Bring the thread down the front of the machine from the take-up lever, run it behind the needle-bar guide, then through the needle guide as shown in the photos on page 22.

With most industrial machines, the needle is threaded from your left to your right. Double-needle machines thread from the right for the left needle and from the left for the right needle—hardly confusing at all!

Let's digress for a moment and talk about the needle position. Look at it closely. One side of the needle has a long groove from the top of the shank to its eye. The other side has a half-moon indent at the eye. This indent must face

Shuttle-cover plate lets you access bobbin. Bobbin case is placed vertically directly under needle. Compare Nakajima shown here with Pfaff at right.

Pfaff has easy access to bobbin. Slide cover plate back, flip up latch and bobbin case with bobbin can be removed. Singer machines have the same arrangement, but have no removable bobbin case. Bobbin case is part of the shuttle.

the bobbin. The indent allows the shuttle to pass close enough to the needle to pick up the top thread, which then loops around the bobbin thread. If you get the needle in wrong, the shuttle will not pick up the top thread.

Installing the Bobbin

After you've successfully threaded the needle, install a bobbin. Select a bobbin loaded with the same color. Slide back the shuttle-cover plate, lift the bobbin-case latch and remove the bobbin case.

Look at the bobbin. To prevent the bobbin thread from unwinding, the end of the thread is tucked into one wind of itself. Catch the exposed end and give it a pull. This will free it and the bobbin can unwind. Place the bobbin in the bobbin case and feed the bobbin thread under the bobbin-tension spring. It doesn't matter if the bobbin thread feeds into the tension spring or is turned over to feed away from the tension spring. After you begin to sew you will discover that when the thread feeds away from the tension spring, it *increases* bobbin-thread tension. If tension is excessive, turn the bobbin over so it feeds into the tension spring. You'll have to learn the idiosyncrasies of your machine.

With the bobbin in the bobbin case and 8 to 10 inches of thread pulled out, return the two to the

shuttle. Make sure the bobbin case is seated correctly and the bobbin thread pulls out freely. Push the bobbin-case latch down to lock the bobbin case in place. Now you must get the bobbin thread to feed up through the hole in the feed dog.

Hold the top thread snug with your left hand. With your right hand, rotate the handwheel *toward* you a full turn. This will cause the needle to pass down through the feed dog. The shuttle will rotate, pick up the top thread and wrap it around the bobbin thread. Because you were *pulling gently* on the top thread, you will automatically pull the bobbin thread up through the hole in the feed dog. Now your machine is threaded and you're ready to sew—well, almost ready.

Before you do any serious sewing, you must first learn how to adjust tension of the top and bobbin threads. Unfortunately, you can't adjust this tension until you can sew a seam. Therefore, you'd better learn to sew a seam so you can see where your machine needs to be adjusted.

SEWING

Sewing a Straight Seam

You are going to sew a straight seam down two layers of material of equal length. Both ends must be even at the finish. For the first

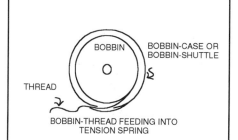

Adding bobbin tension: Standard procedure for feeding the bobbin thread through the bobbin case or shuttle is to feed the thread into the tension spring. You may wish, however, to feed the thread away from the tension spring, as seen in bottom illustration. This causes a little more bobbin tension and can compensate for humidity, bobbin thickness, thread lubrication, or thread type (nylon, dacron or cotton).

Begin threading machine by passing thread through spool pin. Extra hole is for very light threads that require more tension than upper tensioner can provide. In this case, pass thread through top hole, then through bottom hole. For now, use top hole only.

Every machine has a guide to get thread into tensioner. Yours may look a bit different, but will serve the same purpose.

Be sure thread is secured *between* tension plates. Knee lift should be actuated to open these plates. Of course, you can also use presser-bar activator.

Look for lip behind guide. Thread must pass behind lip, then under guide spring . . .

. . . through take-up lever . . .

. . . down behind needle-bar guide . . .

. . . through needle guide . . .

and into needle from left to right.

Machine is threaded and ready to sew.

USING THE BOBBIN WINDER

Most of the time you will be sewing with prewound bobbins purchased in 1/2-gross lots. But you won't always be able to find an exact thread match in a prewound bobbin. Most machines are equipped with a bobbin winder. On an industrial machine, this is driven by rubbing against the drive belt. On commercial home machines it is usually built into the machine.

To use this tool, have two spools of thread of the same color in the thread-tree. One color goes to the machine to stitch the job you're working on. The other spool will feed the bobbin. Bring the bobbin feed thread up over the thread hanger on the spool tree and down to the bench. The bobbin winder has a tensioner just like the upper tensioner on the machine. Bring the thread through the tensioner and wind the end a few times around the metal bobbin spool. (Two or three of these spools should come with the machine. If not, they may be purchased at a local sewing machine repair shop.)

Slip the bobbin spool onto the

Bobbin winder in "OFF" position: Note that bobbin-winder drive wheel does not touch drive belt.

Cam lever has been pushed forward, pressing drive wheel into machine drive belt. Now, whenever machine is sewing, bobbin spool will wind thread.

bobbin-winder shaft, keeping the thread tight between the tensioner and bobbin spool. At the forward-most end of the bobbin winder is a cam lever. When pushed forward, it presses the bobbin-winder drive wheel into the drive belt. When you press on the treadle and the belt moves, the bobbin-winder drive wheel turns. This rotates the bobbin spool pulling the thread through the tensioner and onto the

bobbin spool. When the bobbin spool fills up, pressure is exerted against the thread sensor on the cam lever and the bobbin stops winding. All of this happens as the project is being sewn.

Repeat this process: as one bobbin spool empties in the machine, another is ready on the winder. This is a convenient way to handle bobbin requirements.

---

few seams, don't worry about the edges matching or whether the seam is truly straight. Let's just get some stitches in the material.

Drop by your trim-supply house and buy a couple of yards of expanded vinyl. Any color you like will do. This will serve you for this and the next chapter. Also, pick up a spool of beaver, taupe or natural-colored nylon thread and 1/2 gross of corresponding bobbins in the size your machine will use. More than likely, this will be a G-size bobbin. The next most popular size is E. If you are using a home machine, you will have to wind your own bobbins. Consult the owner's manual for these instructions. There are many ways to wind bobbins on a home ma-

chine.

From your two yards of expanded vinyl, cut a 4-inch strip across the roll. Cut this strip into four equal pieces. You'll have four pieces of material measuring about 4 X 13-1/2 inches. Place two of these pieces together, face-to-face. If they are not the same length, trim the longer ones to equal the shorter. Sit down at the machine, lift the presser feet with the knee lift or the presser-foot actuator behind the machine. Place the two pieces of material under the needle foot so the forward edge of the two pieces are just under the needle. Now lower the feet.

It doesn't matter now how much material there is to the right or left of the needle. Later I will

talk about seam allowances, that's the amount of material to the right side of the seam.

Now comes the sewing. Do you remember the first time you drove a car with a stick shift? You probably did what your instructor called a *jackrabbit start.* You punched the accelerator and the car leaped forward. You quickly took your foot off the pedal and the car slowed down. Repeating this process made the car jump forward in fits and starts. The sewing-machine motor, like a car engine, is very powerful. The machine will also jump right out unless treated with care. So be careful that your fingers don't get pulled into the needle.

With one hand through the

Bobbin case out and sitting on bench.   Pass thread under tension spring and out to front.

FAST CHANGE OF THREAD COLOR

It's time-consuming to stop and rethread a sewing machine when the need comes to change thread from one color to another or for whatever reason. To speed this process, trimmers have developed a quick method. Here it is:

Cut the thread you're using in the machine about 12 inches behind the spool pin. This is about halfway between the spool pin and the top of the spool tree. Tie the end of the new thread to the end of the old thread hanging from the spool pin. With the knee lift, raise the presser feet and hold them there. Remove the thread from the needle and pull on it. Because the other end is attached to the new thread, it will easily pull the thread through the machine's mechanisms.

Now, all you have to do is cut the old thread off at the knot and thread the needle. The whole operation should take less than 10 seconds.

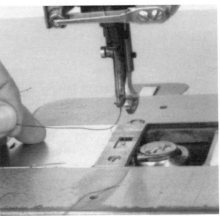

Pop bobbin case back in and push latch down. Just let thread hang there. Don't close cover plate, though, until bobbin thread has been pulled up through feed dog.

OK, now you can close the cover plate and not worry about thread being caught.

throat of the machine, pull the top and bobbin threads snug. Lay your other hand on top of the two pieces of material about 4 or 5 inches in front of the needle to guide them. *Very gently tap the treadle* until the needle goes into the material and takes two or three stitches. You may wish to switch hand positions as soon as you start to sew. Generally, your left hand passes around the front of the machine while the right hand guides the material in front of the needle. This is not carved in stone, so guide the material through the machine in whatever manner is comfortable for you.

Always oil your machine before beginning a day's work. Oil bobbin shuttle every time you change the bobbin. Use a light, self-cleaning oil such as WD-40. Oiling your machine regularly will help ensure its long life.

The result of regular oiling: Pfaff above is 20-years old, has been used every working day, often three shifts a day. It runs as well as the day it was purchased, yet has never been overhauled.

Hold threads snug while you make first three or four stitches. Forget to do this and you'll spend 15 minutes trying to get thread out of shuttle.

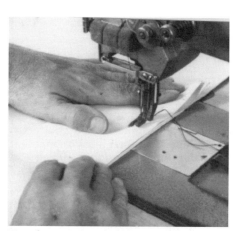

First few stitches look good. Flip reverse lever and back-sew over what you've done to lock stitch and prevent it from unraveling. Note hand position. I'm right-handed and guide material into machine with my right hand. My father, who taught me how to sew, was also right-handed, but he did just the reverse, guiding with his left and pulling with his right. Do what works best for you.

To sew backwards, lift reversing bar.

If you did everything right, you should have a few perfect stitches. If you failed to hold tension on the threads, they will have balled up under the bottom layer of material and wrapped themselves around the shuttle about three times. If this happened cut the threads loose, remove the material, cut the thread from around the shuttle and try again.

If you started off too fast I hope your fingers are still intact! In addition to possibly running over a finger (and a big industrial machine *can*) starting too fast only messes up the seam. Practice starting until you can sew three or four stitches to begin without tangling the thread or roaring across the material.

When you can do a good start, learn how to backstitch next. This locks the seam and prevents it from unraveling. If your machine has a reverse, reach over with your right hand and lift (or push) the reversing bar. Again, tap the treadle to sew back over your first few stitches. It's not necessary to maintain tension on the threads while backstitching. Practice until you can start a seam, then backstitch it neatly.

If your machine has no reverse, here is the procedure for locking a stitch. After the first three or four stitches, lift the feet by hand or by knee. Rotate the handwheel to get the needle out of the material and give a little slack in the thread. Pull the material back until the edge of it is directly under the needle where you began. Lower the feet and make a few stitches. Now your stitch is locked in and you can begin to sew a seam.

Tap on the treadle to get the machine started. Let the material move through at a leisurely pace. *Don't push or pull the material.* This will stretch either the top or bottom piece. Sew until you reach the end of the material, then backstitch again. Always start and stop with the backstitch. Release the feet, rotate the handwheel to release any stitch remaining on the shuttle and pull the material out of the machine. Clip the threads flush with the material and admire your handiwork. You just finished your first seam!

For now don't concern yourself about whether the seam is straight or crooked. There are only two things to be concerned with now, locking the stitch when you start and finish, and making sure the two pieces of material are the same length at the end of the seam. Does the material lie flat on the table or does it pucker up? If it

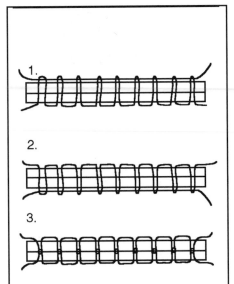

Adjusting the tension:
Top to bottom: 1. Top-thread tension is too tight. It has pulled the bobbin thread up to the surface of the top material. 2. Opposite of first illustration, bobbin-thread tension is pulling top thread all the way through. 3. Just right—tension on top and bobbin threads is correct and the looping of the two joins in the center of the material.

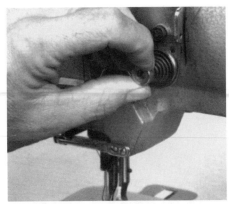

To adjust top-thread tension, rotate adjusting nut one full turn, then run sample seam. If this isn't enough, adjust it further by half turns.

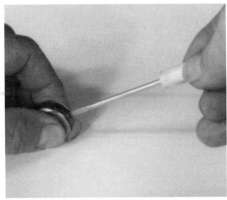

You may have to buy a jeweler's screwdriver to adjust bobbin-spring tension.

puckers or one piece is longer than the other, you pushed or pulled the material rather than letting the machine do the work for you.

Adjusting Tension

Whether or not your seam is satisfactory at this point, stop and adjust tensions. Then you can go back to practicing.

Look at both the top and bobbin threads in the seam. When looking at the top seam, can you see the bobbin thread pulled up to the level of the top thread? Looking at the bobbin thread, has it pulled the top thread into view? If either of these conditions exist, adjust the tension to correct it.

To tighten the top thread, turn the adjusting nut on the upper tensioner clockwise. This

clamps down on the top thread as it passes through. To reduce tension, turn the adjusting nut counterclockwise.

To tighten bobbin thread, remove the bobbin case from the machine. Note the small adjusting screw on the bobbin-tension spring. Again, clockwise tightens, counterclockwise loosens. Make tension adjustments in quarter-turn increments. This adjustment is pretty fussy, so don't overdo it.

Now, replace the bobbin and run another seam. Are both top and bottom threads secure without being pulled to the opposite side? Are both threads tight? If you loosened the top thread so it doesn't pull the bobbin thread, is the top thread too loose? Continue adjusting tension until both threads lock in the middle of the material and do not show on their opposite sides. See accompanying drawing. Both threads should be tight, but not so tight as to bind, break or pucker the material.

If, when you check thread tensions for the first time, everything looks OK, put the machine *out* of adjustment so you can see what it looks like when it's not OK, then correct the problem you created. Being able to adjust tension is a very important part of sewing.

Sewing Curves & Making Turns

In your sewing career you'll sew far more curved seams than straight ones. You'll also make more turns than you will curves. Let's see how these are done.

Cut some more practice pieces, put two together face-to-face and insert them into the machine as before. Lock your stitch and begin sewing. With your favored hand in front of the needle and the other behind, move the material to the right and to the left to get the feel of control. Most turning is done with the hand that's in front of the needle.

When you get near the end of the material, stop. Lift the feet, turn the material around and begin again. Pull the material to one side and then the other, sewing sweeping curves then tight curves. Try sewing a few circles. Soon, both hands will begin to coordinate and you will be able to guide the material where you want it to go.

To prevent boredom from setting in, try some 90-degree turns. Sew a straight seam for about 2 inches. Be sure the stitch stops with the needle *through* the material and all the way down. It may be necessary to use the handwheel. When using the handwheel, *don't push on the treadle.*

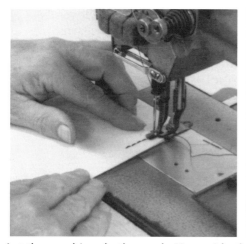

Let the machine do the work. You guide the material and let machine do the pulling. If you pull, stretches, wrinkles and puckers will result. Just swing material around and get the feel of things. Keep even pressure on the treadle or tap on it as you go. Stay limber and don't tense up. It's similar to driving a car. Let it take you there; just point it in the right direction.

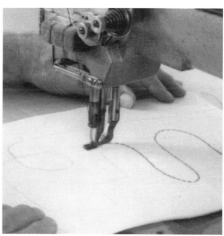

Following a randomly drawn line is great exercise for control. Do a number of them and do them often. Such practice will quickly develop your skills at the machine.

It would be like sticking your hand into the fan belt of a running car engine. With the needle all the way through the material, raise the feet with the knee lift and rotate the material 90 degrees. Now, release the feet and begin sewing again. Try both right and left turns, always with the needle through the material acting as your pivot. Try your hand at making a few four-sided boxes with all four sides being even. This requires a lot of eye-hand control, and it's good practice.

Soon your practice piece will be filled with stitches, so cut some new ones about 10-inches wide this time. On one piece of material, using a lead pencil, draw a "scribble picture" like you might have as a child. Include several hard turns along with the curves. With two pieces of material together, face-to-face and the "picture" on top, try to sew directly on top of your lines. Follow these lines carefully, trying to put the thread seam directly on top of them. Yes, you'll wander around a bit, but you'll be surprised at how accurate you will become in just a short time. Now it's time to learn to sew a seam with a uniform 1/2-inch seam allowance.

Sewing With A Perfect 1/2-inch Seam Allowance

Seam allowance, or *selvage*, is the distance between the edge of the material and seam. This is measured from the right side of the fabric to the seam.

If the seam allowance is too narrow, the material might pull away from the seam. This is especially true if you are sewing fabrics. If the allowance is too great, excess bulk will show under the cover when the job is finished. Therefore, 1/2 inch is the optimum allowance from the seam and edge of the material.

When sewing your material, whether a practice piece or full seat cover, the bulk of it should lay on the bench to your left and the seam allowance to your right. Now, all of this talk about seam allowance has probably made you think it's going to be a real project. Not so! It's simplicity itself.

Remove the material from the machine. Using a small ruler—6- or 12-inches long—measure from the tip of the needle *to your right* 1/2 inch and draw a small line. Along that line lay about 2 inches of masking tape. Now you have a guide for your seam allowance. How simple can it get?

Again, cut two pieces of mate-

Use handwheel to plant needle into the material when making 90-degree turns. Use it to make two or three stitches when you're working in a tight area, too. It will move a little easier if you give treadle just the *tiniest* nudge. Be careful! If you push too hard on treadle, machine will start to sew with your hand and fingers resting on drive belt. This may result in nothing more than a pinched finger or as bad as a broken hand.

rial into equal sizes, lay them face-to-face and staple them together. Along the edges cut some fancy scallops and designs. Include a few 90-degree turns. Beginning with the top right edge, insert the material into the machine as before, but this time lay the right edge of the material next

A 1/2-inch seam allowance is standard in the industry. If you have experience with sewing clothing, you used a 5/8-inch allowance. This is too much for trim work. And, although I recommend using tape as a guide for maintaining the 1/2-inch seam allowance, get rid of it as soon as possible so you won't become dependent on it.

This is like the scribble exercise, only now you must do it while maintaining a 1/2-inch-seam allowance. Keep your eye off the needle and on the edge of the work. This will help.

to the masking tape so it just touches.

Begin sewing, locking the stitch as before. Keep the edge of the material next to the edge of the masking tape as you sew your seam. At first it will seem like patting your head and rubbing your stomach at the same time. It will, however, become natural.

Hint: Don't look at the needle. Concentrate on the edge of the material and let the needle take care of itself.

There is one exception to this: with the 90-degree turn you must stop sewing within 1/2 inch of the end of the material. Set the needle into the material by hand as before, making sure you are 1/2 inch from the end (and edge) of the material. Again, lift the feet and turn the material 90 degrees. If you stopped accurately, after the turn you will again have a 1/2-inch seam allowance to the right just as you did before.

Continue to practice sewing

with the correct seam allowance. This is the only way to learn. Leave the masking tape on the machine as long as you like. But if you have thoughts of someday turning professional, you should get rid of your "training wheels" before you move into a shop! When you get bored with one seam, practice another.

Decorative Seams

There are two decorative seams you must learn to make. The first is the *flat-fell* seam and the other is the *French* seam.

To sew a flat-fell seam, cut two 4 X 10-inch pieces of material and sew them together with the correct seam allowance. (After the seam is sewn, the seam allowance is called the *selvage edge.*) Remove the material from the machine and clip the threads. Open the two pieces and lay them in front of the needle. Turn the selvage edge to your *left* under the left piece of material. Insert this under the needle. Set the right edge of the presser foot directly along the seam edge. This will give you a 3/16- to 1/4-inch seam allowance between the needle and folded seam edge.

To review: the two pieces are opened like a book. The selvage edge is tucked under to the left so that when you sew the seam, it will keep the selvage edge tight to the left piece of material and there will be about 1/4 inch between the original seam and the top seam.

Lock the stitch and begin to sew. Keep the right edge of the presser foot as your guide. Pull both pieces of material taught from side to side. This will help keep the seam straight.

When finished, you will have sewn through three layers of material; the top piece and both edges of the selvage. Notice that the two pieces now lay open and flat. You have also added some strength to the seam. Now let's look at the stronger, decorative seam, the French Seam.

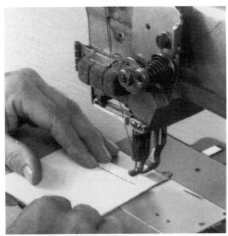

90-degree turns are easy to make as long as the needle is in the material. Judging when to maintain your 1/2 inch comes with practice.

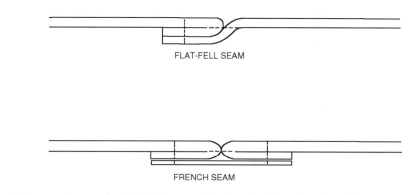

FLAT-FELL SEAM

FRENCH SEAM

Cutaway views of a flat-fell seam (top) and a French seam: The construction of both begins by sewing a 1/2-inch seam allowance. For the flat-fell seam, fold the selvage under to your left and top-stitch the entire length. For the French seam, open the selvage to both sides, sewing them down with a cloth backing strip.

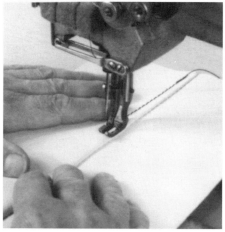

Flat-fell seam is used a lot in the trim business. Look at edge of seat cover in your car. If there is no welt, you're probably looking at a flat-fell seam.

To sew a French seam, sew two pieces of material together with the correct seam allowance. Then cut a 2-inch-wide strip of any soft, thin cloth the length of the seam. When doing production work, keep a roll of unbleached muslin around for this. For now, an old piece of bedsheet will do.

Open the two pieces of material in front of the needle as you did for the flat-fell seam. This time, fold the right edge of the selvage under the right piece of material and the left selvage under the left. Under this fold place the 2-inch piece of material and keep the selvage folded flat. Now, as with the flat-fell seam, begin sewing down the left side of the seam using the presser foot as guide.

When you reach the end of the seam, backstitch to lock it. Instead of removing the piece, swing it around without cutting the thread and sew down the other side. Be sure to lock the stitch before you start.

The finished product will have the two top pieces lying flat with each of their edges tucked under. A piece of reinforcing material will be sewn to the bottom. There will be a top seam on each side of the connecting seam. If yours looks like the one in the pictures here

you did it right.

Welting

By now you should be accomplished at this sewing business. It's time to add something new to your abilities. You must learn to sew a *welt.* The term *welt* has become interchangeable with the word *cord* or *cording.* Generally, *cording* is used in the dressmaking business and *welting* is used in auto trim. However, I hear them used interchangeably in both industries. For this discussion I use *welt.* What is this welt business, anyway?

Flat-fell seam gives a nice finish and keeps selvage edge where it belongs.

French seam is the strongest you can make. It must be sewn very neatly, however, or it will look ugly, especially if you use contrasting thread. Sew carefully!

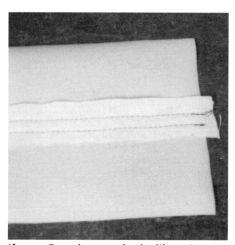

If your French seam looks like mine—or better—you've got the hang of it. Now, if you only had a double-needle machine . . . .

Trick to sewing a welt is keeping all three edges aligned. If you cut face straight and welt even, it should fall into place. You may need to adjust width of welt material to compensate for welt-cord size or material thickness. In curve, clip welt material three or four times ahead of needle. If turn is tight, make clips closer together, in some cases 1/8 to 1/4 inch. Just be careful not to cut into area where seam will fall.

Be careful in the turn not to ride up on welt with your stitch. It will show when you sew on boxing. Be careful not to pull on welt material.

A welt is that round tubing covered with material that is found in the seam between two pieces of material. It is strictly decorative and has no functional value. It is used, however, extensively throughout the trade. Let's try sewing welts.

Go back to the trim-supply house and pick up a roll of 5/32-inch plastic, hollow-welt cord. If it's not available, ask for 1/8 inch. And if hollow-welt cord isn't available, solid cord will do. Avoid paper-welt cord, twine, string or any other thing they may try to sell

you—or by which you may wish to save a buck. Stay with quality.

Back home, cut another piece of material 4 or 5 inches wide across the roll. Be sure the edge is straight. Also, cut a strip exactly 1-1/2 inches wide across the roll. You're now going to sew this together.

Be sure you have the welt foot in the machine. This is the foot that has been rounded-out on the inside and follows the needle foot on the left. It is quite different from the presser foot which is completely flat and follows the

needle foot on the right. Some machines come equipped with a universal presser foot. This foot follows on both sides of the needle foot. It will do the job, but makes it hard to sew the welt tightly.

At the machine, lay the 4-inch strip of material *faceup* in front of the needle. Lay the 1-1/2-inch strip—now called *welt material*—face down on top of the 4-inch piece. Be sure the right edges align. Now, lay the welt cord on top of the welt material and fold the left side of the welt material around and over the cord. Align all three edges and move this bundle up to the needle. Lift the feet, insert the bundle and be sure the edges meet the masking-tape guide. Drop the feet.

The needle should now be positioned just to the right of the welt cord and directly above it. You should have a comfortable 1/2-inch allowance to the right. Because expanded vinyls differ in thickness, you may have a little more or a little less than the 1/2-inch allowance. Don't let this bother you for now. Just begin sewing.

Keep the seam tight against the welt. Be careful not to let the seam climb up and over the welt.

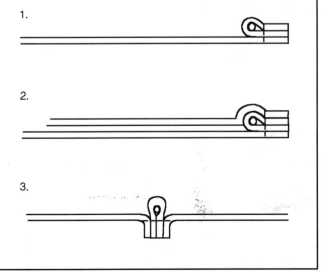

Cutaway view of welt: In step 1, welt material has been wrapped around welt cord and sewn to a face-piece. In step 2, second face-piece has been sewn to bundle. In final step, two face-pieces are opened. Welt stands up in center of face-pieces.

1.

2.

3.

Of course, it will the first few times you attempt it. Stop, get back on track and keep sewing. When you come to the end, check your work. Did you keep all three edges aligned? Did you run over the top or too far in? Did you get too far away? These are the basic mistakes. If you pulled on the welt material, it will be stretched and longer than the face material.

Do another practice welt. Set your project on the bench and, using your long stick, mark a line the length of the material just in front of the welt. Cut along this line and throw away the welt. Cut another piece of welt material and start over. If your seam allowance was too great before, cut the welt material down by the amount you judge to be correct. If it is any less than 1-1/4 inches wide, you're doing something wrong. Go back and reread the preceding paragraphs. When you have it all down, move on to the next section.

Sewing Curves & Making Turns with Welting

You didn't think it was *all* going to be straight stuff, did you? Cut a face-piece about 15 inches square. Then round one corner of this. You can use a 1-gallon or larger paint can as a template for drawing the circle. Now cut a piece of welt material that's 45- to 50-inches long. Sew the welt to the square face with the rounded corner.

Begin halfway down one side of the material before the corner, starting as you have before with the welt material wrapped around the welt cord. When you are within 1/2 inch of the end of the material, stop with the needle planted through the material. Using the knee lift, raise the feet and hold them there. With your scissors, cut a slit in both edges of the welting material right up to the needle. *Don't cut the face material.*

Tip: If you have trouble getting your trim scissors in far enough to clip up to the needle—this can happen if you're using a universal foot

Finished product: It lays flat, no puckers, and maintains an even 1/2-inch seam allowance.

Boxing is handled just like welt. It, too, must be clipped to prevent stretching.

Pull material tightly around corner, drop foot, then release tension you were holding.

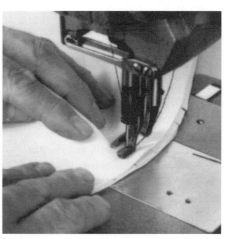

If radius is large enough, you'll not need to clip boxing as you did welt. If it looks as though material is stretching—indicated by selvage edge curling up from strain—clip it to release strain.

rather than a welt foot—get a pair of 4-inch scissors for use at the machine.

Turn the face 90 degrees, welting material and welt cord all together, exposing the next side of the face piece. While you hold the face with one hand, pull the welt material and welt cord around sharply to align with the new edge of the face material. Release the feet and begin sewing.

When you reach the rounded section, clip your welt material just as you did for the 90-degree turn, only do it about every 1 inch for the length of the curve. After

you finish the curve, clip the welt and threads and remove the piece from the machine. It should lie flat with no puckers and look like the one in the illustration. If you like what you did, go on. If you need more practice, cut some pieces and work on your corners or curves.

Sewing the Boxing

Above I indicated that welting was a decorative object between *two* pieces of material. The larger piece of material is usually called the *face* and the smaller, or narrower, piece is the *boxing*. You

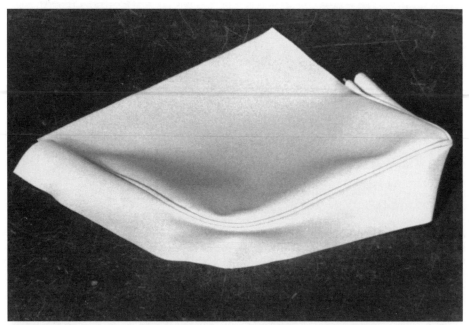

Finished product should look like this. It incorporates all procedures for making a seat cover. All you need now is to learn how to fit your work.

will also hear it called the *band or border.* For our use I use the term *boxing.* You have been practicing sewing a welt to the face. Now you can add the boxing. Cut a 4 X 45-inch piece. This will be your boxing.

Again, lay the face piece with its welt in front of the needle. Lay the boxing *facedown* on top of this assembly. Align the right edges, adjust for a 1/2-inch seam allowance and sew the boxing to the face as if you were just sewing two pieces of material together.

Once more, take care not to run over the welt or get too far away from the welt seam. If you do, the seam you sewed to hold the welt in place will show.

Just as you did with the welt, clip the boxing in the corner. Be careful not to stretch the boxing as you go around the curve. If you discover you're stretching the material, clip the boxing as you did the welt.

When you reach the end, lock the stitch and remove the piece from the machine. Open it up. You should have two pieces of material with a nice tight, round welt between them. Pull hard on each edge of the material. Can you see

the seam you sewed to hold the welt to the face? You shouldn't be able to. Did you run over the top of the welt? Sure you did. Everyone does while they're learning. Continue practicing until it all works together and there are no stretches, puckers, wrinkles or visible threads.

CONCLUSION

Although the boxing and welt are not joined in this project, you have the elements of a cushion. The goal of this chapter was to cover the basics. With them you can sew anything, even the most complex projects. Practice each type of seam until you're comfortable and proficient.

In the next chapter I show how to make a complete cushion with a zipper and how to fill it with polyfoam. Kids love these for sitting on the floor while watching television.

3 *Making a Stadium Cushion*

A stadium cushion doesn't seem like it has much to do with auto trim, which indeed is true. It does, however, incorporate almost all of the techniques used in the auto-trim trade in one small project. In addition to the experience, you'll have a useful item when it's completed. Before you run to the bench to begin, you must make two decisions.

The photos in this chapter show a cushion covered with vinyl. When you sit on this type of cushion, air leaks out as it slowly compresses. Conversely, when you stand up, it takes considerable time for the air to return, slowing the expansion of the cushion. Now, this may be a problem or totally irrelevant. It wasn't a problem for me. I gave the finished cushion to my 5-year-old grandson and he loves it the way it is.

But if you want your cushion to "breath" quickly, make the top, bottom or boxing (sides) out of a breathable fabric. If you really get involved in this trade and begin to make cushions for profit, invest in a tool for installing metal breathers in the *zipper plaque*. For now, though, keep it simple.

Making a basic stadium cushion incorporates almost all of the techniques used in the auto-trim trade.

MEASURING & CUTTING

Your second decision involves how big to make the cushion. Chair cushions can be found in many different sizes, but 22 inches square is about standard. I made the project cushion 24 X 24 X 4 inches simply because I had a piece of Polyfoam filler that fit. If you plan to use your cushion at the stadium, 18 X 18 X 2 inches is the size concessionaires rent. So, assuming your two decisions are made, let's get started.

Layout
On a piece of paper write out the following list:
1. Two faces.
2. Two pieces of welt material.
3. Boxing.
4. Zipper plaque.
5. Zipper tape and slider.
6. Polyfoam or Nimbus.

Using my dimensions or substituting your own, let's determine the materials you have to purchase. The first thing on the list are the two faces. These are cut 24

Consider economy when cutting materials. Work to keep longest parts to one side. This will leave a long full piece on other side. If the pieces are short—under 54 inches—layout cutting so longest parts run right to left. Then, when you have to square up material for the next project, there will be little waste.

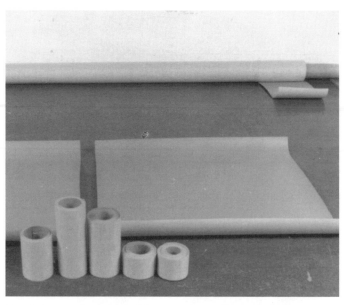

Don't leave vinyl folded for very long (especially face-to-face) because it will wrinkle. If rolling up material is inconvenient, lay each piece flat and write the identification on back. Use pencil or chalk only. Ballpoint-pen and ink marker will bleed through over time.

inches square. Next is the welt. This will be 1-1/2-inches wide—standard width for welt material—by the length of all four sides: four sides multiplied by 24 inches equals 96 inches. Now, add 2 inches for a seam to finish the welt and you'll find you need 2 pieces of welt material that measure 1-1/2-inches wide by 98-inches long.

The boxing, if you plan to use 4-inch foam, should be cut 4-inches wide. The length is the sum of the three sides of the face, but less about 6 inches to allow for the zipper plaque—it comes across the back and around the corners about 4 inches. So, the boxing will measure 4 inches wide by 3 multiplied by 24 inches, or 72 inches less 6 for the zipper, giving a total length of 66 inches.

The zipper plaque is made in two pieces. One will be 6-inches wide and the other 3-inches wide. If you peek ahead in the chapter you'll see how the wider piece is made to fit over the top of the zipper, hiding it from view and giving the installation a nicely fin-

ished appearance. Zipper-plaque length is determined by the width of the rear of the cushion plus 10 inches. In our case this makes it 34 inches. It follows, therefore, that the zipper tape will also be 34-inches long. In all of these measurements you may notice that I get more material than needed. This is to allow for any possible mistakes. It's always better to be a little too big than too small. ("Gee, I've cut this boxing off three times and it's still too small!")

Finally, you must determine the size of the Polyfoam filler. The rule of thumb is the foam is the exact dimension of the unsewn face piece for length and width and the same thickness as the width of the unsewn boxing. Let's see why.

To make a cushion fill out and puff up, the foam must push evenly against all surfaces, yet it must be smooth and wrinkle-free under the material. When you sew the cushion with a 1/2-inch seam allowance, the finished size—on the inside—will be 1-inch smaller

in all dimensions. Therefore, the foam will now be 1-inch larger in all dimensions than the cavity into which it must fit. So, when the foam is inserted in the cushion, it will fill it out correctly. Remember this as you move on through the book: The foam should always be 1/2-inch larger on all sides than the finished product.

All of these measurements can now be transferred to your list:

1. Two faces, 24 X 24 inches.
2. Two pieces of welt material, 1-1/2 X 98 inches.
3. Boxing, 4 X 66 inches.
4. Zipper plaque, one piece 6 X 34 and one 3 X 34 inches.
5. Zipper tape and slider, 1 yard.
6. Polyfoam or Nimbus, 24 X 24 X 4 inches.

Items 5 and 6 need further explanation. Zipper tape comes in a continuous roll to be cut off as needed. It comes in a number of sizes. For your cushion choose either a #4 or #6. These are available in aluminum or brass, aluminum being the cheaper.

Also available are zippers

made of nylon and Delrin. These are used where exposure to the elements might be a problem. Boat covers, sleeping bags and foul-weather gear all incorporate these products, Delrin is used for protection against extreme conditions. Because these zippers are quite decorative, you might want to use one in your project. They are, however, considerably more expensive.

There are dozens of styles and sizes of zippers for all applications. For light work, the sizes suggested will do.

I suggest either Polyfoam or Nimbus for filler. As a review, Polyfoam is an open-cell, polyurethane foam. Nimbus combines foam rubber with the polyurethane to make a denser, longer-lasting product. But it's also more expensive. Maybe you'd like to use Polyfoam for your first attempt and Nimbus for something you want to last longer—such as lawnchair pads.

With your list complete, determine how much material you must buy. If you want one-piece welts—no seams all the way around— you must buy 98 inches of material. Vinyls and fabrics are generally sold in 1/3-yard increments, so you will need 2-2/3 yards. Yes, that's only 96 inches, but the person cutting the yardage always cuts generously and our figures are generous, although they don't provide for a seam allowance around the face pieces.

You have all the information needed to buy your materials now, so it's off to the local trim supplier. When you get back, you can begin cutting.

Cutting

Sharpen a piece of chalk, get out your 60-inch-long measuring stick and *framing square*—as used by carpenters—and go to work. Begin by squaring the edge of the material facing you as it lays on the bench with either the right or left edge. Lay the long side of the framing square along the selvage

Use a combination foot or welt foot when hemming. On this zipper plaque I'm "eyeballing" the 2-inch hem. Mark it anywhere you like to help with maintaining correct dimensions.

It's very easy to stretch zipper tape. Be careful not to push or pull it. If you push tape, it will make waves. If you pull zipper tape, it will bow in direction of pull. Like all pieces you've sewn, piece should lie flat when finished.

edge, either the right or left side. Lay the long stick against the short leg of the square and chalk a line. Cut along this line to square it up.

The following instructions are all based on a 24 X 24 X 4-inch cushion. If you elect to do a different-size cushion, such as the 18 X 18 X 2-inch one mentioned earlier, adjust the dimensions accordingly. This is especially true in the case of the zipper plaque. It will need only a 1-inch flap over the zipper rather than the demonstrated 2-inch flap.

Generally, a trimmer works from the left side of the material to the right, just as you read from left to right. layout your longest piece first. This will be the 1-1/2 X 98-inch welt. Remember to cut two pieces. Next is the boxing at 4 X 66 inches. Cut these pieces carefully. Any wavering will show up as waves in the finished product.

Layout the faces one above the other. There is plenty of room to lay them out side by side, but one above the other is less wasteful.

The zipper-plaque pieces should be cut from the material directly above the second face. Again, this is the most efficient use of the material. There will be

enough material now for a second cushion just in case you make a mistake or want to make another one. Roll up the pieces as shown in the photo on the opposite page. If you fold them, particularly face-to-face, the vinyl will wrinkle. These can be impossible to remove.

After rolling up each piece, tape the loose end to the body with masking tape and write its name there. Although it's unlikely you would confuse the parts on a small project like this, you would for a project using 10 or more pieces. You're now ready to sew this project together. Get a cup of coffee, put something good on the radio and let's make a cushion out of these pieces of vinyl.

MAKING ZIPPER PLAQUE

Sewing Zipper Plaque

Unroll the 6-inch piece you cut for the zipper. You're going to make a 2-inch hem down the right side. Lay it *facedown* on the table and make a 2-inch fold on the right edge. (The fold will actually be 2 inches wide.) If it helps, make a line 2 inches in from the left edge all the way along the material. Fold the left edge over to meet this line. Insert the right edge of this hem, or

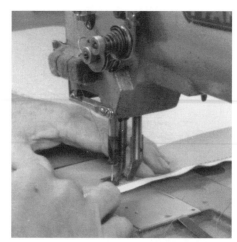

By top-sewing plaque over zipper tape, finished product lies flat and even.

Slide two zipper pieces together. Keep hem to your right, ends even and edges straight.

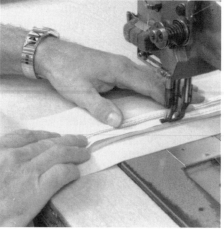

"flap," under the needle. Give yourself about a 1/8-inch seam allowance, or about the width of the foot.

Sew a straight seam all the way down while maintaining the hem at a consistent 2 inches. Remember to lock the stitch at the beginning and end of the seam. Be careful not to stretch the vinyl by pulling against the machine as it sews. And don't push it, either. Let the machine do the work; you just guide it.

Check to see if you've stretched the material by measuring the seam side and comparing this with the unfinished edge. If the seam side is more than an 1/8 inch longer, you've done some stretching. If it's stretched, cut out the seam and sew it again. But if everything is fine, clip the threads close to the material and set the piece aside.

Pick out the narrow, 3-inch zipper piece and yard of zipper tape. You're going to sew these together. If you have one, install the zipper foot on the machine. Then lay the material face up in front of the needle. Lay the zipper tape on top of the material with about 1 inch extending over the end of the vinyl.

One side of the zipper tape has little red or black arrows printed along one edge. These must face up when you lay the tape on the vinyl. The two right edges should be together and even. Sew the zipper tape to the vinyl.

Did you do it correctly? Is the zipper tape straight and even along the edge? Does it stay in line with the edge of the material? Did you stretch either piece, tape or

A finished zipper plaque.

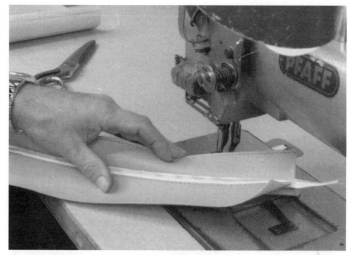

Open it up to see how flap hides zipper tape. This is the same way most zippers are handled on pants and skirts, only this is slightly larger.

vinyl? Did you *push* either piece? No? Great! It must not have been too hard after all. The next step is to top-stitch the seam you just made.

Turn the whole thing over face down. The top of the material and zipper will be lying on the bench in front of the machine. Hold the zipper tape in this position and fold the material over along the seam. Sew through both layers of vinyl and zipper tape. When completed, the vinyl should show a nice finished edge, top-sewn to the zipper tape. The other side of the zipper tape will be free so it can be sewn to the previously hemmed piece.

Follow this carefully to avoid confusion. Retrieve the first piece you sewed—the 2-inch hemmed piece. Lay this face down in front of the needle with the hem to your left. Also face down, lay the piece with the zipper tape *on top of the first piece.* Align the two ends. Adjust the zipper tape so the right edge is about 1/4 inch to the left of the 2-inch, hemmed edge. This is the free edge that hasn't been sewn. Check the position against that in the photos at the top of the opposite page.

Sew the right edge of the zipper tape to the 2-inch hemmed piece, lock-stitching each end. Clip the threads and turn over the finished zipper plaque. The finished product should have the zipper tape sewn between the two zipper-plaque pieces with the 2-inch hem covering the tape. If it doesn't look quite like the illustration, backtrack to where you went wrong, cut the seam and sew it correctly. If you did it right the first time, that's great. Move on to the next step.

Trimming Zipper Plaque to Correct Width
During the course of the above explanation I use some general terms such as *about 1/4 inch.* Three or four of these *abouts* can add up to 1 inch (or more) variation in the finished piece. That's part of the reason for cutting the

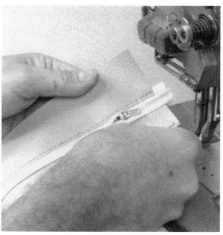

Zipper slide should point in the same direction as arrows. Slide will go on the wrong way, but will work very, very stiffly at first, then will bind after a few attempts.

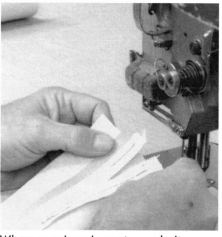

When opening zipper tape, do it slowly and carefully. If tape opens all the way, you'll have a hard time rejoining pieces. Should this happen, lay the two zipper-tape pieces on the bench side by side and faceup with arrows pointing toward you. Carefully work zipper slide onto tape, both sides simultaneously.

plaque pieces extra large. The other part is to allow some room for error in sewing.

Lay the finished zipper plaque on the bench facedown with the length left to right. Be sure the zipper tape is in a straight line. Lay the yardstick against the zipper teeth and adjust up and down until the tape is "arrow" straight. Use an imaginary centerline between the two rows of teeth for your centerline across the plaque. Measure off 2 inches on each side of this centerline at each end of the plaque and mark it with a pencil. Connect these marks with two lines, one on top of the plaque and one on the bottom. Cut along the lines with your scissors and you have a 4-inch-wide finished zipper plaque. The zipper plaque will be completed after you install the zipper slide.

Installing the Zipper Slide
If you sewed the zipper tape to the first piece with the printed arrows facing up, they will now be visible on the backside of the zipper. If you missed on this step, pull the seams back until you find one of these arrows. The arrows point in the direction the zipper slide should go.

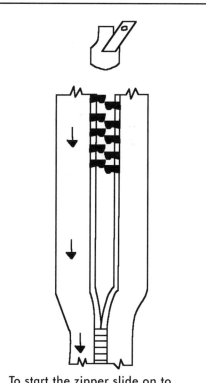

To start the zipper slide on to the zipper tape, open the first few teeth. Be sure the arrows are pointing toward you. If there are no arrows printed on the tape, check the individual zipper teeth. Slide the two sides of the tape on to the front of the zipper slide and pull it down. If you start from the wrong end, the zipper slide will seize.

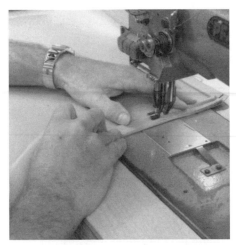

Keep stitch close to cord. It's easy to wander, either away from cord or over it. If you go over it, it'll be obvious in the finished product. If you wander away, it makes welt too large and uneven.

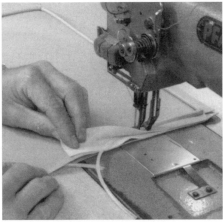

Accuracy is important. If you can't come very close to estimating 1 inch, measure it. Nobody's looking.

Same is true for a 1/2-inch-seam allowance—measure it if you can't make an accurate estimate. Remember to lock stitching.

With the back of the zipper plaque facing you and the arrows pointing down, open the zipper tape about 3 inches. Now, turn the zipper plaque around to the front side. Guide one or two teeth of each side of the zipper tape into the front of the zipper slide—slide should point down. Grasp the pull tab and gently pull the slider down. Notice that it closes the zipper as it slides along while opening it from the front. Pull the slide about halfway down the tape and leave it. You've finished the zipper plaque for now, so turn your attention to the face pieces. The next step is to sew the welt to the face pieces.

SEWING WELT TO FACES

Get the two face pieces and two pieces of welt material. Use the leftover welt cord from your original practice pieces. If you have a zipper foot on the machine, change to a welt foot. Sewing this phase of the project will be just like sewing the practice pieces, only this time it's for real.

Wrap the welt material around the welt cord and lay the bundle along one edge of the face piece in the center. Begin sewing 5 or 6 inches from the end. This way, you will allow yourself room to work when you join the two ends.

Keep both edges of the welt material together and those two edges in line with the edge of the face piece. Stop your stitch with the needle through the materials and 1/2 inch from the edge of the vinyl as it faces you. Clip the welt material—both edges—right up to the needle. Rotate the face piece 90 degrees, then pull the welt material and welt cord around to line up with the new face edge. Sew down this side and repeat the clip-and-turn action at the next corner.

Repeat this process for all four sides of the face. When you're between 5 and 6 inches from where you started, stop.

Joining the Welt

Cut the welt cord 8 to 10 inches

from the needle. Lay both ends of the welt material along the edge of the face, being careful not to stretch them. Make the end you're working on overlap the end from where you began. Estimate the overlap at 1 inch, then mark and cut. *Cut only the material, not the welt cord.* You'll cut the welt cord later.

Remove the whole bundle from the sewing machine and clip the threads flush. Fold the face piece in half, face-to-face. Pull the ends of the welt material out and lay them face-to-face. Align the ends of the welt material and sew them together with a 1/2-inch seam allowance. Remember to lock the stitch. Now check to see if you did it all correctly.

Open the face, fold back each end of the welt material on itself and see if the finished welting is the same length as the face material. If there's too much slack in the welt material, it won't lay flat against the face—it will make a little hump. If you cut too short, there will be a pucker in the face material and the welt will stand above it. If everything was done just right, the welt material will lie straight and flat along the edge of the face. If it isn't correct, clip the seam and adjust it. If you try to force-fit the welt, there will be major puckering in the finished product. When it's correct, finish it.

Open up the welt material again and lay the seam allowance out flat the way it was when you removed it from the machine. Fold the material in half *lengthwise* and notch the seam allowance up to the seam. When opened, you'll have a deep V-cut in it. This will remove bulk from around the welt cord at this union.

Open the face material again and lay it under the needle about 2 inches behind where you stopped. This lets you sew 2 inches over the seam, locking it down.

Lay the ends of the welt cord into the welt material, smoothing them out so they're both flat.

Reach in with the tip of your scissors and cut both pieces at the same time. This will make a butt-joint that will be invisible under the welt material. Be sure the welt-material seam allowance is folded back and the welt cord is snug inside the welt material. Sew the bundle closed and remove it from the machine. The finished product will now lay flat on the bench. The welt will be straight and smooth. Did you run up over the top of the welt anywhere? Check closely for this problem. It happens with the best of us.

The second welt is sewn to the second face in exactly the same manner. It's the next step in the project. Finish that part and you'll be ready to assemble all of the separate pieces into a cushion.

SEWING BOXING & ZIPPER PLAQUE TO FACES

You're on the final leg of the project. Get your finished zipper plaque and boxing material and sew them together.

Lay the boxing on top of the zipper plaque face-to-face and sew them together with a 1/2-inch seam allowance. In this case it doesn't matter which end of either piece you sew together. Later, when a pattern in the material is involved or there is an up-and-down situation, you'll need to make a decision on which end goes where. For now, just sew the boxing to the zipper plaque.

Be careful as you sew over the zipper tape. I usually move the needle with the handwheel when I get close to the metal teeth. This prevents breaking a needle, knocking out a zipper tooth or cutting the thread. If you want to add some strength, sew back and forth over the zipper teeth a couple of times. The metal zipper teeth working on that one stitch can cut the thread over a period of time. When this happens the zipper tape will open up. With the boxing sewn to the zipper plaque, you're ready to sew this assembly

V-notch eliminates bulk around joint. If you could count the layers of material on finished product, you'd come up with six. If your project is going to be a "throwaway," clip one welt piece this way and leave the other. Compare unions after cushion is filled.

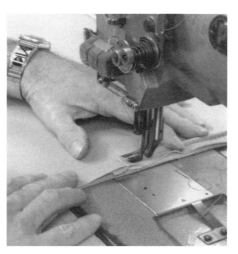

Sew boxing to zipper plaque. You can also turn it over and sew zipper plaque to boxing. There's no right or wrong here. Just maintain a 1/2-inch seam allowance.

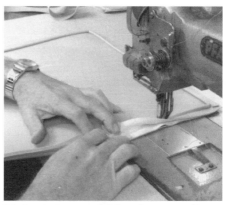

It's important to fold welt-seam allowance back on itself while sewing. This eliminates bulk on one side.

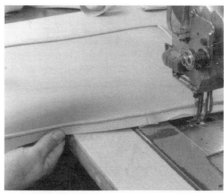

Finished product will lie flat if sewn correctly. If it lumps or bumps, correct the problem. If you move on without doing this, the problem will get worse as you continue until it simply won't go together at all.

Left: Test your welt before sewing it. If it doesn't lie flat, open seam and take it up or let it out.

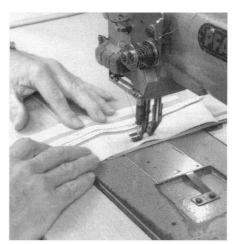

Begin sewing about 3 inches from end of zipper plaque. This is fairly standard. Remember to clip material at corners.

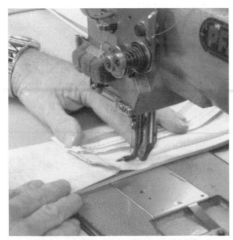

As you sew zipper plaque to face, seam allowance at union of boxing and zipper plaque will try to lie in one direction. This is OK. Don't open seam allowance and sew it down as you did with the welt. If you do, zipper tape will try to poke out the side and make a big lump. The trade-off is a little bulk for no big lump.

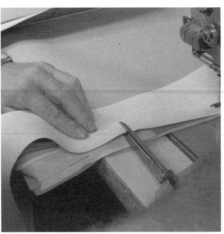

This 1-inch overlap comes up again. It must be accurate and cut perpendicular to edge. If you angle either way, second face piece won't fit. Use a framing square to be sure of your accuracy.

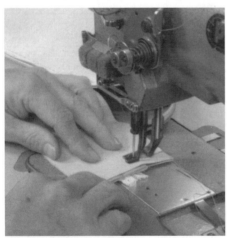

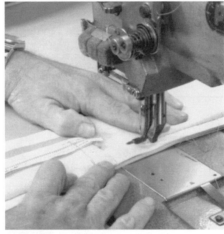

Finish boxing. As with the welt, it must be accurate and trial-fitted before it is sewn to the face.

to the face piece.

Lay one face piece down in front of you with the welt seam (where the ends came together) facing you. This will be the rear of the cushion. The welt seam *always* goes to the rear or side, never to the front. A job with a welt seam in the front looks unprofessional. Center the zipper plaque over the face piece with the edges even. There should be about 5 inches of overhang at each end of the zipper plaque.

With a pencil, make a mark on the zipper plaque at the right corner of the face piece.

Rotate the zipper plaque around the right corner of the face piece and insert the bundle under the needle—the welt foot should still be on the machine. Be sure your corner mark aligns with the corner and the edges are even. Set the needle foot down on the material about 3 inches from the end of the zipper plaque and take note of where everything is.

If all is positioned correctly, the face piece is under the machine with the welt seam facing you. And the zipper plaque is face-down against the face piece with the edges aligned and the corner mark directly over the corner of the face piece. The boxing sewn to the zipper plaque is trailing off somewhere down to the floor. You have a 1/2-inch seam allowance ready and the needle about 3 inches down from the end of the zipper plaque. If all checks out, you're ready to sew.

Sewing & Finishing Boxing

Run a seam down to the corner of the face piece and sink the needle there. Clip the material up to the needle and turn as you did with the welt. Turn the face piece, then the zipper plaque. Sew all the way around until you reach the point where you started. The boxing finishes off just as the welt did.

Stop the stitch about 5 inches or so from your starting point. Lay the boxing over the zipper plaque, allowing for a 1-inch flap. Cut away the excess boxing. Remove the assembly from the machine, place the boxing and zipper plaque face-to-face and sew them together with a 1/2-inch seam allowance. Double-stitch over the zipper teeth for security and return the assembly to the machine. As you sew this finished assembly to the face piece, don't open the seam allowance as you did for the welt. Let the seam allowance lie flat, pointing toward the needle. After you've sewn the assembly closed, remove it from the machine.

Sewing Boxing to Second Face Piece

For convenience, I refer to the boxing and zipper plaque assembly now as just the *boxing.*

Now we come to the tricky part. You must sew the boxing to the second face piece so all four corners are aligned. Yes, there is a trick, and you're about to learn it.

With the nearly finished

cushion cover out of the machine, position it, inside out, face up in front of you with the boxing standing somewhat erect. Turn it a bit until one of the corners is toward you. Push the right and left sides of the boxing down against the face piece. This will force the boxing material in the corner in front of you to push up. Work your hands together, sliding them across the boxing until the corner becomes tight. Hold that corner with one hand and, using your scissors, clip a small notch there. If you did the job correctly, the notch you just cut will be directly above the corner. Repeat this at all four corners. Now you can sew the boxing to the face piece and keep the corners aligned.

Lay the finished assembly face down on the second face piece with the welt seam under the zipper plaque. Partially align the two notches on the zipper plaque with the corners of the face piece and insert this under the needle. Now, carefully align the notch facing you with the corner of the face piece and drop the foot to hold it there.

Begin sewing 5 to 6 inches back from the corner. When you reach the corner—notch still aligned—clip and turn. Before sewing farther, check the next notch. I hope it is directly over the corner. You can adjust up to 1/4 inch either way with some gentle pulling. If it's off more than 1/4 inch, go back and check things out.

One of the most common problems is a less-than-vertical seam where the boxing and zipper plaque join. If either of these ends was cut on a diagonal, there will be a difference in length from one side of the boxing/zipper plaque to the other. So check there first.

The second biggest error is stretching the boxing when it is sewed to the face piece. This may be seen by closely observing the work. A less likely but occasional problem is a stretched face piece. This is more likely to happen if

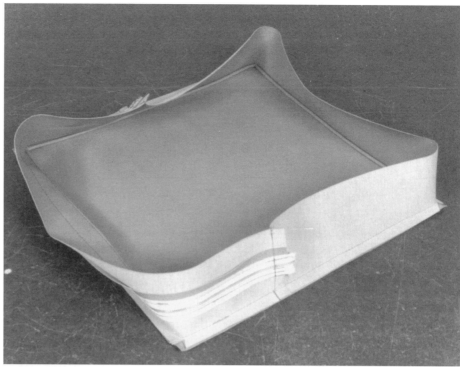

Boxing/zipper plaque is now fixed to face piece. By pushing in on the sides you can find where corners line up.

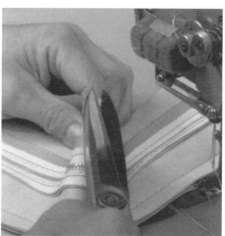

Be sure corners align accurately. Try marking them with a pencil before you cut notch. If you make some dry runs and corners are consistently in the same place, you're doing it right.

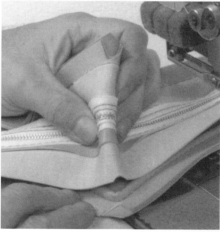

Alignment of first corner is critical. This establishes location for remaining three.

you're using fabric for one of the face pieces. So check it and correct any error.

Sew to all four corners, clipping them as you go. Tug a little here, push a little there so all corners align. The last side should fall smoothly into place. Be sure to sew over the start of your seam

a few inches to lock it in place. Now, somewhat frustrated but much the wiser, you've finished sewing your first project! It's now time to fill it so you can use it.

FILLING CUSHION COVER

Before you can fill the cushion cover, it must be turned right-side

After turning corner, *check before you sew.* You must be accurate. About 1/4 inch off is all you can get away with on vinyl. For a longer cushion, say over 48 inches, less accuracy can be tolerated. The same is true for some other fabrics.

Coming down the final stretch, check that all pieces lie flat without stretching.

has a bit of a saw-tooth edge. A hacksaw blade does wonders, too. Pull it across the foam with the teeth pointing toward you. Even a handsaw works well if you keep it straight and pull it rather than push it. A bandsaw is the very best tool for cutting foam.

Things that don't work well for cutting foam include a razor blade, paring knife, saber saws and X-acto knife.

The main area of concern while cutting foam—besides safety—is to get a smooth, perpendicular cut. If the top and bottom of the finished product are not the same, the cushion may not fill out nicely. So, take your time and cut carefully. Remember: the foam is cut the same size as blanks for the face pieces and should be the same width as the boxing.

Putting that oversized hunk of foam in the cushion cover may seem like putting 10 pounds of sugar in a 5-pound bag, but it's really not that bad. Begin by folding the foam in half and holding it there with one hand while you open the cushion cover with the other. If you have small hands or

out. To do this, start by lifting the zipper flap. Find the slide. By pulling sharply on the two sides of the tape *in front of the slide* you can open the zipper up to the seam. Then pull the zipper slide back until it reaches the opposite seam. You can now turn the cushion cover right-side out.

The next step is to cut the

foam. There are as many ways to do this as there are tools to cut with. As shown, I'm using a professional foam saw, a tool you can get along without until you have your own shop. Except for the last one, the following are less-expensive options: Use an electric knife; it works exactly like a foam saw. Sharpen an old butcher knife so it

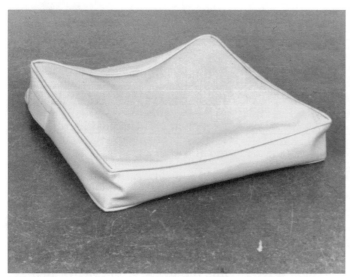

Finished product can be filled with anything that makes it stand out. Besides polyfoam, you could also use springs and cotton, down (feathers), dacron or any of these in combination.

Your search for accuracy continues even to the filler—polyfoam in this case. Measure carefully. In this case I use a felt-tip marker to draw lines. This felt tip makes a 1/4-inch-wide line. Before marking, decide whether to cut on inside or outside of lines. In this case, cutting on one side versus the other makes as much as a 1/2-inch difference in finished size of foam.

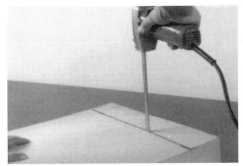

Before I got the fancy foam saw, I used all of the tools mentioned in the chapter at one time or another. My first power-cutter was a used electric knife I got at the Thrift-Shop for $1.

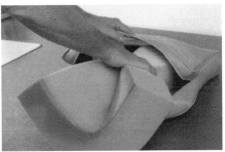

If you can't manipulate foam in this way, there's another way. Turn cover inside out. Place front edge of foam against front edge of cushion cover. Turn cover right-side out over foam, then adjust from inside.

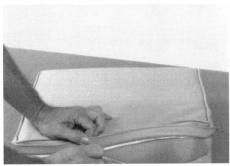

As you close it, push down on foam to take strain off zipper tape. You can pull a zipper tooth if force is too great.

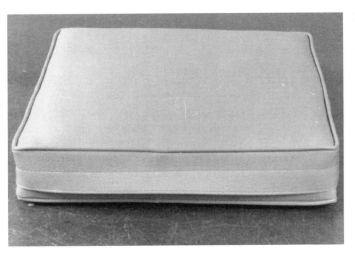

Two views of finished product: If yours looks like this—and it may—move on to next project..

insufficient strength in one hand to hold the foam this way, use both hands and have someone hold the cushion cover open for you.

Push the foam in as far as you can, then let it go. Reach in, grab a corner of the foam and force it into the corner of the cushion cover. Do this with the other corner. The foam should be somewhat flat inside the cover with about 2 inches sticking out. Reach in, grab a front corner with one hand, hold the cover with the other and pull the foam into the

corner of the cushion cover. Try pushing on the rear of the foam while pulling on the cover, gradually working the foam into the cover. Continue to work inside. Make the foam stand up with its corners directly in line with the seams. *Make the selvage edges of the seams point down* with the foam holding them in position. Work until the cushion looks fully filled out, then close the zipper.

Congratulations on a job well done! You should have enough material left over to make another cushion if you think this one was

not satisfactory, you had to cut it apart so many times it looks like Swiss cheese, or you just want more practice. If you're happy with it, go on. If not, try it again. Practice makes a professional out of an amateur.

The next chapter takes us into the mysteries of making a bench-seat cover. From here on you should be able to go to any of the projects that interest you as one project does not necessarily build on another. But you should read through each chapter to pick up hints and techniques.

MAKE IT SLIPPERY

If you have a lot of trouble getting the foam into the cushion cover, use this trick. Silicone spray will act as a lubricant between the foam and jersey-backing of the vinyl. It is available in aerosol cans from your local trim supplier. Or, you may find it at your local Sears store as Silicone Spray, part number 55763.

Note: *Don't confuse silicone spray with vinyl-treatment products such as Armor All. They are two distinctly different products and should not be used interchangeably.*

Spray silicone liberally over the foam and inside cushion cover before inserting the foam into cover. Silicone is odorless, colorless and non-staining, but try to keep it off the outside of the vinyl. Silicone will make it so slippery that you won't be able to get a good grip anywhere to work the cover over the foam!

Another handy application for silicone spray is to use it under the needle when sewing leather. Leather tends to stick to the bench, thereby, making it difficult to sew. Also use it where you need one material to slide over the other. If you ever make clear-plastic seat covers, you'll "die" for this stuff.

4

Making a Bench-seat Cover—Part 1

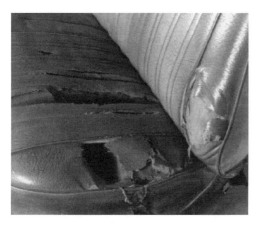

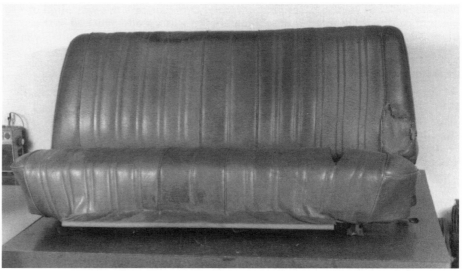

A bench seat in this condition is the kind of job a trimmer sees every day. These are the "before" shots of our bench-seat cover project. Peek ahead for the "after."

About this time you should be quite comfortable with the sewing machine, measuring materials, doing layouts and those things we discussed in the preceding chapters. In this chapter you'll use all of these newly developed skills to complete your first automotive-related project—making a bench-seat cover.

A bench seat is any seat that isn't a bucket seat. That should make perfect sense! Seriously, a bench seat is generally an undivided seat extending across the width of the vehicle. It seats at least two people. This describes the rear seat of many of today's small cars. Although it may be scooped out to give the appearance of bucket seats, if it's one seat or cushion designed to fit two—albeit small people—it's a bench seat.

The back of a bench seat may be attached to the cushion, as in our example. Or it may be a separate piece as in the case of the rear-seat example. On most rear bench seats, you can remove the cushion independently of the back.

In our example, the entire unit came out. It was then separated on the workbench. Knowing what a bench seat is, let's look at what we'll do with it in this chapter.

Because this is a rather extensive project, I've divided it into two parts. In this chapter you'll

learn how to measure for materials, cut and bond vinyl and polyfoam, then layout and sew decorative stitching. In Chapter 5, you'll finish up by fitting and sewing all the pieces together. You'll then install them to the frame to complete the project.

In describing the step-by-step process of making a bench-seat cover, our demonstration will center on the project seat. Where necessary, I explain certain steps that would occur if the design were a bit different. I also demonstrate techniques to use on your own project. But, as we go, I

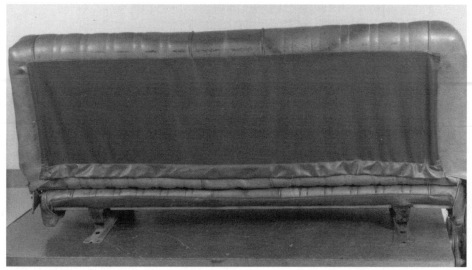

Outside back has curtain covering seat frame. On older cars this was often a piece of cardboard covered with seat material. It was usually attached to the frame with sheet-metal screws.

Seat back hinges at sides so it can be laid forward for access behind it. To separate back from cushion, C-clip or cotter key is removed and seat back "hockey stick" is pried over pivot pin. A large screwdriver or small crowbar was required to do this.

also describe how a professional might do it differently to save time. So, read on as you begin your first auto-related project—the bench-seat cover.

MEASURING THE JOB

Start with the Cushion

Our project seat is from a 3/4-ton Ford pickup. It's seen a hard life being used for parts pickup and delivery in a southern California salvage yard. The driver's side is basically destroyed but salvage-

able. The rest of the seat is in relatively good shape.

You should have some idea of what materials you want to use on your project before you begin. The project seat was originally a two-tone tan expanded vinyl. The customer wants to change to a blue-and-gold expanded vinyl, so we'll oblige him. Before proceeding, we'll start by removing the back from the cushion. Don't remove the cover from the cushion or back,

though. Why? Always do your fitting with the old cover in place unless you're using it for a pattern.

If you take the old cover off and work from the polyfoam or cotton, the cover will be too big. Why? Remember the stadium-cushion project? You cut the foam 1 inch bigger than the finished cover to get a tight-fitting cover.

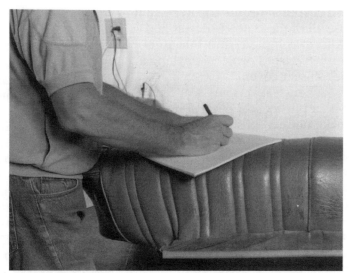

Measurements are always made from front-to-back or up-and-down, then side-to-side. Following this procedure will make measuring and cutting go quicker and smoother.

Record your measurements as you make them. Some trimmers write directly on the old seat material. This is fine if there are only a few measurements.

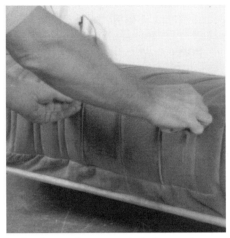
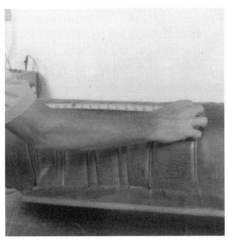

Each piece of seat material must be measured separately. Don't forget to add seam allowance—at least 1/2 inch on all sides. I usually add 1 or 2 inches to the width when making pleats. This allows for "shrinkage" caused by the material being pulled toward the pleats as they're sewn.

Don't forget to measure stretcher at rear of cushion. You can save time by making cover large enough to incorporate stretcher, but do this only if appearance is not a concern.

Seat foam is made the same way. Usually it's 1 inch or more larger overall. In this case the foam already exists, so you must make allowances in the cover. If you don't, your cover will be 1 inch or more too big.

Now, get out your tape measure, pencil or pen and a sheet or two of paper. Start by measuring the cushion depth. Add 2 or 3 inches to be on the safe side. This seat design is sometimes described as a *waterfall* seat because there is no division between the top and front. It simply "falls" over the front. Another style would have the facing come all the way across the front of the seat with or without a welt. On the project seat you can see there is only a facing at each end. If yours has a facing, *don't* include it in the depth measurement; measure it separately.

The project seat is made in three sections with two end caps. To get the seat width I measure each of these sections. Here I add 2 inches to each piece for seam allowance and shrinkage created from sewing the decorative top-stitching. (The more top-stitching you do, the narrower the finished piece becomes.) If this had been a single-piece cover I would have added 2 inches for an overall

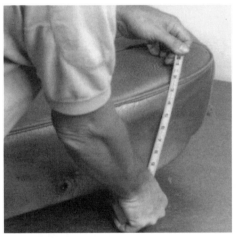

After measuring pleats, measure facing. Again, measure up and down, then side to side.

measurement.

Now we have three measurements: a center piece that measures 38-inches deep X 11-inches wide and two side pieces measuring 38 X 23 inches. In back of the cushion another piece is sewn the complete width of the seat. This is called the *rear stretcher* or *rear pull*. The stretcher must be measured and cut as a separate piece. Some covers, however, don't have a stretcher. When this is the case, the main body of the cover wraps around the back edge and is hog-ringed in place. More on hog-rings later. For now, we have a stretcher measuring 5 X 56 inches.

The end caps are measured the same way as the body: back to front, then up and down. Results are two 2 X 7-inch end pieces and two 13 X 29-inch end facings. Allow lots of extra material for the end facings because there is usually a two-way curve to deal with. Also, the material may need to be brought under the seat to be fastened to the frame. So give yourself plenty of leeway.

Hog-rings, J-hooks & Other Fasteners

Let's look at hog-rings and other fasteners for a minute. As discussed in Chapter 1, hog-rings are used to fasten seat-cover material

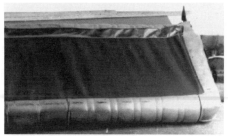

The final measurement will be the outside-back-curtain. If your seat looks like this, be sure to add the 2-inch fold-over you see below my left hand.

This is what you'll find under that fol-dover flap; a listing with a wire passing through it. I'm cutting hog-rings that retain curtain at bottom of cushion . . .

. . . and at top of cushion.

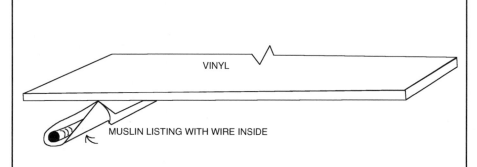

VINYL

MUSLIN LISTING WITH WIRE INSIDE

A listing is a 1-1/2-inch-wide strip of muslin folded in half and sewn to piece of vinyl or fabric. Rod or wire can be inserted through loop. If you use a fastener such as a hog-ring to loop over wire, material can be fastened to a frame so fasteners can't be seen. This is a very common way to pull material down into a groove, such as on a bucket seat.

to the seat frame with hog-ring pliers. (You should have these pliers by now.)

Some covers from late-model cars don't use hog-rings. Instead, a hard-plastic J-hook is sewn to the bottom of the cover. This hooks over the edge of the seat frame and is held in place by the force of the springs and padding in the seat. As you'll see, this is the case with part of the project seat. The front and rear of the cover is held this way while the sides are held by hog-rings. If your seat uses a J-hook, its location must be considered when you fit the pieces. I cover this when I talk about fitting the cover on page 59.

Yet another way to hold a seat cover to the frame is with *cushion-wire clips,* a particularly popular fastener with British and German manufacturers. It requires no installation tool. You snap it on by hand. The cover is pulled tightly over the frame and one or more of these clips is snapped over the material to secure it in place.

You don't have to make the cover the same as the factory. If you have a simpler way to attach it, do so. I did this with the project seat by eliminating the J-hook at the front and by adding a stretcher so I could use hog-rings. The J-hook, as illustrated by the first photo, broke and no longer served its purpose. So, as you measure your cover, allow for how you'll fasten it to the frame.

Measuring the Back
The back cover is constructed much like the cushion cover: three pieces at the center and caps at each end. Unlike the cushion, the back cover has a back called an *outside back.* The outside back of our project seat is called an *outside-back curtain* because it is not fastened at the sides.

Measure the back as you did the cushion. Then find the dimensions for the outside back.

To help get the correct measurements, remove the outside

back. From the photos, you can see how the outside back anchors. A listing, or folded piece of muslin, is sewn to the bottom, inside of the outside back. (There's a mouthful!) There's also a listing with a wire sewn to the bottom edge of the back cover. The back cover is ringed at the bottom to the frame and the outside-back curtain is then ringed to the back cover. When the outside back is removed, you can get a good look at the end cap. Note the J-hook fastening the end cap to the frame. I finish measuring the back by measuring the end pieces and end facings. When you finish measuring the back, you'll layout those measurements to determine the amount of cover materials to buy.

LAYOUT FOR MATERIAL PURCHASE

You probably decided long ago what cover materials you'd like to use for your bench seat. Although the example seat is all vinyl, this doesn't mean you must use all vinyl. You may wish to use a combination of vinyl and fabric or all fabric. There are so many materials to choose from it's easy to get confused when making such a decision. Assuming you've crossed this hurdle, you must now figure out how much to buy.

Rules to Consider

There are a few things to consider when buying and laying out seat-cover materials. The type and pattern of the covering materials you selected will determine how much you need. These are rules you need to know, but, with one exception, they aren't carved in stone.

1. Generally, stripes should run up and down rather than side to side. If you're dealing with a plaid pattern, the boldest stripe runs up and down, too. The sometime exception is a fabric insert in a bucket seat. Up and down means the stripe starts at the top of the back, runs down to the bottom of the back, then picks up at

the cushion and travels from the back to the front. Note how this is the same way we measured the job—top to bottom, back to front.

2. The nap of a material, such as velvet, lays down on the back and down from rear to front on the cushion. On a finished job, you should be able to wipe your hand down the back, then out to the front of the cushion, pushing the nap down and making it feel smooth.

3. If there's a design in the material, such as a flower, be sure the flower points up on the back and lies front to back on the cushion.

4. Heavy fabrics designed for furniture use will work well, but other than these, stay away from materials meant for clothing, draperies or uses other than auto trim. Generally, these materials are too light and will not wear well.

5. Black vinyl can get hot enough in the summer to burn bare skin. Use it accordingly.

The rule governing the direction of napped material is the only one you should never break. The nap will get "fuzzed up" if you run it in the wrong direction. Also, it will appear to change color from the back to the cushion if the nap direction isn't the same on both parts.

Now, with those points in mind, layout your measurements and decide how much cover material to buy. The best way to do this is to draw little boxes on a piece of paper. Each box should include the name of the piece and its measurements. Be careful not to exceed the width of the material, generally 54 to 56 inches. Adjust these boxes to the best advantage of the material. If you're using striped material, be sure the stripes on the back align with the stripes on the cushion.

Centering Stripes & Pleats

Centering stripes and pleats is easy if you remember one rule: Work from the center out. Select the dominant stripe for the center. You must cut the material so the

With outside-back curtain off, you can see how end caps are retained. A plastic J-hook is used. This must be carefully removed from the old cover so it can be reused on the new one.

stripe falls exactly in the center. If your piece is 18-inches wide, the *center* of the stripe or pleat must fall along the 9-inch centerline mark. No matter how wide the stripe or pleat is, its centerline must match, or be, the centerline of the material. Then, if the cushion piece is wider than the back piece, the stripes or pleats will align because the centerlines of the two pieces align.

When all of your measurements are laid out as demonstrated, add up the inches from top to bottom, divide by 36 and you'll know how many yards of cover material to buy.

For the project seat, the widest piece is the stretcher at 56 inches. Fortunately, the piece of material we used was 56-inches wide. This allowed us to cut everything *across* the roll rather than *up* the roll, which saved quite a bit of material.

If your bench seat has a welt around the front edge which measures over 56 inches, or typically between 80 and 90 inches, you'll have to layout the pieces going up the roll. This means purchasing a length of material equal to the length of your welt.

If you're using all-vinyl with no pattern, you can layout your

Right: Sample measurement list. Once you have all the measurements, you can begin cutting.

Left: A cutting diagram. All measurements are transferred to boxes representing the pieces to be cut. Cross-hatched area is selvage and can be used for welt or stretcher. By adding inches on the left side and dividing by 36 inches per yard, you know exactly how much material in yards to buy.

In this illustration, we have 22 + 8 + 48 + 24 + 10 + 10 = 122 inches. To convert to yards of material, divide by 36 inches per yard. This gives 3.39 yards, or 3 yards plus about 14 inches. Buy 3-1/2 yards of material for this job.

CUSHION		
Center	38 X 11	
Side	38 X 23	cut 2
End	27 X 7	cut 2
End facing	13 X 29	cut 2
Stretcher	5 X 56	
BACK		
Center	38 X 11	
Side	38 X 23	cut 2
End	30 X 8	cut 2

pieces anyway you like. Up and down or left to right doesn't matter.

My shopping list for materials for the project seat follows. Yours should look something like it.

2 1/2-yards blue vinyl
2 1/4-yards gold vinyl
1/2-yard unbleached muslin
2-yards 1/2-inch scrim-back polyfoam
1/2-pound hog-rings
1-pint contact cement
1-gallon lacquer thinner or contact-cement solvent
3-yards 85/15 cotton batting
1-pound-spool blue nylon thread and matching bobbins

Review Chapter 1 for a thorough understanding of the above materials. A quick review here should help to refresh your memory. Unbleached muslin is a cotton material used for listings. These hold the wires through which hog-rings are installed. Scrim-back polyfoam has a backing that prevents the threads from pulling through. 85/15 cotton is a cotton batting composed of 85 percent linters—seeds, chaff and short-fiber cotton—and 15 percent pure,

long-fiber cotton.

Now, list in hand, go to the fabric house, pick up the materials you'll need and prepare to cut.

CUTTING THE MATERIAL

Roll out the cover material on the bench, sharpen your chalk and get out the little diagram you made for cutting out the materials. You didn't make one? Then, you'll have to start from the top. Besides, professionals don't make cutting diagrams anyway!

Look at your measurements. Find the piece(s) that, when laid side by side, come as close as possible to the width of the material, or 54 inches. These pieces should also be about the same height so there's no big piece of waste above one or the other. After squaring your material, layout your measurements with the yardstick and cut them out.

Find the next measurements that come as close to 54 inches as possible. Lay them out the same way and then cut. Repeat this process until all the pieces are cut out. You should end up with a piece left over that is pyramid-

shaped with the point facing you and the base at the top. If it is over 54 inches long, you'll cut your welt material from this piece.

Remember, if you're cutting stripes, each piece should have a common centerline. *Never line up stripes working from the left or right of the piece you're cutting.* The stripe always aligns from the center out to each side. This allows the cushion section to be larger than the corresponding back section and still have the stripes lined up.

If you are using listings or stretchers, cut them now. You should develop the habit of doing all your cutting at one time, all the fitting and sewing at one time and then the installation. This saves time by avoiding repeating steps.

Cutting Materials in a Production Shop

If you ever have the opportunity to hang around a trim shop for a while and watch the trimmers work, you'll see they rarely cut the way I've just described. Even though the method is accurate, it's not efficient. Wasted time means lost income. So here's how the "pros" do it.

Instead of working from a cutting diagram, the trimmer takes off the old cover. Then, with a razor blade or scissors, he cuts the cover apart at the seams. Each of these pieces is laid atop the new material and used as a pattern. While holding the pattern tightly against the material with one hand, the trimmer then cuts out the new piece, allowing for a 1/2-inch seam allowance. Finally, the trimmer makes little nicks here and there in the pattern and in the new piece so he'll know where to align the materials to begin sewing.

This is very fast and efficient, but represents an unseen problem. If the old cover material stretched or shrunk, it will be reflected in the new cover when the material is assembled. To avoid this the trimmer must make adjustments in the pattern while cutting. This calls for a great deal of knowledge gained from years of experience.

This process is best left to the pros for now. At the earliest, avoid it until you've made a few pieces as demonstrated in this book. When you've mastered the knack of cutting, fitting and sewing, then you can start working on the shortcuts.

Cutting Polyfoam

If, like the project seat, yours has pleats or designs sewn into it, you'll have to back up the cover material with polyfoam. This is cut next. Layout the foam on the bench, scrim-side down. Lay the pieces that will have foam under them on top of the polyfoam. Arrange them so there's a minimum of 4 inches between each piece. This allows you to cut each foam piece at least 2 inches larger around the periphery than the corresponding cover material. This will give you plenty of room to work with when you get to the gluing stage.

Generally, only the main pieces are backed by polyfoam.

CONTACT CEMENT PRECAUTIONS

Contact cement is highly volatile and should be handled accordingly. Most contact cements are thinned with lacquer thinner or similar products which, when exposed to a spark or flame, may cause an explosion! Some things to avoid when using contact cement are burning cigarettes, pilot lights on gas water heaters, any type of heater or furnance, something as seemingly innocent as static electricity. The simple solution to this problem is to use a lot of ventilation when spraying contact cement. If you smoke, don't while spraying. And don't leave any smoldering cigarettes lying around. A flash fire in your face could spoil your whole day.

There are non-flammable contact cements, but they are very expensive and slow-drying. Because I prefer the flammable type, I eliminate potential "spark plugs" and ventilate my workspace with a large fan in a door or window.

If you buy contact cement in bulk—quarts or gallons—as opposed to aerosol cans, it will be thinned to a consistency suitable for brushing or rolling. It must be thinned further for spraying. Although manufacturers recommend their own thinner, if the cement is petroleum-based, any inexpensive lacquer thinner works just as well. Give the cement a sniff. If it smells like lacquer, you're in business. If it smells like a swimming pool, it's a chlorinated, non-flammable product. With non-flammable cement, you *must* use the manufacturer's thinner.

To reduce with lacquer thinner, buy the cheapest you can find. This is generally *wash thinner* which is available at your local auto-paint store. Bring a metal container; it's sold from bulk. For some odd reason, the expensive thinners don't seem to work as well. Some just float on top of the cement and won't mix in. This is one of those rare cases where cheapest is best.

I can't give you a good rule of thumb on what ratio of thinner to cement you'll need because there is such a difference in products. Begin thinning with about 25 percent thinner/cement. Test this mix with gun pressure set at 40 to 60 psi. If it sprays nicely you're in business. If the cement spits out in globs, add another 10 percent thinner and test it. If you get something that looks like cobwebs as you spray, the mixture is too thin or your gun is set at too high a pressure. So reduce one or the other (or both).

Facings are left plain. The idea of using polyfoam is to give body to the main pieces, particularly when pleats are incorporated as is the case with our project. So there's no need to waste polyfoam on the facings. Once the foam pieces are cut out you can glue your vinyl pieces to the polyfoam.

BONDING VINYL TO POLYFOAM

Vinyl or cloth is bonded to the polyfoam with contact cement.

You can use cement specifically formulated for this purpose, available from the fabric-supply house, or you can use any good, general-purpose contact cement.

If you select a general-purpose contact cement, select one without a coloring agent. Coloring agents let you see where you've sprayed the cement, but unless it was formulated with a coloring agent for trim work, the color may bleed through the material. If the cement is designed for trim work, you can be fairly sure it won't

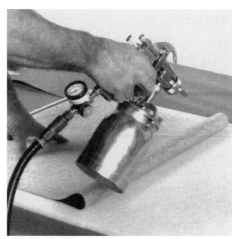

Photo illustrates three things: A covered bench to protect it from cement overspray (I'm using masking paper); material laid out in a fold to expose back for cement and to protect face from overspray; and finally, air pressure set at the gun. Note gauge at gun. Regulating pressure at gun is more accurate than using gauge at tank. Keep air pressure fairly low, or 40 to 60 psi.

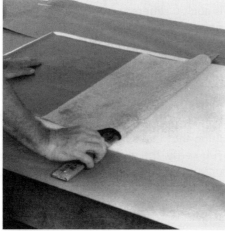

Wiping freshly cemented material over polyfoam prevents wrinkles in material.

bleed. The following are some additional precautions to remember when bonding cover material to polyfoam.

Solvent in contact cement dissolves polyfoam. This is necessary to make the cement adhere to the foam and material. It will, however, turn the foam to jelly if the cement is used too heavily. So don't brush or roll cement onto the foam. You must spray on the cement to control the amount.

If you think you'll be doing a lot of trim work, buy an inexpensive spray gun. These may be purchased new at any commercial auto-body or paint-supply house as a *primer gun*. This, as the name implies, is a gun intended for spraying primer. The opening in the nozzle is larger than in a gun used for enamel or lacquer work. This is because priming pigments are larger and heavier than lacquer or enamel paint. Therefore, a *primer gun* serves better as a glue gun (and is less expensive) than a top-of-the-line paint gun.

If you're into saving money, you can probably find a good used gun at a yard sale or swap meet, or from the classified ads. If you buy a brand-name gun, rebuild kits are available for replacing wornout parts.

For a 'one-shot deal,' use contact cement from an aerosol can. These should be available at your fabric-supply house. Generally, the cement in aerosol cans is not as good as bulk cement. But if your project will be top-sewn, this is of little consequence. If you're going to bond a large surface area with no stitching, experiment with the "rattle can" before you commit to the big job. Once you've selected the means of application there are some other things to consider.

Contact cement must be applied to both the polyfoam and the cover material. You can't spray one piece, then stick the two together as you might when gluing two pieces of wood together. Keep the layer of cement thin and apply it to the faces of each piece.

Contact cement adheres—just as the name suggests—on contact. After you've put the two pieces together, especially after a little drying time, attempting to peel the "sandwich" apart usually tears the polyfoam. To avoid the need to pull apart the pieces—usually because of a wrinkle—we'll look at how to make the bond *without* creating wrinkles.

Finally, once you've finished bonding the material and poly-foam, avoid folding the assembly face-to-face. It will leave a visible line along the fold. This is caused by the cells of the foam being forced together and bonding to themselves by the contact cement. If the bonded panel must be folded, do it so the back of the polyfoam folds against itself.

With these prohibitions in mind, let's go over how to do it.

Cementing

Keep cement overspray off of your bench. To do this, cover it. I use masking paper purchased from a paint-supply house. If you'll be doing a lot of spraying at the bench, use some inexpensive vinyl. You can use it over and over, plus it holds up well under abuse from seat frames which you may set it on.

Lay the piece of polyfoam faceup on the bench. Lay the vinyl on top of the polyfoam, also faceup. There should be an even amount of polyfoam extending out (about 2 inches) from the periphery. Without moving either material, fold one side of the vinyl back over itself. It should be folded in half with its underside exposed. This fold will protect the face of the vinyl below it from overspray.

Hold things in place with one hand and spray an even coat of cement over the back of the cover material and exposed polyfoam. Now comes the trick. Slide a yardstick or dowel into the fold of the vinyl. Use this to wipe the folded-over vinyl out evenly and carefully back over the polyfoam. If you do it slowly and with care, there should be no wrinkles or stretches.

Repeat this process with the other side. Fold the unbonded half over the half you just cemented. Cover this and the corresponding half of the polyfoam with another thin, even coat of cement. Again, wipe the freshly cemented half of the cover-material back over the polyfoam with your yardstick or dowel.

Work opposite side the same as you did first half.

Finished product should lie flat with no wrinkles or bubbles.

As in the photo top right, your material should now be bonded flat and even to the polyfoam. Repeat this process for all the pieces you've cut except for the facings, then set them aside for marking.

DECORATIVE STITCHING & SEWING SUB-ASSEMBLIES

When making decorative stitches or pleats, such as stripes, the back and cushion pieces must line up. Nothing looks as unprofessional as pleats or stripes that don't match. Use extreme care and thoughtfulness when doing this layout.

To make everything fall into place correctly, *always work from the center out.* In your mind—sometimes on the cover material—make a line at the very center of the project and work simultaneously to the right and to the left. Peek ahead at the finished project seat to get an idea of how to go about centering things.

Notice the panels on the seat cushion are the same size as the panels on the back cushion. Only the end caps are a different size. This is where the difference in seat dimensions are made up—at the ends. As long as each piece in the cushion, except the end caps, corresponds to its mate on the back, everything will line up in the finished project.

Let's begin with the gold side panels because this is where the

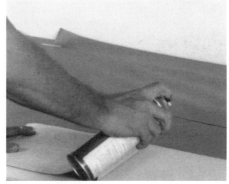

Aerosol cement cans can be convenient and effective. Buy the most expensive brand for best results.

most work is. The pattern will be 1-inch pleats every 2-1/2 inches. Here's the process: Find the exact center of the material. In the example, the panel is 23-inches wide, so the center will be 11-1/2 inches in from either end. With very sharp chalk I make marks at 11 inches and 12 inches. This is 1/2 inch to each side of the center. I repeat this at the top of the and then make lines to connect the marks. The finished panel has five 1-inch pleats with 4-inch borders left over at each side (see photo top left).

By marking the side pieces 3-inches wide, I'll have another 2-1/2-inch pleat with a 1/2-inch seam allowance. After finishing the layout of all the panels, I top-sew along each of these lines to create the pleated effect.

Stitching the Pleats

Now you're ready to sew the pleats.

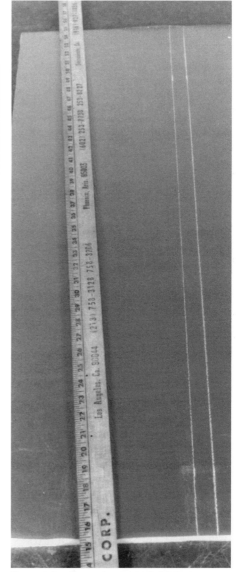

Seams for first pleat are laid out. Center line is directly between the two chalk lines. This will help ensure that cushion and back pleats will align.

Finished layout should look similar to this. Only size and pattern will be different.

Remember to allow for "shrinkage" by adding 1 or 2 inches to width of material. After pleat seams are sewn, there should be some excess at each side. Trim it off.

Panel is now ready to be added to others to become the top of the cushion or inside back.

Trim excess polyfoam from around center panel to prevent foam and material "sandwich" from bunching up under needle while it's sewn.

Then you'll sew the pleated panels and center panels into sub-assemblies.

To sew pleats, thread the machine with a color that matches the fabric and install a universal foot or welt foot.

Start with a full bobbin. The finished project will look very tacky if you run out of bobbin thread in the middle of a pleat seam, then have to restart the seam. You'd have to top-sew for about 2 inches to lock the threads in place, so the seam will stand out as a glaring error. Check your bobbin thread after every few seams, too. When it looks like there's not enough thread left to make another seam, throw the remainder away and put in a new bobbin.

Begin sewing on the line to your *right*. Sew slowly and evenly, using both hands to keep the seam line directly under the

needle. Lock the stitch at the beginning and end. This is a pretty tense-jaw operation. If you stray off the line the seam will be wavy. It will look even worse if you cut out the seam and stitch it over again.

If you're worried about your abilities, cut out a few pieces from scrap and practice sewing them first. When you're feeling good about your technique, sew the panels immediately. Wait too long and your small motor muscles will forget what they were doing and you'll lose it.

After you've made four or five seams, the right edge of the material will start to rub against the neck of the machine. To prevent this, *roll* up the material as you proceed toward the middle of the panel. Remember about not folding the cover material-and-foam sandwich to prevent permanent creasing? Well, don't roll it back

over on itself, either. It will try to roll this way, but force it to roll the other direction—with the cover material on the *outside*. When you've passed the center, turn the panel around and start working in from the other edge. This will prevent getting too much material rolled up in the throat of the machine.

When all seams have been sewn, remove the material from the machine and trim right up to the outside seam. In the example I allowed 1/2 inch for seam allowance. Any selvage is trimmed away. By trimming this selvage you prevent it from rolling up under future seams when the panels are sewn together. Any remaining panels are sewn next. In the case of the project seat, there are a total of four panels.

To finish the preliminary stitching I trim the selvage polyfoam from around the blue panels. Then I top-stitch around all edges. This is not a have-to step, but it keeps things neat and prevents any peel-back or separation of the vinyl and foam.

Final sub-assembly
The goal now is to sew a pleated panel to each side of a center panel with a welt between them.

Again, we'll start with the right edge of the cushion-pleated panel. Although it was an arbitrary

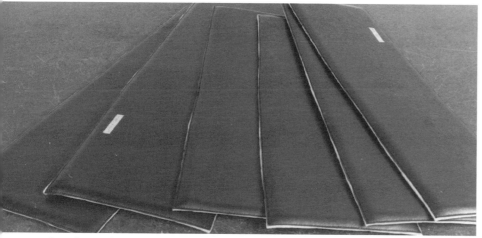

nter and end panels are ready for final assembly.

Sew welt to either panel first, then join panels.

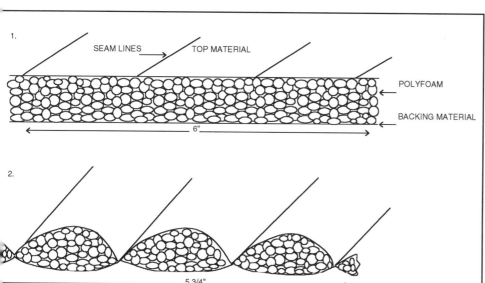

Before and after sewing pleats: When sewing pleats you'll find the assembly tends to shrink a bit. What started as 6 inches of pleat panel here shrunk to 5-3/4 inches after sewing three, 2-inch pleats. Some large panels can be stretched back to size. On smaller panels it is necessary to make the pleats about 1/16-inch larger. I just increase the width of the pleat by the thickness of the chalk line so that a 2-inch pleat becomes 2-1/16 to 2-3/32 inches wide. Do this by eye; if you try to work with measurements this fine you'll go crazy!

Start of spiffy new cushion top.

blies to the shape of the seat. To do this, now go to the following chapter.

decision, I sewed a blue welt to the panel. I could have started with the center piece instead. As for color, it didn't matter whether the welt was blue or gold. What matters is that all welts are the same color. Be sure you use the same color welt throughout on any project.

After the welt is sewn to all in-board edges, the pleated panels are sewn to the center panel. Lay the center panel down faceup. Lay a pleated panel facedown over it with the welt between the two. Sew the pleated panel to the center panel. Stay on the *inside* of the welt seam. If you sew outside this seam, it will show when you open up the finished product.

Now turn the center panel around to expose the unsewn edge. Sew the other pleated panel.

When the major sub-assemblies have been sewn together, begin to fit the pieces and assem-

About our Author

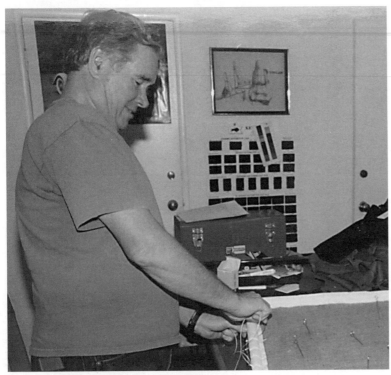

Don "at the bench" hand-sewing "fox edging" to the back cushion of a rumble seat for a 1932 Cadillac V-16 convertible coupe. Today, seats with "fox edging" have been replaced with molded polyfoam.

Don Taylor grew up in the auto trimming business: his father was a trimmer, Don is a trimmer, and his two sons were trained as trimmers as they grew up. As an expert author, Don created the *Automotive Upholstery Handbook* for Fisher Books and five automotive books on engine rebuilding, restoration and paint and body work for HPBooks. He is co-author of *Custom Auto Interiors,* a book described on page 214.

With his brother, Alan, at Taylor-Made Van Conversions in San Diego, California, Don created numerous van conversions. And they created several exciting vehicles, including Toyota's "Yamahauler" (later made into a Revell model), and the "Huskyhauler," the Husquvarna Motorcycle team's mobile garage. One interesting job was trimming a steam-powered taxicab with seating for the physically handicapped. It was done for the Federal Department of Transportation (DOT) through San Diego Steam Power Systems. The vehicle was displayed for a year at the Smithsonian Museum with a Taylor-Made sign.

Just prior to hanging up his trimmer's tools for a 14-year "retirement," Don's work on the interior of a 1932 Auburn Coupe won Best of Class, People's Choice, and Best of Show awards at the International Auburn/Cord/Duesenberg Show.

Currently, in addition to book-authoring and illustrating, Don is temporarily "un-retired," working again with his brother Alan's Design Engineering restoration and custom trim facility in Escondido, California. Collectible cars in the shop as this was written included three Bugattis, three Rolls-Royces, a Bentley and a 1932 Cadillac V-16 convertible.

5 Making a Bench-seat Cover—Part 2

We ended the last chapter by sewing the pleated sections of the seat cover to the center-piece. This was done for both the cushion and back. You should now be ready to join those assemblies and corresponding end pieces to make a cushion and back cover.

SEAT-COVER ASSEMBLY

Fitting

Place the seat cushion on the bench. The old cover should still be securely fastened to the frame. You should always do your fitting with the old cover in place unless you're using it for a pattern. Otherwise you'll end up with a cover that's too big unless you make allowances as you did when making the stadium-cushion cover.

As shown in the accompanying photo, I clamped the pleat assembly to the seat cushion after making sure it was centered left-to-right and front-to-back. Centering is very important, especially left-to-right. If the cushion and back covers are centered correctly, the pleats will align when the cushion and back are assembled. If the centers are off, the pleats will also be off. So measure carefully.

Use clamps to hold things in place as you begin fitting. Be sure everything is centered. Measure front and back as they relate to the seat frame.

I use clamps for the initial fitting so I can move the cover easily. When I'm satisfied with the placement I pin the cover in place. This is more secure than clamps. As shown, I placed a pin in the front and back of the welt where it meets the end caps. Mark these locations with chalk. When you remove the cover, make a *nick* or *V-notch* with your scissors

at the chalk mark. This is to position the end cap to the pleats when you're ready to sew them together. Remember how you made nicks in the corners of the facings on your stadium cushion? This assured that the face-piece corners were correctly aligned.

Next fit the end caps. If you're doing a similar piece, pin the new end piece to the old, allowing

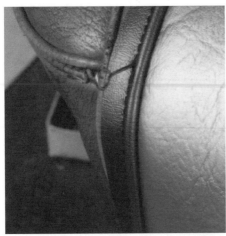

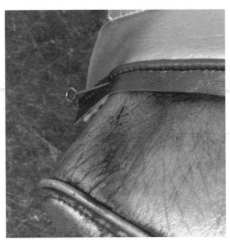

After centering cover, secure with trim pins. They hold the position of the cover better than clamps do. Indicate welt and frame locations by V-notching pleat selvage at both places.

Photo at left shows V-notch that indicates where end cap welt should meet pleats at front. Photo at right is for aligning pleats to rear frame.

New end piece is positioned directly over old one and is secured with trim pins at both ends and in center.

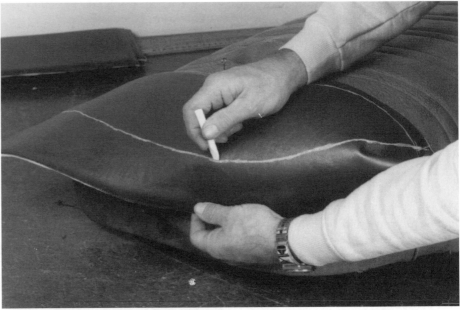

With one hand I pull end piece tightly over edge of seat. This helps me "see" original welt so I can follow it with chalk. If in doubt, I could also feel it through the end piece. Because it was securely pinned, new piece stayed in place while I was chalking line. Always work for accuracy while you're fitting new pieces.

plenty of overlap. As shown in the photo above, mark the seam lines with chalk. You can see the welt beneath the new material if you pull it tight over the corner of the cushion. Chalk a line directly on top of the original welt. If the old material is loose or torn, adjust your line accordingly to make the new piece as accurate as possible.

One reason I seldom use old material for a pattern is because it may have shrunk or stretched. If you make new pieces identical to the old ones, you risk having the new cover fit like the old. So until you've reached the professional level, or at least have become an advanced amateur, fit your work to the job.

Here's one place you can use a pattern: After you've fitted one piece to your satisfaction, use it to make the corresponding piece on the other end—the one that's symmetrically opposite.

After the lines have been chalked, trim away the excess. Remember to keep the 1/2-inch seam allowance. Place the trimmed piece *facedown* on its counterpart piece of material (which is faceup) and chalk a line around it. Then, cut along this line. Don't add the 1/2-inch seam allowance; it's already in the pattern piece.

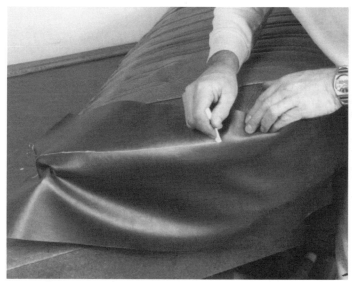

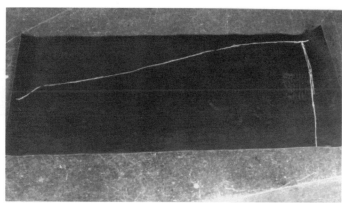

End facing is marked and ready to be cut. Remember to cut 1/2 inch outside line to provide needed seam allowance.

Fitting facing: Notice that there are no wrinkles in material at front corner. Wrinkle in back will come out when I cut around frame member.

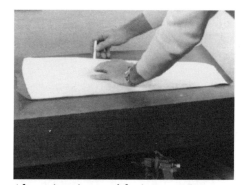

After trimming end facing, use it as a pattern for making opposite-end facing. Place it face-to-face onto piece cut for opposite end facing, chalk around it and then cut it out. This saves time and ensures both end facings will be trimmed to the same size, but symmetrically opposite.

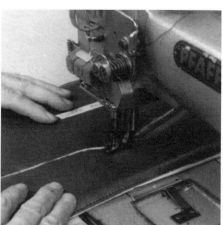

I sew around edges of pieces bonded to polyfoam. It makes sewing multiple layers of material much easier and prevents getting selvage edges twisted up under needle. This would leave a lump and can prevent welt from lying straight. Trim off excess, but leave the 1/2-inch seam allowance.

For this project you need to determine where to sew the stretcher to retain the cover at the front and J-hook at the rear. Do this by measuring from the center out on both the cushion frame and pleat assembly. To be super accurate, place the pleat assembly back on the cushion, pin it back in the exact location you had it—simply match the notches—and determine where the stretcher and

J-hook should go. When this is done you should be ready to sew the pieces together.

Sewing

Begin with the right-side end cap assembly. Look at the photo above to see the stitch I sewed around the chalkmark—leaving the usual 1/2-inch seam allowance— on the end piece. I then trimmed off the selvage. This stitch is not a have-to operation. It's only made on pieces

bonded to polyfoam only for the sake of neatness. It makes the job neater and easier when sewing all of the pieces together if the edges of the material and foam are sewn. If you don't do this, the polyfoam may get twisted around and stitched over, leaving a lump. This step is not used in a production shop because the job goes faster without doing it. Your situation is different. You have lots of time,

Question: Do you sew welt to end piece first or to facing first? Answer: Always sew welt to main body first, never to facing.

Sew facing to end piece. This is the same process you followed in making your stadium cushion. Follow this up by sewing welt to top and bottom of cushion, then facing to these pieces.

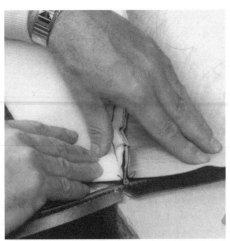

Here's where the V-notches I cut as reference marks come into play. Position end-cap welt directly over notch to indicate where old end-cap welt met pleats.

Hold welt to notch while you sew. If "stretch" is too great, pin or staple pieces together.

so make your work as easy and as neat as you can.

Next, sew a piece of welt to the outside edge of the end piece. Remember to lock the stitch at both ends. Trim the welt flush at the front edge, but leave a 5 to 6 inch "tail" of welt at the back. This will come in handy to pull on when you install the cover.

The last step with the end cap assembly is to sew the end facing to the end piece. Lay the end facing on top of the end piece, align the front edges and sew the assembly together. With this done, you can sew the left end cap

assembly.

Steps to sew the left side are the same as the right; but start at the opposite end. When you sew the welt to the end piece, begin by sewing that 5 or 6 inch "tail." Then, place the end piece *under* the welt and continue sewing. Trim the welt *flush* with the front edge of the end piece.

When you sew the end facing to the end piece, align the front edges, hold the pieces together and begin sewing from the back. I suggest that you pin or staple these pieces together to hold them in position. You should now have both end-cap assemblies completed so they can be sewn to the pleated section.

On the project seat I went back to the right side to sew the end cap to the pleats. Here's where those locating nicks paid off. In the photo (top right) you can see how I aligned the welt on each end cap to the nick in the welt material of the pleats. Keep these aligned while sewing and your cover will fit.

Holding everything in place, flatten out the facing over the welt and begin to sew. As you proceed, check frequently to see that the welt and nick are still aligned. When you reach the welt turn the selvage *away* from you. This is so

the selvage will point *down* when you install the cover. This, in turn, will force the welt to stand up. Finish the seam and go to the left side.

Once again, the process starts with alignment. Align the nick and welt and keep them there while you sew the left end-cap assembly to the pleats. To finish the job I fudged a bit.

On the old cover the J-hook and rear stretcher were in very good condition. I used a a razor blade to cut the threads holding the stretcher to the old cover and reused this assembly. This saved some material and time. The reused standard-weight vinyl will stand up better to the additional perforations caused by additional stitching than will the hard-plastic J-hook. I can do this because it won't be seen once the seat is installed. This is perfectly acceptable if it improves the finished product.

Finish the cushion cover by sewing a stretcher to the front edge.

In a production shop the trimmer would continue by fitting and sewing the back. For now, though, see how the cushion cover fits. If you made any mistakes on it, you can avoid repeating the same ones when you finish the back cover.

Right: The finished cover: Photo at top shows old J-hook sewn to body. *Below:* shows stretcher sewn to front to replace broken J-hook.

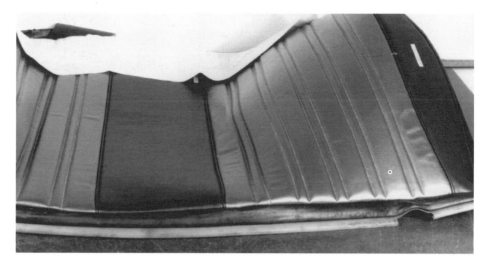

SEAT-COVER INSTALLATION

Removing the Old Cover

All you'll probably need to get the old cover off is a pair of diagonal wire cutters, commonly called *dikes.*

Turn the seat cushion over, start in one corner and cut or twist off all of the hog-rings. Then, release any J-hooks the seat may have. On a late-model car, it may have only a J-hook(s) or similar hook(s) held on by the cover tension. Once you have everything disconnected, turn the seat cushion over and remove the old cover. I hope your project is in better condition than this truck seat, which suffered considerable abuse. Such abuse will continue once it's back in service.

Seat Repair

As you can see from the photo at the far right, I had to do some work on the cushion before covering it. Otherwise the holes in the foam will "telegraph" through the cover in a short while and the customer "will be after my neck." There are three ways to correct this damage: find a similar seat at an auto re-cycler and use the foam from it, rebuild the foam by cementing in new pieces or do it the way I've done—fill the holes with cotton.

The customer didn't want to spend a lot of money on this seat, otherwise I would've used one of the other two options. So, a judicious use of cotton will save the existing cushion foam at minimal cost. If your project will be done this way, begin by filling in with layers of cotton, packing them down as you go. Fill the hole to the top, then add one layer out over the edges.

To avoid a noticeable division line under a cover at the edges of the cotton batting, *featheredge* (taper) its edges. With one hand,

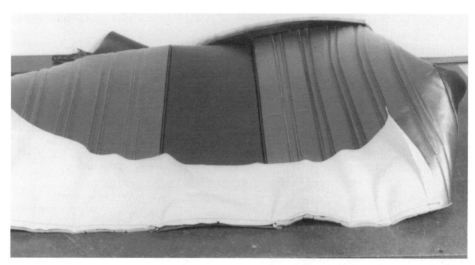

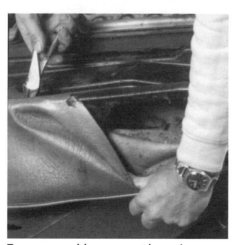

To remove old cover, cut hog-rings holding it to frame.

No, this is not the Grand Canyon, it's what happens to polyfoam after the cover wears out and seat continues to be used. Foam must be repaired or it will show under new cover.

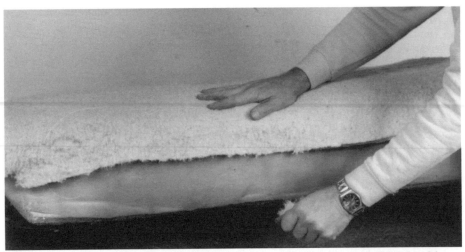

One acceptable method of foam repair is to fill voids with cotton. Notice also foam scraps stuffed under end of cushion. Driver of truck is a *big* guy, so I gave seat extra support.

Adding layer of cotton batting is good practice when polyfoam cushion is old and worn. Don't forget to featheredge the front of the cotton batting so you won't see division line under new cover.

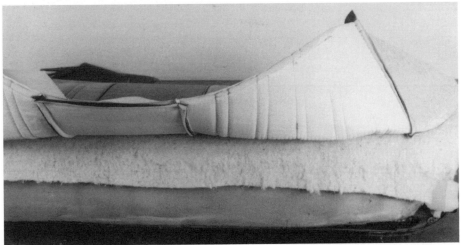

Position cover on seat very carefully. Cotton batting will tear with the least effort. If cover must be moved, lift it first. *Don't slide cover on batting.*

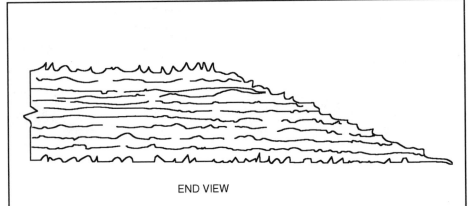

END VIEW

Featheredge cotton batting—taper to a knife edge—as shown in drawing.

hold the layer of cotton in place. With the other, strip off the edges of the cotton back about 1/3 of the width of the piece. The accompanying illustration gives you a better idea of how a feathered edge should look. Taper the edges gradually as you would a knife edge.

Placing a single layer of cotton over the seat is standard practice on any old seat that's to be covered. This is because use over time compresses the foam rubber and the new cover will need extra material to fill it out. This is not always the case with new foam. Sometimes the addition of cotton makes the new cover appear ill-fitting. So you'll have to make a judgment call when working with a relatively new seat. There's no question in the case of this old truck seat. I used a layer of cotton to cover the entire top of the seat.

Putting on the New Cover

Turn the cover inside out. Carefully position it on top of the cushion so the corners of the cover align with the corners of the cushion. If you misalign it, *lift* the cover before you move it. It won't slide on the cotton. It will tear the cotton if you try. So lift first, then move.

If you're right-handed, place

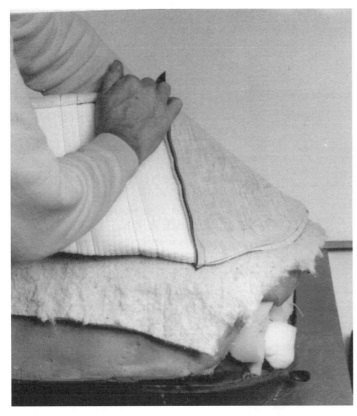

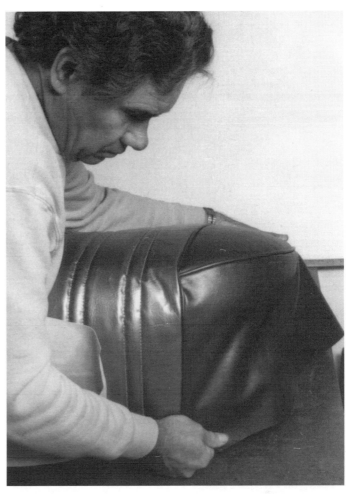

With cover turned inside out, hold cover tightly to seat with one hand. Then turn it right-side out over cushion with other hand. By measuring, or in some cases using special reference marks on frame, you'll be able to position cover accurately on seat.

your left hand on top of the cover on the seat's left (driver) front corner and hold it there. With your right hand, pull the cover right-side out down over the corner as shown. If you pull the cover over the corner without holding it in place, it may move out of position, tearing the cotton as it goes.

Use a trim pin or clamp to hold this corner in place and repeat the process again at the rear (left side) of the cushion. Now you have the left side positioned and pinned, turn your attention to the right side.

If you find that the cover appears 2 to 4 inches short of meeting the right edge, don't panic. There's lots of stretch in vinyl, particularly when it's pleated. The first thing to do is be sure the left side is pinned securely; you're going to pull it to the right. This time hold the front corner of the cover with your

Cover should look something like this after you've pulled it over seat.

Hog-ring cover at locating marks first. Here, I'm ringing welt between pleats and end facing. Do the other side next.

Below: Note how nicely J-hooks hold seat cover to frame. Fitting and sewing must be accurate here because "pulling harder" won't remove a wrinkle.

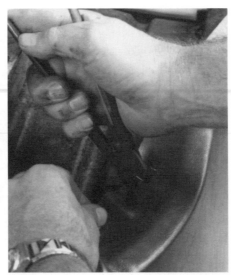

Go back and install two more hog-rings in corner to help hold things together. Space rings about 1 to 1-1/2 inches apart.

fasten the cover to the frame.

Turn the seat cushion upside down on the bench. Check first for pins, hog-rings or other sharp objects that could puncture your new cover. Put a hog-ring in the ring pliers and set it within reach on your bench. Push the seat down into the cover at one corner until it looks like the right *depth.* Usually you've gone deep enough when the wrinkles *just* pull out. While you're holding things together with one hand, grab your ring pliers with the other and clamp a ring over the welt. If you have no welt to ring to, double-over the vinyl or fabric and hog-ring directly into the material. Now let go.

How deep should you push the seat into the cover? That's up to you. Whatever looks good. Try not to collapse the front edge of the cushion, though. The seat needs springing action here. So, if you must pull the cover until the front edge collapses to get out wrinkles, you made the cover too big. Take it off, refit the cover, sew it back together and reinstall it. Don't do a cobble job by adding more cotton or foam to correct the problem. Fix it the right way. Then you're doing the work of a craftsman.

Move to the other side and repeat the process. Be sure both corners are of equal depth. Check it with a tape measure to be sure. On the project seat I set the J-hooks next. If your cover has any such hooks, set them now. If you have no hooks to deal with, set the rear corners. Generally there is little or no springing action at the rear corners, so you can pull them very tight. This is helpful if you have minor wrinkles that didn't come out on the initial pulling at the front corners.

Move back to the front of your cushion and hog-ring everything between the corners. Start from the center and work out to the corners. If you put a welt along the front of your cover, use your tape measure to be sure it stays

right hand. With your left hand, force the corner of the seat cushion into alignment with the cover corner. Using your right hand to hold everything in place, pull the cover down over the corner with your left hand.

What you must do is keep the corners of the cover in line with the corners of the seat cushion and peel them down. Do this while you're being careful not to tear the cotton or foam. Yes, it's difficult, but not impossible. Finish cover placement by pinning the right-front corner, then

peeling the right-rear corner into place. If you did everything right, the cover will be correctly positioned on the cushion and the welts will be standing up—welt-selvage edges pointing down—with no tears or lumps underneath.

If you must remove the cover to change its position, repair the cotton or make other adjustments, be careful! Use the same handwork described above to remove it. Hold the corner tightly in place with one hand while you peel up the cover with the other. When everything is in order,

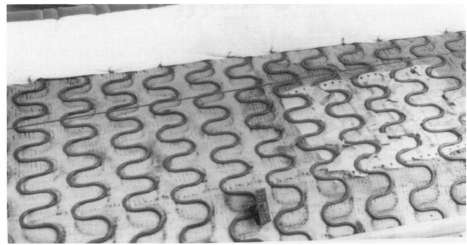

Normally there will be a wire inside the frame to which you can hog-ring cover. This seat, however, uses a J-hook at front as well as the back. Because I used a stretcher, I had to hog-ring to the springs. It works, but is not always the best solution because seat springs are in constant motion, which can cause excessive wear.

Heat gun does a great job at removing little wrinkles. *Be careful.* It's easy to burn or melt vinyl. To get an idea of how much heat the cover material will tolerate, cut a scrap of vinyl and put the heat gun to it. It is better to melt a piece of scrap than your cover.

straight and level in relation to the bottom of the frame. Here is one place where craftsmanship is noticed. Work to make the front edge "arrow-straight." If you have to cut out hog-rings in various places to make that edge straight, do it and take up or let out slack. If you think the bottom edge of the frame is bent or warped, use a straightedge to check that the welt is straight. Spend some time on the front edge and make it as straight as possible.

Finish up by hog-ringing the sides between the front and back corners. Check one side against the other to be sure they're the same height and shape. Be sure the welts stand up straight. If an area of welt is lying in the wrong direction, use a trim pin to turn the selvage. Do this by reaching in with the trim pin between the welt material and the vinyl face at the seam line. There should be no mark where the pin was inserted.

Removing Wrinkles from Vinyl

When everything is complete, remove small wrinkles with a heat gun or, lacking such, a hair dryer. If you're using a heat gun, hold it

about 10 to 12 inches from the offending wrinkle and turn it on. Direct the flow of hot air by slowly waving the heat gun over the wrinkle. Don't concentrate the heat in one spot. *Be very, very careful that you don't overheat the vinyl.* A heat gun can melt vinyl in a heartbeat if you get too close or fail to keep the flow of hot air moving. I move the heat gun with my right hand and constantly touch the vinyl with my left. When the vinyl gets too hot to touch, I know that's enough. Just short of getting things that hot, stop. If the wrinkle hasn't disappeared, it should as the vinyl cools.

The family hair drier won't begin to get as hot. It can be used within 1 or 2 inches from the vinyl and often does a satisfactory job.

Removing Wrinkles from Fabric

Removing wrinkles from fabric presents a different problem. You'll need steam. You can buy a plastic, portable hand steamer at a dress-fabric store at a reasonably low price. It can be used in a vertical position, unlike a regular steam iron. Also, unlike a steam iron, the sole plate won't get too hot. This

is an advantage because most trim fabrics are synthetic and melt easily under the heat of a steam iron. If you can't find one of these beauties, try this method. Spray a little clean water on the wrinkle, then use a hair dryer to heat it. This will generate steam in the wet area, removing the wrinkle.

Don't use this method on velvet. It will make the nap go every which way. A steamer, however, does wonders with velvet nap. It makes the nap lie down beautifully.

MAKING THE BACK CUSHION COVER

Fitting & Sewing

The back cushion is fitted just as the seat cushion. End pieces and end facings are fitted first. Turn back to page 59 to see how the end facing is fitted for the project seat. Here, I'm faced with fitting a compound curve. To develop the curve, I cut a giant *dart* in the corner. This term comes from the shape the fold makes. Darts are used in all sewing trades.

After sewing the darts, I sew the end pieces and end facings together to form end caps just as I

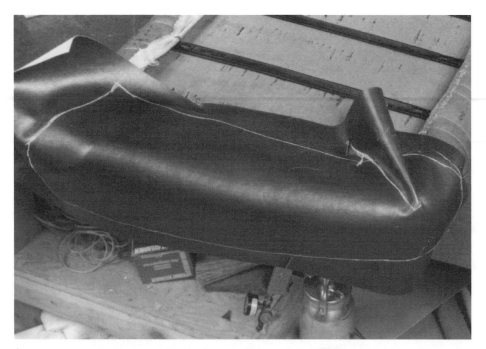

Top to bottom: Things are getting a bit more complicated now in the seat-cover-fitting process. Vinyl end piece is pulled around curve and excess is gathered into a *dart* then cut away.

Fitting is finished. Sew edges of dart together first. Note seam allowance bordering chalk line.

As with the seat cushion, pieces will become back-cushion end caps when sewn together.

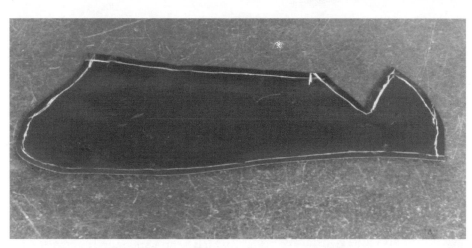

did for the cushion cover. Then, I sewed these to the pleated section.

To finish sewing, *hem* the outside back on three sides. Fold the edge of the material over about 1/2 inch and sew a seam along it. It gives the vinyl a finished edge. Then, sew a listing to the bottom inside edge to finish.

Installing the Cover
The trick now is to put a layer of cotton on the back and pull on the cover. The project cover presented little problem. As with the cushion cover, I laid the back cover on, held it in place with one hand, and peeled it over with the other. *However,* to get the end caps wrapped around the top, I had to warm the vinyl with a heat gun. This made it limp and stretchy, allowing me to to peel it around without tearing the vinyl. Again, if you don't have a heat gun, use a hair dryer; it's the next best.

You may run into another problem with your seat back. Many back cushions, especially those with a *split back*— a bench seat with separate back cushions that tilt forward to allow access behind it from each side—have a cover made somewhat like a sock. The cover, closed on all sides except the bottom, is pulled down over the back just as you'd pull a sock over your foot. Two things to help you do this are cheesecloth and silicone spray. Silicone spray is for spraying on foams and fabrics to make them slippery. It's available at your local trim supplier or Sears.

Cheesecloth is available at most hardware and auto-paint-supply stores. After placing a layer of cotton over the back cushion, wrap it well with one layer of cheesecloth. Use masking tape or other light tape to hold the cheesecloth together. Turn the cover inside out. Spray the inside of the cover and outside of the cheesecloth. Now, pull the cover on over the back cushion. The cheesecloth will hold the cotton in place and protect it from tearing while the silicone spray provides lubrication. The cover should slide on nicely. Production shops use a very thin plastic film similar to the plastic bags put on clothes at the dry cleaners. This film does the same job as the combination of cheesecloth and silicone.

Returning to our project seat, I next insert a wire through the listing sewn into the outside back. This provides a concealed place to hog-ring. I hog-ring the material to the frame starting at the corners, then fill in from the center out. Finally, I ring the edge wire on the outside back to the edge wire at the bottom of the back-cushion cover, then use the heat gun to remove any wrinkles.

The last step is to assemble the back cushion to the seat cushion, put the seat back into the vehicle and, in the case of our project seat, call the customer.

CONCLUSION

No matter how simple your first project may have been, you should have learned a lot—how to fit, sew and install a seat cover. In many quarters this is called *upholstering* a seat rather than *making a seat cover.* Upholstery connotes a more sophisticated,

Finished end caps: Note J-hooks sewn to sides.

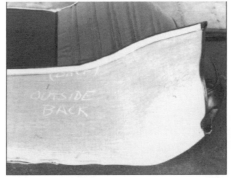 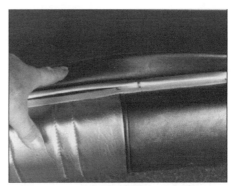

A 3-inch strip of muslin is folded in half and sewed to outside back, another to bottom of cover. After cover is installed I insert a stiff wire into both listings and hog-ring them together, right. This holds cover on and gives outside a finished appearance.

better-fitting, finer-crafted piece of work. So, let's call your job a newly *upholstered* seat.

In the next chapter I detail a more difficult seat project. It includes rebuilding the seat from the springs out.

Finished cover on assembled seat. Even the "big guy" can sit on it in comfort.

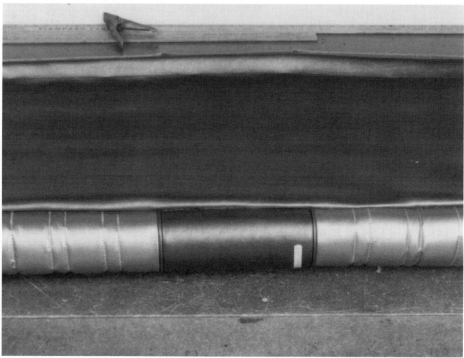

Finished back as viewed from the top.

6 Advanced Seat Building

In Chapter 5, I showed how to complete your first genuine auto-trim project; upholstering a "simple" bench seat. At the time it probably didn't seem very simple. But you survived and should now be ready to move on to more advanced work. Now you can try your hand at a few new tricks.

This 1963 Studebaker Hawk bench seat presents some new problems. Rather than being top-sewn, the pleats are *blind-stitched,* that is the seams are hidden from view. In addition, each pleat panel is set low into the seat to give a "bucket" appearance. This is accomplished with the use of a listing and listing wire. Finally, as with most seats that are this old, this cushion must be rebuilt from the springs up. Let's dig into the project and see what you can learn.

MAKING THE CUSHION TOP

As usual, I begin by measuring, then cutting my pieces into rectangles, or blocks. Again, this cover will be fitted to the seat as opposed to cutting the old cover apart and using it for patterns. Can you imagine all that work only to have the seat look just like it did before you started?

Refering to the photo above,

This is the seat-cushion cover we're replacing. It was a "quick-and-dirty" replica of the factory original.

note that the top of the cushion is made from one piece of vinyl. Cutouts were made for the pleated sections. From the car's owner I learned this was not exactly how the original cushion was made. The factory made the top from five pieces. A French seam joined each corner and a French *V-seam* in the center—see photos on the next page.

I made up the term *V-seam* for descriptive purposes. There are an infinite number of seam patterns. To name each would require an infinite number of names. Most trimmers are far too busy to spend time defining the pattern of each seam. I create my own names, hence the V-seam.

To establish seam location on new material, I first make a few measurements from the centerline out. These measurements define end points of the seams. I then fold the vinyl on lines that join these points. If your project is something like this and you're unsure of your measuring abilities, try the following.

On the old seat cover, find the centerline and mark it. At each corner of the pleats make a dot. At the center of the radius of each front corner, make a dot. If you don't think you can eyeball the center of the curve at the front edge, cut a piece of chipboard about 30-inches square. Connect any two opposite corners with a

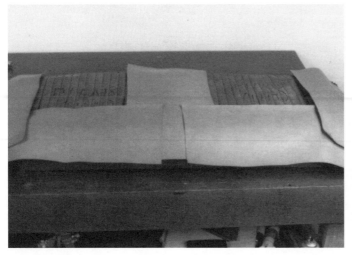

Begin fitting cover by laying out five pieces in their respective positions, then follow up by marking the seam lines. Each piece is folded over where a seam will be.

Use plenty of pins to hold pieces in place. Place pins where holes won't be seen in finished product.

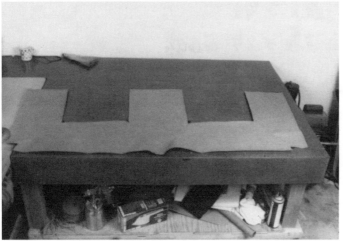

Finished cushion top: Note French seams and reinforcing tape that can be seen at ends of seams. Strength is primary reason for using French seams.

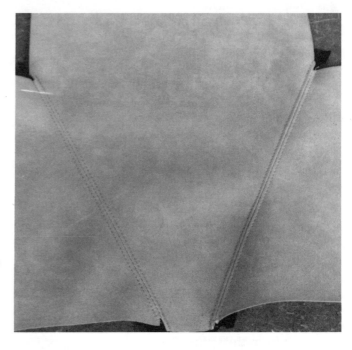

line. Lay this on the seat and align the front and side edge of the chipboard with the front and side edge of each pleat panel. The diagonal line should lie directly over the radius of the corner of the seat. Shove a trim pin through the chipboard where the diagonal line crosses the center of the corner radius. Now you have a pin prick that should be close to the center of the radius. Draw a line from the dot at the corner of the pleats to the dot at the corner of the seat edge. Do this on each side.

At the centerfront edge of the seat where the centerline meets the welt, measure 2 inches out from each side of the centerline and make a dot. Connect these dots with the corresponding dot at the inside corner of the pleats. Now you have the location for each of the four seams.

Fold and pin the vinyl along these seam lines. Make sure the material lies flat and smooth. Pull the material tight, but not so tight that the seams open or pull away from their mates. Now, chalk a line on each piece along the

fold(s), making a few marks to indicate where each piece goes and where you should start the seam(s).

Sew the five pieces together with reinforced French seams just as you practiced in Chapter 2. The accompanying photos show how the finished product should look. Now let's make the blind-stitched pleats I mentioned at the beginning of this chapter.

**Blind-stitched Pleats—
Things to Consider**
Whether you're top-stitching or blind-stitching pleats, as in all

HOW TO LOCATE SEAMS ACCURATELY

On the old seat cover, find the centerline and mark it. At each corner of the pleats make a dot. At the center of the radius of each front corner, make a dot. You may want to cut a piece of chipboard about 30-inches square. Connect any two opposite corners with a line.

Lay this on the seat and align the front and side edge of the chipboard with the front and side edge of each pleat panel. The diagonal line should lie directly over the radius of the corner of the seat.

Shove a trim pin through the chipboard where the diagonal line crosses the center of the corner radius. Now you have a pin prick that should be close to the center of the radius. Draw a line from the dot at the corner of the pleats to the dot at the corner of the seat edge. Do this on each side.

At the center front edge of the seat where the centerline meets the welt, measure 2 inches out from each side of the centerline and make a dot. Connect these dots with the corresponding dot at the inside corner of the pleats. Now you have the location for each of the four seams.

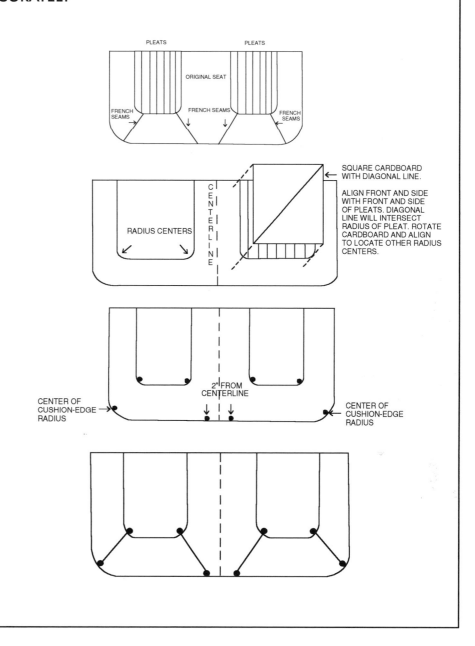

cases in this business, you must start with a centerline. When the panel has an odd number of pleats, this centerline will fall in the middle of the center pleat. When there is an even number, it will fall *between* the two center pleats. If you don't adhere to this rule, the pleats will not be the same on each side of the panel.

When blind-stitching pleats, allow 1/2-inch extra material for seam allowance to make each pleat. This is not the case with top-stitched pleats where no seam

allowance is necessary.

Blind-stitched pleats tend to "shrink" even more than top-stitched pleats. After marking out and sewing 10 2-inch pleats, the finished panel should measure 20 inches. Right? Wrong! It will measure anywhere from as little as 18 inches to 19-1/2 inches.

A 19-1/2-inch-wide blind-stitched pleat panel can easily be stretched to 20 inches. At 18 inches it's impossible. I solve this problem by making a 4-inch-tall panel from scrap before I begin. If

I have to add anything, I simply measure the sample panel to find out exactly how much. On the 18-inch example, I found I needed to add about a 3/16 inch to each pleat. To be completely honest, though, because 3/16 inch is too hard to measure, I added 1/4 inch to each pleat. I then fudged a little when sewing each seam to use up the extra 1/2 inch.

The final consideration is the stretch of the material. Most materials, vinyl in particular, stretch more one way than the other. To

Working out from centerline, layout lines for folds in blind-stitched pleats. Use centerline even if it falls in middle of center pleat. As with our project, centerline fell between two pleats because there was an even number of them.

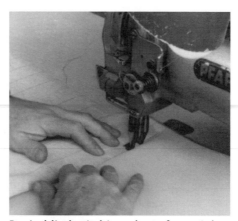

Begin blind-stitching pleats from right edge of material and left edge of foam as you view them. As you fold over each pleat one by one, left edge of material will finish along right edge of foam.

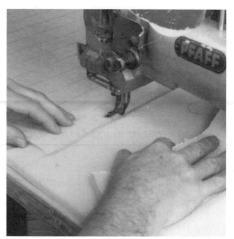

First seam is finished. Note 1/4-inch seam allowance rather than the usual 1/2-inch allowance.

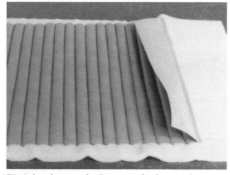

Finished panel: Sew end pleats down so insert will be easier to handle. Top-sew along outside edge to prevent stitching from showing on finished product.

determine which way a material stretches most, simply try stretching it! You should see that it stretches easier in one direction than the other. On vinyl, the direction of maximum stretch is usually *across* the roll. Run the length of the pleats in the direction of *least* stretch. This places the stretch where it's needed—across the panel. This also gives finished pleats a neater appearance.

Let's make some pleats.

Fabricating Pleats

Making blind-stitched pleats is both a science and an art. You can lay them out to within a 1/16 inch, but it takes real care to sew them correctly. Do it as I described above and make at least one short practice panel before you attempt to make a panel for your project. Why chance ruining your $80-per-yard mohair? Ruin some $1-per-yard material first!

The factory seat had 16 1-1/2-inch pleats with 1-inch pleats at each end. This made a total of 18 pleats in a finished 26-inch-wide panel. After making my 4 X 26-inch sample, I discovered I needed to add about 1/8 inch to each pleat. My final measurement for each pleat was 2-1/8 inches: the pleat width of 1-1/2 inches, plus a 1/2-inch seam allowance, plus the 1/8-inch additional needed to make up for the short-fall.

I began with a centerline and measured out eight 2-1/8-inch pleats on each side. If there'd been an odd number of pleats, I would have measured 1-1/16 inch on each side of the centerline for the center pleat, making it 2-1/8 inches wide. I left plenty of material for the two outside pleats, but didn't lay them out. They will fall into place on their own when I fit the panel for welt.

The 1/2-inch scrim-back foam for backing is laid out next. A centerline wasn't needed here. I laid out 16 1-5/8-inch pleats—1-1/2 + 1/8 inches—leaving about 2 inches on each side for the outside pleats. I added about 2 inches to the top and bottom. This way my material didn't wander off the top or bottom of the foam. At this point I sewed the vinyl to the foam.

At the sewing machine, lay the material face down on the table. At the right edge, fold the material together so it's face-to-face along the first seam line. Crease this line firmly using the handle of your scissors. This will help keep it folded while you sew.

The first step is to sew the right edge line of the material to the left edge line on the foam. It will be easier if you roll up the foam and push it under the throat of the machine. Use a 1/4-inch seam allowance—sew in to your left, 1/4 inch from the line you just creased. Center the material over the foam which should have been cut a total of 4 inches larger than the material. Be sure to lock your stitch at the beginning and end.

The first full pleat is completed by folding the material over to the next seam line and repeating the above procedure. Either continue creasing the line as you did to start the first pleat or just press it down with your fingers. Sew and fold, sew and fold until you reach the last seam line. To keep the end pleats from "flapping in the breeze," sew down the end pleats. I let mine flap because it's just two less seams to sew when I'm trying to hustle along.

Making a Panel Pattern

To fit the new pleat panels I made a pattern. I did this because I had four places to use it, making the job easier and more accurate. The four places included the two panels and the areas into which they fit. To make my pattern, I selected a piece of scrap vinyl and pinned it to the seat. I then marked out the exact line of the panel beneath it using the welt as a guide. This will be the seam line *with no seam allowance.*

If you make a pattern like I just described, remember to *add* the seam allowance when you cut out the finished piece. I cut directly on the line, then added the seam allowance to the finished piece.

Tip: If pattern piece is to be symmetrical, fold it in half so its edges align. If the two halves aren't exactly the same, trim the larger half to match the smaller one. This will give you a finished piece that's symmetrical about its centerlines. While you have the pattern folded, mark its center. This will help in future alignment. Unless both of your panels are identical, mark the pattern for the right and left sides. Now, transfer your vinyl pattern to chipboard. This gives further assurance that all pieces will be the same. Chipboard is easier to trace around.

Using the Pattern

Take the pleat panels and panel pattern you just finished to your bench. Stretch out the pleat panel and tack it to the bench. (If you don't want to mar your bench top with tack holes, tack to a piece of plywood instead.) Make sure the panel is square and the exact size you want.

It's important to make sure the panels are square. I use a

framing square to check alignment as I tack down the panel. If it's not square, the pleats will be at an angle relative to the frame of the job on which you're working. Be careful here.

Lay the pattern on the pleat panel and match the center lines. Chalk a line around the edge of the pattern. Because you transferred the vinyl pattern to chipboard, the chalk line should come out smooth and accurate. Flip the pattern over and layout the second panel.

Because the pattern is frequently uniform on all sides, you could make the other side without turning the pattern over. Unfortunately, this is not always the case. Suppose, for instance, the inboard radius was narrower than the outboard radius. If you fail to turn the pattern over, the narrow radius would be on the outboard side. Make it a habit to always turn the pattern over for a "mirror image."

Stitching the Pleat Panel

Your first tendency will be to cut on the line you just drew. *Stop!* There are two things you must do first: add the 1/2-inch seam allowance and top-stitch the outboard pleats so they don't open. This is done in one operation.

With those two points in mind, top-stitch a seam 1/2 inch *out* from the chalk line. Then trim away the selvage right up to the seam. The panel will now have the correct seam allowance and your pleats will not pull out at the edges. OK, now the pros will jump on me. They'll ask, "Why not just sew the welt to the panel on the chalk line and trim afterwards?" Well, they're right. That's the way it's done in production shops. But again, you're in no hurry. Neatness is king and the method I describe is the best way to learn.

Here's a sewing tip. As you make your top-stitch seam, stretch the pleats the same as they were on the bench. This will maintain

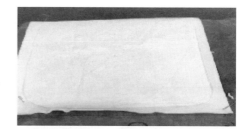

Top to bottom: Step 1—Make pattern for pleat insert. You could fit each insert individually, but this ensures each panel and cutout will be the same. Step 2—More accuracy is possible if you transfer pattern to a piece of chipboard. Step 3—Pattern made from chipboard is easy to work with, allowing you to draw accurate chalk lines. Note end pleats tacked down. I didn't sew them down as I suggested you do earlier. Step 4—Remember when you're using such a pattern, that chalk line is the seam line, not the cutting line. Maintain the 1/2-inch seam allowance.

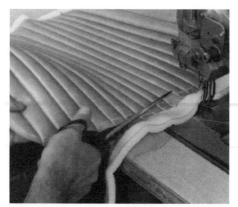

Trim right to seam line, but don't cut through it.

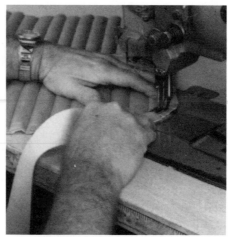

Left: Sewing on welt is a snap now. None of the threads will unravel, allowing pleats to open. When sewing welt to panel, remember to clip welt material so it will round corner. This will allow it to stay flat and not stretch.

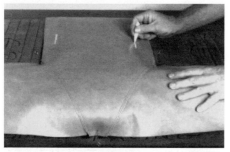

I'm using chalk marks as reference to position pleat-panel inserts at inboard edges. Other reference marks are French seams at each corner. Finally, I lay a 60-inch measuring stick along front to ensure correct front-edge alignment.

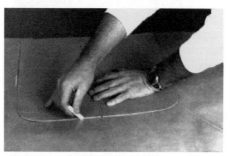

Use same cardboard pattern for making cutout that you used for making pleat panels. Note side and corner alignment of seams.

Chalk line is again the seam line.

the correct finished size and it will keep the pleats from puckering under the needle. Now you can sew welts to each panel. Remember to make a few slashes in the corner to release tension on the welt material so it will be easier to turn the corner.

Fitting Pleat Panels to Cushion Top
Set aside the finished panels and put the seat cushion on the bench. Place the new cushion top on the seat cushion and align it in the position in which it was fitted. For the project seat I aligned the seams so they fell directly on the centers of each radius to which I fitted them earlier. I then pinned it in place. This is done to position the pleat panels exactly where you want them.

On the project seat, I marked the location of the inboard welts and got a rough location of the front welts. I refined the front location later with a straight edge after I had the cushion top on the bench.

Remove the cushion top and lay it flat on the bench. Lay the pleat pattern on the cushion top and align it with the reference marks you just made. Chalk a line around the pattern and do the same with the other one. Be sure to mark the centerline of each panel on the cushion top. This is very important because you'll use it to align the pleats and begin your sewing.

After you've finished sewing, trim off the selvage, but don't cut on the line. Remember to leave the 1/2-inch seam allowance. I keep emphasizing this because I've forgotten it myself more than I wish to remember. So be wise.

Don't cut on the chalk line. Flip over the pattern and do the other panel.

Sewing Pleat Panels to Cushion Top
At the machine, lay the left pleat panel faceup on the table with the centerline pointing to the left side of the needle. Turn the cushion top left side facedown on the panel and align the notch in the cushion top with the centerline of the panel. Lift the sewing-machine presser feet and place this bundle under the needle. Keep everything aligned. Starting at the center mark, begin sewing.

When you reach the corner of the panel, set the needle into the material and make a slash in the cushion-top selvage right up to the needle with your scissors. Begin the turn; sew a few more stitches; plant the needle; make another slash, then sew a few more stitches. Continue this until you've made it around the corner.

Be careful not to stretch the cushion-top material as you round the corner. This is why you need to make the slashes; to relieve stretching. Finish sewing down the side. Lock the stitch at the end of the seam and remove the cover from the machine. You've finished one side.

Turn the bundle over and place it back in the machine at the same place you started the first seam. Back up about 2 inches to lock the stitches, then start sewing. This time when you reach the corner, you won't have to slash it because the cushion-top material is on the bottom. The feed dog under the needle prevents the material from stretching. Ease around the corner and finish off by sewing along the outboard side. You now have a pleat panel sewn into the cushion top. But you're not quite finished.

You must sew a listing to each pleat panel. For the project seat I cut a 4-inch-wide strip of muslin, folded it in half and used a 1/2-inch seam allowance. This made it finish 1-1/2 inches deep.

On your project, measure the old listing or measure the distance from where the listing connects to the frame or springs to the top of the padding. This will give you your finished measurement.

To sew the listing to the cushion-top assembly, arrange the assembly so the pleat panel is faceup and the cushion top is facedown. From the rear edge, insert the seam under the needle as if you were going to sew the whole thing together again. Fold the listing material in half with the folded edge pointing to your left. Lay it on the seam and begin sewing. Be sure to maintain a 1/2-inch seam allowance. Now the cushion-top assembly is finished.

Above: With pleat panel positioned to cushion top, start sewing in middle and sew across half of front and down one side. Turn the whole works over and sew other half of front, then the other side.

Top right: Finished insert without wrinkles or stretches in corners.

SEAT BUILDING

Before I could finish fitting, sewing and installing the cover for the project seat, I had to rebuild the seat. The padding was more than 25 years old and had compacted, disintegrated and moved around. A cover fitted to a seat in this condition wouldn't have looked good. So follow me as I rebuild this seat cushion, then finish fitting the cover.

To start with, everything had

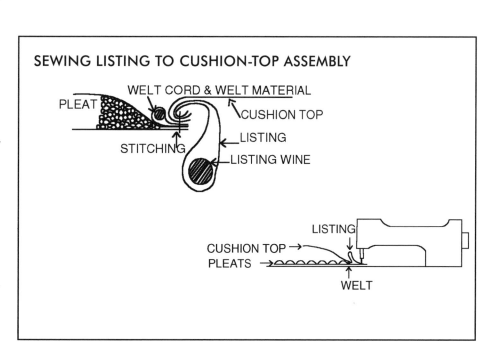

Finish by sewing listing to selvage of each panel insert. Determine width of listing by thickness of seat padding. On some boat seats I've had to use 6-inch-wide listings. This accommodated 6-inch-thick foam on a plywood base.

SEWING LISTING TO CUSHION-TOP ASSEMBLY

PLEAT

WELT CORD & WELT MATERIAL

CUSHION TOP

LISTING

STITCHING

LISTING WINE

LISTING

CUSHION TOP →

PLEATS →

WELT

With everything stripped off, it can no longer be called a *seat cushion*. Now it's a *spring unit*. Be sure to check everything carefully and replace any broken parts. Springs may be hog-ringed to edge wire. Originally they were attached with a fastener called a *Baker clip*. These clips and the tool to install them are very difficult to find. I lost mine, so if you find two pairs, I'm interested in one of them.

Rebuilding spring unit begins by adding new layer of burlap over springs.

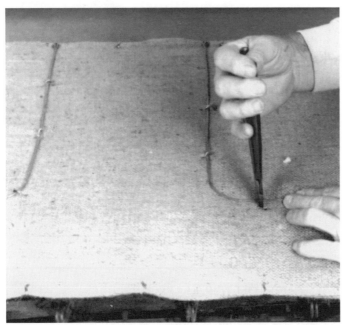

Replace the anchor wire for the listing. Be sure you position new wire correctly or you won't be able to fasten the pleat panel to the spring unit. Mark its location before you remove the old one.

When you add jute felt, leave grooves so you'll have room to anchor the listings. To prevent jute from moving, stitch it to spring unit. Use an 8-inch curved needle and nylon button twine. Take several big stitches through jute, into burlap and around springs. Tie it off when you're done.

to be removed down to the springs. When you reach this point it's no longer a seat; it's simply a *spring unit*. I then removed the wires to which the listings were fastened. If your spring unit has such wires, mark their locations so you can put them back in the same place. Check for broken springs, broken wires and bent or damaged frame members. Repair anything that's broken.

The easiest way to make repairs is to buy an old seat from the auto-salvage yard. It needn't be an exact replacement unless the frame of your seat is destroyed. Use parts from the old seat to repair your spring unit. If a frame member is broken, have it welded. For a really neat job and to prevent rust, paint the spring unit before covering it. Gloss black in an aerosol can is the usual color.

Covering Spring Unit with Burlap
When repairs are finished, cover the top of the spring unit with a

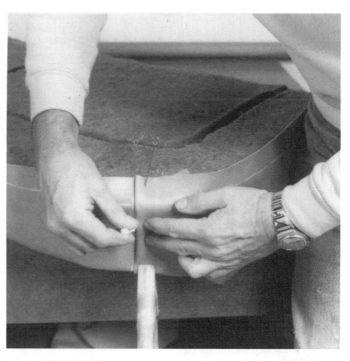

Cushion-top assembly is fitted to spring unit after first layer of jute has been attached.

Right: Although it's hard to see in photo, this is a compound curve at the corner. A seam here prevents bunching. This was also the way it was done by the factory, so seams must be duplicated in new cover.

layer of burlap. As with all such materials, you can get this at your fabric-supply house. Use hog-rings to fasten it to the top. Generally, you'll only cover the top, not the sides.

After covering the project-seat spring unit with burlap, I hog-ringed the anchor wires back in place. It's to this wire that I fastened the listings on the pleat panels. I was careful to mark their locations to ensure they went back in the right place.

The next step is to place a layer of jute felt over the burlap. Make cutouts or grooves for the listings—see photo on left. The jute felt is fastened to the spring unit with hog-rings.

There's still a lot of padding yet to be added. In the case of the project seat, because it was mostly cotton and, therefore, quite bulky, I finished fitting the cover to what I had at this stage. This gave the cover a good fit. Then I added padding as I went and fastened the cover to the seat.

Final Seat Cover Fitting
Clamp and pin the cushion-top assembly to the partially padded spring unit. Make certain the pleats are aligned over the wires

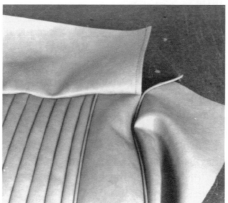

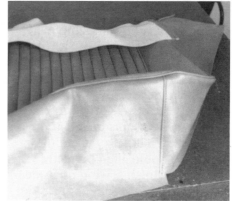

Close-ups of finished cover.

to which the listings will be fastened. Now chalk a line all around the edge. Make as many reference marks as you may need.

On the project seat I marked the spring unit with a centerline and each corner where the seam crossed the center of the radius. When I joined the facings, I wanted the corner seams to align with the top seams.

I fitted the cushion facings in three pieces as was done by the factory. One piece went across the front and two at each end. The customer gave me the factory location of these seams. I measured out from the centerline the same distance on both sides so both seams would end up in the

same relative positions.

I pinned and clamped the three face pieces to the spring unit, marked the location of the seams, marked the center, then chalked a line around the top edge. This corresponded to the line I drew on the cushion-top assembly. After this I sewed everything together. (All of these lines are seam lines.) When I trimmed the selvage I *instinctively* left a seam allowance.

Final Seat Cover Sewing
Begin final assembly of the seat cover by sewing a welt to the cushion-top assembly. Leave a 5- to 6-inch "tail" at each end. This will cover any extension of the

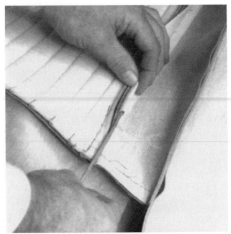

Old listing wire goes into listing. Don't try to hog-ring listing without using a wire. It will "telegraph" the pull of the hog-ring up to the material.

I pad seats a little at a time to prevent tearing cotton as I attach cover. I pad with cotton only the area in which I'm working. If I attempt to pad the entire seat at one time, I usually end up tearing the cotton as I move or adjust the cover.

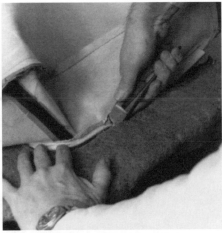

Ring listing to anchor wire all the way around. Place a ring every 4 to 6 inches. One should go at each corner and end.

cushion facing beyond the back edge of the cushion.

Sew the cushion facing to the cushion assembly. Find and match the centerline. I usually start by placing the cushion-top assembly faceup and the cushion facing facedown. Sew from the centerline out. Check as you go to be sure the end seams match at the radius. Pull a little, push a little and they should align perfectly. When you finish sewing one side, flip it over and sew the other side. Remember to overstitch about 2 inches at the beginning to lock the

first stitch in place. Finally, on the project seat, I sewed a stretcher across the back to complete the cushion cover.

Before you can call your cover finished, test fit it to the seat. To do this, lay the cover out, pull the facing down and put a few pins in to hold it in place. Carefully check its fit. If anything is wrong, now's the time to correct it. After the test fit showed everything was in order, I began installing the finished cover.

Padding & Installing Cover

Before I could install the cushion

cover, I had to put the old wire in the listing. This can be difficult, especially if the old wire is rusty. This will often be the case on a seat from an older car. If your wire is too rusty, replace it. Coathanger wire is a perfect replacement. But if the old listing wire isn't too rusty, clean it with steel wool or sandpaper.

If you replace the wire, use a pair of needle-nose pliers to make a tight loop at one end. This is the end you'll insert into the listing. The loop prevents the wire from snagging as you pass it through the listing. To make the job even easier, spray the wire with silicone.

To get the wire into the listing material, push it as far as it will go. Force the listing to bunch up over the wire until it will go no farther. Then *pull* the wire—grab it by the loop—until the wrinkles in the listing material pull out. Repeat this process until you round the corner. The wire can then be pushed up to the next corner. Again, force a bunch of the listing material onto the front of the wire, pull the wire until the wrinkles smooth out and you round the curve.

This process is similar to putting on your socks. You bundle the sock up until you reach the heel. Then you stick your foot in

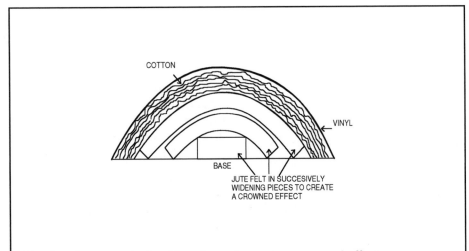

Use jute in successively wider pieces to create a crowned effect.

REINFORCING SEAT CORNERS

Usually, on an old seat such as the project seat, the springs have weakened from use. This is especially true for the springs at the front corners. As the driver and passenger slide in and out, these springs take the brunt of that movement.

Often you'll find one of these springs has broken, particularly the one on the driver's side. Fortunately, this was not the case with our project seat. It was very weak, however. And because considerable stretch of the cushion-cover material may be required to remove the wrinkles at the front corners, it may be necessary to reinforce these springs. Following is a quick, but satisfactory way to reinforce a coil spring.

Begin by wading up a ball of cotton and forcing it into the center of the spring. Be sure much of it hangs out between the coils. In the same fashion, continue packing it with cotton until you can't see the spring. It's very important that the cotton extends out between the coils. The idea is to prevent the spring from compressing excessively.

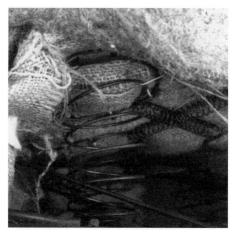

To help it support the corner, pack cotton into coil spring until it won't accept any more. Here you see spring from no cotton to all I could jam into it.

When the spring is full, pack in more cotton around it for added support. Now the spring should only collapse about 30 percent of its original size when it's loaded. You can pull the cover as tightly as you need to remove the wrinkles without collapsing the corner.

and "unbundle" the sock over your toes and up to the heel. Then you bundle the sock again until your toes meet the toe of the sock. Finally, you smooth out the material over your foot and heel and you're "all socked up." Treat the selvage material and wire in a similar manner. Work at it and you'll get the wire around both corners. We do this daily in the shop.

After you've installed the other wire, you should be ready to install the seat cover. As I demonstrated on the project seat, follow along on your seat. I began by putting a layer of cotton over the area where the pleat panel was to be positioned. I did this to the driver's side only so the passenger's side won't get mussed up while I'm working.

I *carefully* laid the cover over the seat, making sure the listing on the pleat panel falls neatly into the groove and is correctly aligned. After double-checking I hog-ringed the front of the listing to its anchor wire on the spring unit. Again, I checked to see that nothing moved or was out of alignment. After I was satisfied that all was well, I hog-ringed the entire listing. When you do yours, be sure you get a ring in each corner. It is tricky to do on the inside corner. You'll probably have to do some considerable pulling.

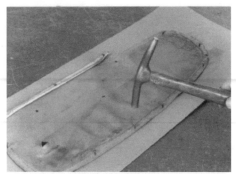

To get a more accurate pattern, tack old piece of material over a piece of chipboard rather than trying to hold it in place by hand.

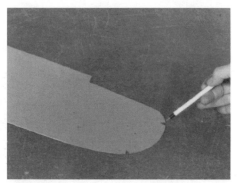

Don't forget to include reference marks on pattern.

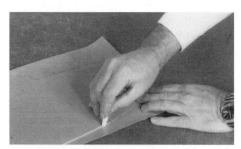

With chipboard pattern, you can obtain better accuracy and symmetrical pieces.

USING AN OLD COVER PIECE FOR A PATTERN

Although you should learn to fit a cover to a seat frame, sometimes there will be no way out but to use a piece of the old cover as a pattern. Following is the most accurate way to do it:

Use a single-edge razor blade to cut the thread around the piece you wish to use. Some pros cut the material at the seam line, but I think its more accurate to leave the selvage on. One reason is you'll get the factory reference marks.

After removing the desired piece, it must be laid out perfectly flat in order to determine its original shape. To do this you can use two processes. First, if it's vinyl, heat it so it will lie flat. If the piece is fabric, use a steam iron to achieve the same results. After the piece is as flat and straight as possible, tack the material to your bench or a piece of plywood with a piece of chipboard beneath it. This holds it in place, keeps it straight and lets you work out any wrinkles that may form.

Finally, mark around the material and include all reference marks on the chipboard. After cutting it out, you have an accurate pattern.

seat. If too much padding was wrapped over the edge of the seat, it would've bulged out beneath the welt after the cover was pulled over.

In the center of the cushion I added two layers of jute felt. This area needed to be *crowned*—raised and rounded—a little more than the rest of the cushion. As a side note, if you wish to build a large crown, start with a narrow strip of jute felt, say 1/3 to 1/2 the width of the finished crown. Make each successive layer of felt a little wider. When the cover is pulled over, you'll have a well-rounded crown.

After building up the jute crown, I covered it with cotton. Two layers did the trick. Then, I placed one layer over the indent where the right pleat panel would go.

The next big step is to pull the cover across the crown and ring the pleat panel to the spring unit. I pulled it across and hog-ringed the inboard listing wire first. I then laid the panel into position, hog-ringing the outboard side and then the front. As before, I paid special attention to the corners and installed a hog-ring at the center of each. To finish, I put a layer of cotton on top of the jute felt. In this case I let it hang over the edge to pad the rough edge of the jute felt and hog-rings.

The final step is to pull the cushion-cover facing down and hog-ring it in place. As described in the previous chapter, page 64, hold the corner in place with one hand while you peel the facing over the edge of the seat. As you can see in the photo (center right), I used a heat gun to warm the vinyl. This made it more flexible, thus easier to pull out those wrinkles in the corners.

This completed the cushion-rebuilding job. How does it look? The customer was happy, which is the final test. How does yours look?

Sometimes you can hold hog-ring pliers similar to how actors hold butcher knives in "grab-'n'-stab" movies, hook the wire with the hog-ring and pull it into place. This works where all else fails. After ringing the panel in place, check to see if it lays smooth and wrinkle-free. At this point I added a lot of padding.

I wanted the pleat panels to be lower than the cushion top so it would have the "bucket-seat" appearance. To do this, I "raised" the cushion top above these panels. I did this by adding more padding under the cushion top by first adding one more layer of jute felt all the way around. I trimmed this layer flush with the edge of the

SUMMARY

By doing the project in this chapter you were able to vastly improve your range of skills. Blind-sewn pleats are about the most difficult sewing operation a trimmer will do. Inserting them is probably next.

Using the chipboard pattern helps, however, especially in getting everything aligned. If you remember to make plenty of reference marks and sew from the center both ways just as you hog-ring from the center out, your work should line up neatly and accurately.

When you install second layer of jute, cut it flush with edge of seat. Don't get too much bulk here because you used cushion edge to fit cover.

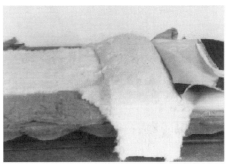

Note built-up crown at center. This was done with jute and cotton. On an old seat, use old-style materials to retain the right "look." A crown of Polyfoam would look and feel "wrong."

Hog-ring inboard edge first. If you try to do front first, you won't be able to get to inboard side of pleat panels.

Thank the inventor of the heat gun! Before we had heat guns, we used heat lamps. Using a heat lamp in winter wasn't too bad, but on a typical summer day it was . . . well . . . hot!

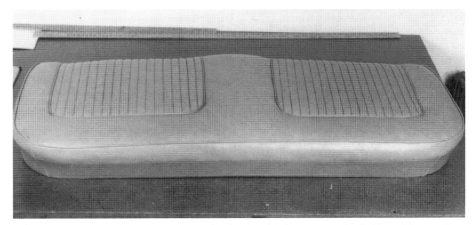

Finished product: The customer and I think it looks pretty good. My critique of the seat is it could've had more padding under the cushion top. Pleat panels would have looked even deeper.

7

Late-model Seat
With Bucket Seats, Headrests & Center Armrests

In the previous chapters, we worked on products of the '60s and '70s. These are excellent learning projects because they're quite forthright and simple, have little or no high-tech engineering or materials, and are readily available to be worked on. Now, we're going to put all your newly acquired skills to work on a late-model interior.

For our example I've selected a 1989 BMW with bucket seats, headrests, and a center armrest in the rear bench seat. This arrangement is common in late-model automobiles.

The customer made one of the common requests heard today: remove the vinyl in the body of the covers and replace it with a fabric. Whether you're a resident of the southwest or the northeast, vinyl can become uncomfortably hot, hot, hot in the summer and cold, cold, cold in the winter.

In the vocabulary of the trade this type of work is called an "insert job." We'll be "inserting" a cloth body into the existing vinyl. Rather than replacing all the materials we'll carefully remove

This looks more like the "after" than the "before," yet this is what the customer wants: new cloth inserts. Trim shops do this all the time.

much of the vinyl coming in contact with the customer's body and replace it with cloth. The remainder of the seat stays. Our project seat will be finished in a gray-black, tweed-style velour.

All of the major techniques you have learned so far will be used in this job. Then, we'll add a few new ones. Contrary to what I said in the last chapters, you'll learn to use the old material as a pattern. You'll see some tricks the auto industry created to do away with listings and discover a number of short cuts that speed things along. So, let's take a look at our job and get started.

ESTIMATING YARDAGE

By now this should be a snap for you. You shouldn't need to make a drawing, just take the face measurements, block them out in your mind and come up with the required number of yards.

The cushions are a bit over 1/2 yard; the seat backs are a bit under 2/3 yard. Each is less than 27-inches wide. Therefore, you should need 1-1/2 yards to do the buckets. The rear bench seat will need another 1-1/2 yards but is right at 54-inches wide in the cushion and a bit more across the back. If you add another yard of material this will give you end caps for the rear cushion with

After removing the reveal molding we can see this is no simple hinge. Before disassembling be certain you can assemble it again. Make drawings, take Polaroid pictures or keep its partner together until you've asssembled this one.

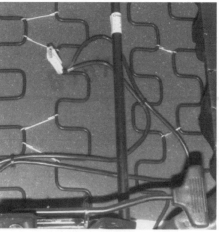

Carefully cut the wire ties holding the electrical wires to the springs. Copy the color code so you can put things back together.

Notice hinge mechanism attached to tracks. This is quite common on late-model cars, less common on some of the earlier models.

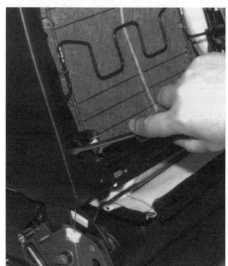

One screw on each hinge bar secures the BMW back cushion. This is only one of the many ways a seat may be assembled.

Check for release cables or rods from the back cushion to the hinge mechanism. Disconnect them before trying to remove the back cushion from the hinge bar.

enough left over for the headrests and rear center armrest. Thus, 1-1/2 + 1-1/2 + 1 = 4. Easy enough; we'll need 4 yards of fabric.

DISASSEMBLY

Seat Removal

Getting the bucket seats out of the car usually requires removing four bolts (or nuts). These are generally accessible from inside the car on models from the late '60s on. Earlier model vehicles were bolted through the floor pan and accessed from under the car. Be sure you disconnect any electrical wires *before* lifting the seat from the car. This "beemer" had two wires: one for the seat-belt-warning light and one to power the seat warmer. Yes, dear friends, an honest-to-goodness bun warmer, built right into your BMW!

The back bench seat is usually removed in one of two ways: lift straight up on the bottom edge or push the bottom edge towards the rear of the car—then lift up. This rearward push unlatches the seat. The rear seat back is usually bolted to the body in two places along the bottom edge. The top is retained by hooks. Remove the bolts and push straight up on the seat back to slide it out of its retainers. Now let's get the bucket seat apart and the cover off.

Bucket Seat Disassembly

My first admonition is to disassemble one seat at a time. These high-tech, umpteen-way seats are true nightmares when it comes to reassembling them. Any child over the age of five can get anything apart. Putting it back together can frustrate an engineer! So, save an assembled seat to look at. If you're only doing one seat, take Polaroid™ pictures to remind you where things went.

This is a real hard point to get across. Most people are positively sure they can remember where a particular part went. Maybe they can for 10 minutes. I know of no one, however, with that photographic memory we're always hearing about. So unless you're that person, keep a *visible* record of the disassembly. Please!

Watch over my shoulder as I take this seat apart. You'll see I

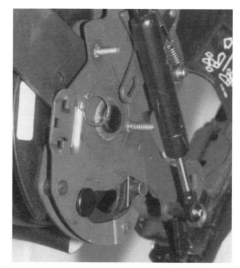

Clockwise from above: 1. Back cushion is off successfully. Now we must get the hinge mechanism off the cushion and tracks. 2. To remove this particular hinge assembly, it is necessary to remove the latch trigger first. 3. Remove the snap ring retaining the hinge to its mounting. 4. The hinge is finally off. Can you close your eyes now and assemble the seat. I don't think so. You'll have to peek first. So keep a drawing or photo to peek at when it's time to do your job. 5. Seat tracks are the simplest of all the mechanisms. When you install the tracks after the job is complete, check to be sure each track is in the same position (one not accidentally shoved forward or back.) If one track is off by even 1/2-inch, you'll have a devil of a time mounting the seat in the vehicle. The holes won't line up.

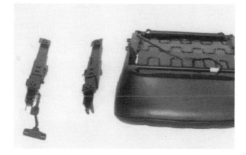

have taken my own good advice later in the chapter as I reassemble it.

Begin by removing any reveal moldings (plastic covers) so you can access the moving parts. Disconnect or remove any electrical wires or motors. Most "power seats" are removed with the motors fixed to the seat and track. Our BMW has wires going to the seat-back warmer and to the seat-belt buckle which came out with the seat. In turn they were tied to the springs with wire ties.

On late-model cars the hinging mechanism connecting the back to the cushion usually incorporates a number of features. These may include letting the seat assembly slide forward when the back is released to allow passenger access to the rear seat. Or, let the seat back down into a reclining position. This is often accom-

plished with a lever on the side of the seat back. Cables or wires go from this lever to the hinging mechanism. These transfer lines must be removed. When all the attachments between back cushion and seat cushion have been removed, the back cushion may be unbolted from the hinging mechanism. Our project back cushion is retained by two bolts through the back-cushion frame and into the hinge arm.

To remove the hinge mechanism from the seat cushion I removed the bolt that attached it to the seat track, removed the trigger (by pulling it out) which lets the back recline, then removed the snap ring retaining the hinge mechanism to its shaft. Voila! It's off. The tracks can then be removed from the seat.

You may have to deal with

power-seat motors. Usually these are fairly straightforward. If electrical wires must be removed, *tag them so you'll know where they go.* Do this even if you only disassemble one seat at a time. Sometimes only the driver's seat will have electrical wiring—the passenger's seat doesn't. So attach little masking-tape flags to the wires indicating where they go. You still have the back cushion to take apart.

Begin with the headrest. The project seat was easy; I just yanked it out. Not very sophisticated for BMW. See the sidebar on page 93 for a more common way to remove a headrest. A tentative rule of thumb is this: if the seat outside back is removable, the headrest locking device will be accessible by removing the outside back;

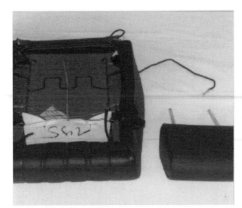

Headrest comes out with a simple tug.

Seat lever is retained by compression only and can be removed with the gentle persuasion of a screwdriver.

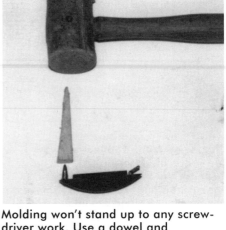

Molding won't stand up to any screwdriver work. Use a dowel and hammer to work the expansion pin out. What appears in the photo to be a broken expansion pin is really a hook. One end is hooked, the other pinned.

Tabs have replaced hog-rings. This type of assembly suggests these covers might have been installed by "robots" at the factory.

Lift tabs and remove cover. Lift tabs only as far as needed to reduce work fatigue in the metal. This will help prevent them from breaking off.

otherwise, refer to the sidebar method. There is an exception: Mercedes Benz has a removable back with a hidden button, usually visible as a small indent up by the headrest area. Push this button (through the leather) and pull out the headrest. Is this sufficiently confusing? You bet! If all else fails, call the dealership and the parts or service manager should be able to help you.

The two levers on the sides of the project seat were pried off with a screwdriver. Before trying this on your seat, check first to see if there's a setscrew. Many manufacturers lock these levers in place with setscrews. To remove the reveal molding, check first for screws. Then remove the plastic expansion pin. Don't try to pry this off. The risk of breaking something is too great. Instead,

with a hammer and a wooden dowel, knock it out from the backside. At worst you'll only break the expansion pin. If this happens and you can't replace it from the dealership, a dab of hot glue will hold it on quite satisfactorily.

A picture begins to develop here. In late-model cars, as much as possible is "snapped together." This labor-saving plan is employed by the manufacturer to hold down costs. In the next section you'll see the manufacturer has even removed most of the need for hog- rings.

Seat-cover removal (Cushion)

The illustration on the next page shows how the seat cover is retained to the frame. Holes are prepunched into the vinyl. These holes are then slipped over metal tabs welded to the seat frame. The tabs are bent down to secure the cover. I wonder how we're going

to attach a seat cover to this frame in years to come when all the tabs have snapped off.

Disengage the cover around the bottom of the seat frame and lift it up. Well, here's a familiar sight: the pleats are retained with old-fashioned listings, wire and hog-rings. Cut out the hog-rings and take the cover off the seat.

Look at the photo on the opposite page showing the underside of the cushion cover. Note three things: first the "foam" (polyester felt instead of polyurethane foam) is larger than the cover. This acts as padding for the sides of the seat. Next, what appears to be stitching for the pleats is actually heat-sealed seams. Those three gray things in the center? They're plastic listings to ring to the seat. Quite a bit different than what we've seen before, yet serviceable and very efficient.

The only problem for us is to duplicate those three plastic tabs that serve as listings. Because they're heat-sealed they can't be removed to use again.

I've carefully removed the heating coils as seen in the next photograph. They're similar to the heating coils found in electric blankets. If your seat has these,

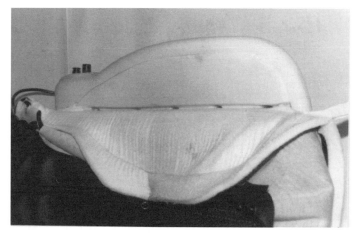

At least there's still a little of the old technology here: a listing retained with hog-rings.

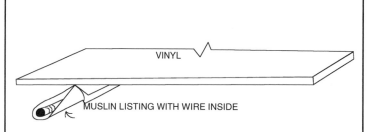

VINYL

MUSLIN LISTING WITH WIRE INSIDE

Listing is a 1-1/2 -inch wide strip of muslin folded in half and sewn to piece of vinyl or fabric. Rod or wire can be inserted through loop. If you use a fastener such as a hog-ring to loop over wire, material can be fastened to frame so fasteners can't be seen.

handle them with care as they're very delicate. When the heating coils have been removed, you've one more thing to do before you're ready to take the cover apart. You must make a number of locator marks.

Using your scissors, cut small notches in the selvage edge about every 4 inches along all the joining seams in your cushion cover. I start in the center and work both ways, being sure to put one where I'll start sewing and one in each corner. These marks are very important to get everything back together the way it was. *Don't bypass this step!* Now you can cut it apart.

I use a razor blade or sharp knife to cut the threads holding the cover together. I find it goes faster than using the scissors. On this insert job I'll be inserting the pleats and end caps so I didn't separate them. As we progress you'll see why.

When you cut the facing from the body, leave the welt attached to the facing. When you sew things back together, sew the facing and welt to the body at one time. This saves the time it would otherwise take to sew the welt first, then the facing. Now let's make the insert.

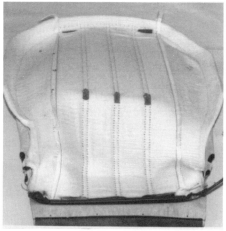

Three gray tabs take the place of a listing to hold down the cover in the center.
Below: Component parts of the seat cushion. Body, seen in the center, will be inserted with fabric.

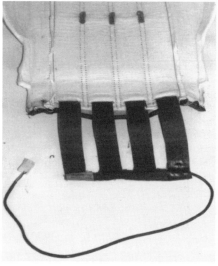

I've pulled the heater coils out a little to give you a look at them. They're very fragile. *Handle with care!*

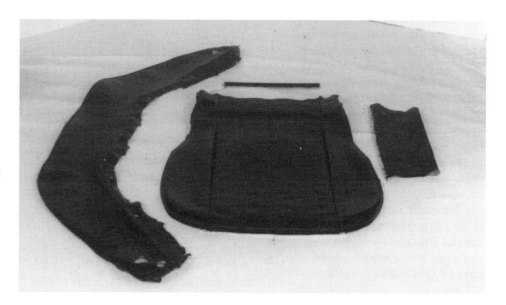

Layout of the pleats for both seat cushions. Notice two seams define the pleats. Though you can't tell from the photo, two outside pleats are 1/4-inch larger than their inside buddies. This will accommodate the seam allowance for blind-stitching the end cap.

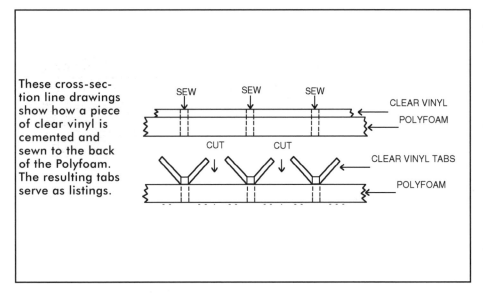

These cross-section line drawings show how a piece of clear vinyl is cemented and sewn to the back of the Polyfoam. The resulting tabs serve as listings.

SEW SEW SEW

CLEAR VINYL

POLYFOAM

CUT CUT

CLEAR VINYL TABS

POLYFOAM

SEAT REUPHOLSTERY

Fabricating the Insert Piece

Essentially you've already done this. You made top-sewn pleats in the second project, the bench seat. This time, though we're going to throw in a twist. If you looked carefully at the face piece in the photos you saw four top-sewn pleats with a separate end piece on each side. Well, we're going to make life a little easier by making the pleats and end pieces all at one time. Here's how.

Measure across the top of the body piece you're going to fabricate to find the overall width. Add a couple of inches for shrinkage, cut the fabric and bond it to 1/2-inch Polyfoam.

As in Chapter 4, when you made your first pleats you added a little for shrinkage. Again, you must add a little on this job. The curve of the pleat uses up the material, making the finished product narrower than what you started with.

Be sure you have the nap going in the correct direction: top-to-bottom for the back cushion, back-to-front for the seat cushion. You can see I'm doing the seat cushion and back cushion at the same time.

Now, layout the pleats as you did in Chapter 4, with one difference: make the last pleat on each side 1/4-inch *larger* than the others. In other words, if the other pleats were 3-inches wide,

make the two outside pleats 3-1/4-inches wide. The finished product should have several pleats in the center, the two outside 1/4-inch larger, and then two large "end caps" (they're not really caps because it's all one piece of material). Before I can sew the pleats I've got to do something about those three plastic listings in the center of the seat. Refer to the drawing at left to see how I solved this problem.

Working from the backside of both the old and new pieces, I draw a line across the pleats at the exact location of the listings. Then, I cut a piece of clear vinyl from a scrap of convertible rear-window vinyl about 1-1/2-inches wide and long enough to cross all the pleats with another 1-inch on each side. I cement this piece, centered over the previously drawn location line, to the back of the Polyfoam. This will hold it in place while I top sew the pleats; and simultaneously, the clear vinyl in place. When finished, I'll turn the work over, separate the vinyl cemented to the Polyfoam, and clip the vinyl down the center of each pleat. This will give me three wing-shaped tabs, which, when trimmed, will become my three listings!

All of the top-sewn seams are in place. We must now make the end caps appear to be blind-stitched to the pleats.

At the sewing machine, fold the material face-to-face along the outboard top-sewn-pleat seam (the one you made 1/4-inch wider than the others). From the back side of the material sew another seam *1/4 inch in from the fold line.* Now you have a blind-stitched end cap. Turn the material over and see what you have. You've got top-sewn pleats and what appears to be separate end caps.

This is a quicky way to do the job when the material for the pleats and end caps are the same. On our bench seat, the pleats and end caps were different

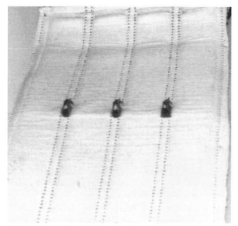

These are the original vinyl tabs.

After blind-stitching the end cap from the backside of the Polyfoam, sew the listing material directly over the top of it.

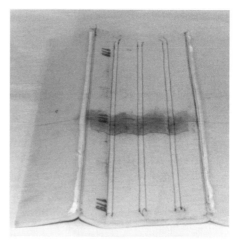

Back of insert showing clear-vinyl tabs, top sewn pleats and blind-stitched end caps with listings.

Align old seat-cushion body *carefully* over newly fabricated insert (body). Weight it down or tack it to the bench.

I've finished sewing and am now pushing the heater coils back into the pleats. If your project has these, install them carefully. Make sure they don't twist on the way in.

Here's the finished cover ready to go back on.

colored materials so they could not be sewn this way.

Turn the material to the backside again and sew in the listing. Now you're ready to fit the old body piece to the new.

Fitting the Insert

Here comes the exception to the rule. Earlier, I stated you should never use the old material for a pattern. If the old material had stretched out of shape, then the new piece would be out of shape also. Well, my reasoning is still correct, but here we have a relatively new car, only 1-year old. There's little chance of copying any distortion from the material.

Lay the old cover face on top of the newly sewn insert, aligning the seams, and in the case of our project seat, aligning the center

listings. Place weights on top of the pieces to hold them in place or tack them in place to the bench or to a piece of plywood as we did before. Carefully chalk a line around the outside of the selvage edge making a mark for each notch cut as a locator mark. *Don't forget the location marks!*

Now, to the sewing machine. You've done the next steps before but here's a quick review.

Sewing Seat Cushion Back Together

Sew a locking stitch around the chalk line and trim away the excess material right up to the seam. Starting at the locator mark you made to indicate where to begin the seam, lay the facing (with welt attached) onto the new insert. Begin sewing through the

facing and welt, maintaining an accurate 1/2-inch seam allowance and matching notches (location marks). Don't forget to lock your stitch at the beginning and end of the seam. Finish by sewing the stretcher onto the rear. Zippo-whippo, you're done!

Reassembly to Frame

Now you've got to get this work of art back onto the seat frame. On the project seat I need to put the heater coils in first. To do this I made a slit through the Polyfoam at each end of the four pleats. Then I ran a yardstick in between the material and Polyfoam to break the glue bond. I knew I would have to do this; so when I cemented the material to the poly, I used very little glue. At the end of each heater coil there is a little

Always begin the installation with the *center* listing.

When all the listings are secured, skin the cover down over the seat. There should only be small wrinkles that readily pull out when the cover is fastened. If you have major wrinkles you probably did not align the cover correctly. Cut it loose, realign it and ring it down again.

Boy, this is easy! Why didn't they think of this before? I got Popeye forearms from using hog-ring pliers!

Looks pretty nice now. A little steam to make the nap go in the right direction and it's all done.

Our finished seat cushion. Now, on to the back.

placket into which a narrow yardstick fits quite nicely.

I placed the placket over the end of the yardstick, pushing the heat coil through the pleat between the fabric and Polyfoam. When the heater coil appeared at the other end of the pleat I grabbed it, held it in place and pulled out the yardstick. From here installation will be just about like the others we've done.

With the cover wrong side out, lay it on top of the seat and align it. If, like the project seat, you have center listings, these must be attached first.

On the project seat I folded each pair of clear vinyl "wings" together. I inserted each of the newly formed tabs into their corresponding holes in the center

of the seat and ringed them to the retainer wire. Any center listing you have must be fastened before the side listings. It's virtually impossible to ring down the center listings after ringing the side listings.

Now, skin the cover down over the Polyfoam and frame of the seat and attach it to the base. On the project seat I'll push the pre-punched holes in the facing over the frame tabs and then knock them down with a hammer.

The interesting tool you see in the photo on the far left is a steamer. This is a little industrial steamer used in most shops to remove small wrinkles and force the nap of the material to lie in one direction after being "abused" by the trimmer during manufac-

ture. Larger trim shops also have a big industrial steamer. You can see this big boy in the chapter on convertible tops. Meanwhile, there is a steamer solution for you.

Your local dress-fabric store carries a small, plastic, hand steamer used primarily by those making clothing. These are priced under $30 as of this writing and do a very adequate job even on auto fabrics. If you don't want to spend the thirty bucks, there's still a way out.

Fill a small spray bottle and fill it with clear, clean water. Spray a medium coat of water over the surface of your fabric. Remember, we're dealing with fabric now, not vinyl. (See Chapter 4, page 52 for preventing wrinkles in vinyl or Chapter 5, page 65 for removing them.) A medium coat of water would be just to the point of run off.

Wipe the nap of the material forward; from the back of the seat cushion to the front. On the back cushion, wipe from the top, down. Now, get out the old hair dryer and dry out the dampened material. This should generate enough heat and steam to do the job. *Never use a regular steam iron for this process.* A steam iron gets so hot it will melt the acrylic fibers of the nap if you should touch it. This is not the case with the plastic steam iron mentioned above. Now let's get the back cushion together.

Fabricating & Assembling the Back Cushion

Although not an exact duplicate, the back goes together much like the seat. On the project back you can see one advantage over the cushion: the listings are accessible from the outside. This makes life much easier for removal and installation. Again, in the photo illustration you can see the back-cushion cover incorporates plastic listings down the sides as it does in the center. They will be fabricated from clear vinyl in a similar manner.

Moving to the top of the back cushion we find two grommets which act as fabric protectors for the headrest. These are generally the same on all cars and can be removed by *carefully* prying the plastic retainer ring from around the grommet. I say carefully because these may be used over again if you don't break or stretch them.

Cut, sew and fit the body of the back cover as you did the cushion cover. If you're faced with plastic side listings as I was, these are sewn on after making the top seam for the end caps. Just go back and sew on a 1-1/2-inch wide strip of clear vinyl. Later, align the old cover with the new and mark the location for the tabs. Cut away the excess material around the tabs and you're ready to go.

The quick way to get those headrest grommets back in is to insert the male portion into the cover, carefully place the female retainer over the shaft and assure yourself it's square with the cover. Place a socket from your driver set on top of the female retainer and gently tap it down over the shaft of the grommet, setting it tightly against the fabric. You're all set now to sew the facing or facings to the body.

Installation of the finished back cover is just like that for the seat cover. Attach the listings first, then the cover to the frame. Just be sure everything is correctly aligned first. If the listings are off,

BMW gave me a break here. I can access the hog-rings in the listings from the outside. Great for removal and installation.

everything will be off and you'll have unbelievable wrinkles. If this should be the case, i.e., big wrinkles when you skin the cover around the frame, go back and cut the rings from the listings. Realign the cover and try again. When you have both the back and seat cushions completed, you're ready to tackle the headrest.

HEADRESTS

Disassembly

All headrests are finished off at the bottom where the finishing is hidden when the headrest is in the lowered position. The difference is in the way the cover is finished off from one vehicle to the next. Most covers, as in the case of our project, have some type of retainer sewn to each end. This is usually a stiff piece of plastic or sometimes a piece of welt (as we'll see later when we get to the center armrest), which locks into a groove in the frame of the headrest.

On some older-model cars the cover was retained variously with staples, listings and hog-rings, zippers and Velcro. I would strongly suggest you make and install one cover at a time so you have an example to follow. I'll let you in on a secret: I still do them one at a time!

I'll remove the project cover by inserting a screwdriver into the retaining groove and carefully pry out one end of the material. In the

After removing the cover, I discovered *all* the listings were plastic.

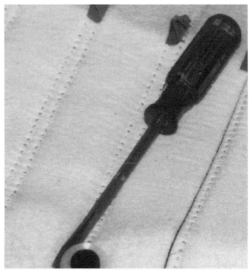

Be careful as you pry these retainer rings from the headrest grommets. If you break one, keep it. When it's time to put it back on, do so. Then hot-glue it together and attach it to the male post.

Because I didn't break mine, I can use a socket to drive it back on over the post. Be sure the socket size just barely fits over the post. If the socket is too large it will simply mash down the edges of the retainer ring, rather than drive it down.

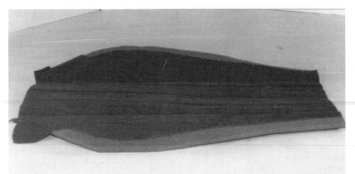

I've left about 3 inches of Polyfoam around the outside of the body. This will add padding to the sides.

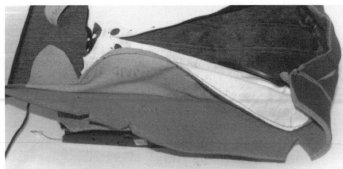

Here, you can see how I've cut "Vs" into the foam so it will fit around the corners without bunching beneath the fabric.

Finished back. Soon we'll have the whole seat together.

First we need a headrest. I've begun to remove the cover by slipping the retainer out of its groove.

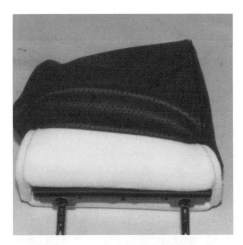

Slide the cover off, being very careful not to tear it, especially where the welts join at the closure.

photo you can see the hard-plastic retainer used by BMW. After removing both ends of the material I slip the cover off the frame. *Be very careful at the union where the welts meet.* This weakest point can easily tear if not handled properly. Squeeze the foam through the cover to relieve any stress in this area as you slide it off.

As in the seat-cover work before it, make lots of locator marks on the various headrest pieces. I mark the front of the body so I'll be sure to get the nap of the new fabric going in the right direction. I mark the sides so I'll know right and left and where the welts finish off. The more

information you have, the less confused you'll become. Because I used the same pieces of welt over again, I even marked them right and left, front and rear.

Cutting, Fitting & Sewing

Check once more to be sure you have enough marks. Layout the body on the new material. If it is a napped fabric, the nap faces down in the front. This will correspond to the back cushion. If you're replacing the side pieces, the nap goes down here also. Now, mark everything, being sure to transfer all of your locator marks, directions and notes. When you're satisfied you have it all, cut out your pieces.

Referring to the project piece, I cut out the two end retaining pieces from the old cover and sewed them to the new piece of material. This is about the only

HEADREST REMOVAL— AN ALTERNATE METHOD

Some headrests, especially '60s and '70s models, have a spring-loaded stop which prevents the headrest from coming out by pulling. If you run into one of these, here's how to get it out.

Buy a kitchen spatula at your local hardware store; one with a blade about 2-inches wide and 8- to 10-inches long. This must be the thin, flexible metal type. No wood or plastic. This will be your "headrest stop-release tool."

At the bench, or in the car if you wish, insert this tool between the headrest post and its runner with the headrest as low as possible. Try it first from the front of the seat. Some units lock from the back, however. Push the spatula in as far as it will go. This will push back the spring-loaded stop from the headrest post. Leave the tool in place and lift the headrest from its runner.

If it doesn't work the first time,

The spatula holds the spring-loaded lock back from the indent in the headrest post. It may take a little work to get it in there, so wiggle it around a bit.

try it again. After a couple of tries, get a friend to pull on the headrest while you hold the spatula in place. It *will* come out!

Note: The above description applies to single-post headrests.

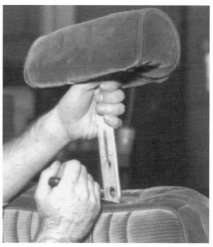

Once the lock is released the headrest will lift right out. It may take a little coaxing.

Double-post models have obvious latches retaining them or are removed with the techniques described earlier.

---

way to do it on this project because these two pieces are specially made to lock together in the frame groove. If zippers or Velcro were involved I'd have used new ones. When you use old parts over, there's always a chance they'll fail or tear. Choose carefully.

Now you must sew everything together. The easiest way is to sew the welts to the body first, then the side pieces. Start at the closure and sew all the way around. For a beginner this sometimes results in twisting the cover. If this happens, cut the threads retaining the side pieces. Instead of starting at the closure, start at the top and sew to the closure. Turn the piece over, start at the top again and sew the other half to the closure. Repeat this for the other side. You should come up with a perfectly "square" piece.

Installation

It's back to the 10-lbs. of flour into the 5-lb. bag! If you made the stadium cushion you remember the fun you had pushing all that Polyfoam into the cover. So, here we go again.

Spray a full coat of silicone over the foam and on the inside of the new cover. This is an important step I wouldn't omit. Insert the foam into the cover keeping things square and making sure the front of the cover is to the front of the headrest. Squeeze the foam through the cover and pull one side down a little. Repeat this on the other side. Continue working the cover down as far as possible. As you did while you were removing the cover, keep an eye on the closure area around the welt. This is still the area most likely to tear.

When you've got the cover down as far as it will go, really

squish the foam together at the bottom of one end and pull the cover over it. Repeat this on the other side and the cover should slip on nicely. Close off the cover in whatever manner of design was used originally.

If it's a zippered cover, compress the foam with your hand as you pull the slider. If you try to just close it, you put all the pressure on the zipper slide and you run the risk of tearing out a tooth.

On the project cover I simply snapped the retainers into the groove with my fingers.

This finishes the headrest. Do the other one now or when you do the second seat. Insert the finished headrest into the back cushion and you're ready to assemble the cushion and back into a seat.

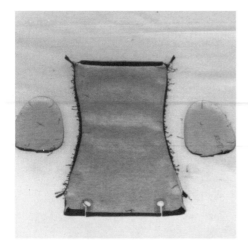

Can you see all my marks? Besides location marks I've noted front and rear, left and right.

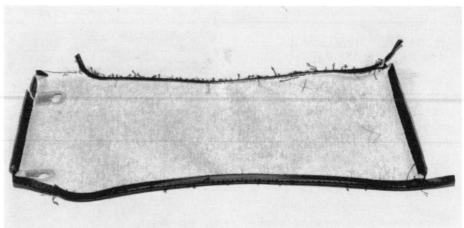

Here's a view of the hard-plastic retainers fixed to each end of the cover body. Save and reuse these if you have them on your project.

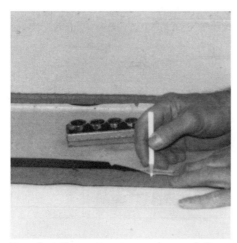

Transfer all your locator marks carefully.

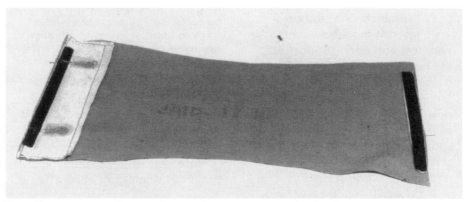

Now I've cut out and sewn the retainers to my new body piece.

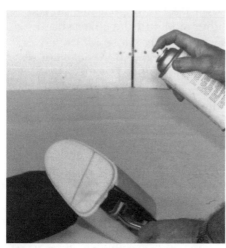

What a boon silicone has become to the trim industry. If you have a problem with silicone or can't find it, wrap the headrest with the very thin plastic film used by dry cleaners to protect your clean clothes. This will let you slip the cover on just as easily.

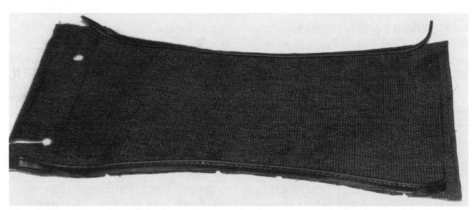

Here's the other side with the welts attached.

ASSEMBLING THE SEAT

If you kept one seat intact, lay it down on the bench on one side or the other. Lay the seat cushion down so the opposite side is exposed. Most bucket seats are mirror opposites. Begin assembling the seat by mounting the hinge mechanism. Next, mount the tracks and attach them to the hinge mechanism if so designed. Mount the back cushion to the hinge mechanism and connect any cables. When everything is assembled, make sure it all works. Test the levers, the tracks and make sure any electrical wires are not pinched. When you're satisfied all is in operable condition, close up the outside back and admire your handiwork! If you

The nice thing about these plastic retainers is they simply snap into place.

Finished headrest.

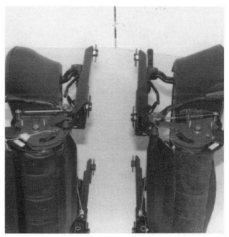

Yes, I do practice what I preach. I've done one seat at a time so I can see how to assemble it.

were only building new bucket seats, you can install them now. The rest of you stand by and see how we handle this center-armrest business.

CENTER ARMRESTS

Removal
They're called *center armrests* to distinguish them from the armrests found on the door panel or rear quarter panel. You can have a front center armrest or a rear center armrest or both. The armrests on captain's chairs are simply called the *right* or *left armrest*. To make life easy, for the rest of this section we'll drop the word "center" and just refer to it as an armrest. For this project we're looking at a rear armrest from the same BMW.

Every manufacturer has its own way of mounting an armrest. Some are mounted to the back cushion and come out with it as a unit. In other cases you'll find the center armrest to be a unit by itself mounted to the body of the vehicle. It comes out independently of the rear back cushion. This BMW has the simplest arrangement yet. It comes out with the back cushion. You just squeeze a set of sliderlocks together and the whole assembly drops out. Remove two Allen screws from each side and the hinge mechanism can be removed.

Most armrests have a flap from the armrest to the back cushion or interior body of the vehicle. This is removed in a number of ways. Our project armrest hider flap was attached by Velcro. Other attaching methods include: screws, snaps, plastic push fasteners and a host of other clever devices just to trick the trimmer. If you run into one of the "clever devices," you may have to ask your friendly parts manager at the local dealership to help you out.

When you have the armrest out and on the bench you must get the cover off. This is a lot like the headrest and has many of the same fastening devices. The project armrest used a piece of welt sewn onto each end of the body piece. These were locked in place by a plastic clamp built into the frame of the armrest. To release them I used a screwdriver to hold open the plastic clamp and then gently pulled the material from the clamp. Again, you may find zippers, Velcro or any number of male/female plastic clamping devices. A little prying and prodding will usually reveal how things are held together.

As with the headrest, make lots of locator marks and indicate front, rear, left and right. Then, razor-blade the cover components apart.

Finished seat looks just like the first photo only now it has nice, breathable fabric. No more burned legs or sweaty backs.

Cutting, Fitting & Sewing
Lay the old body on the material *so the nap lays down when the armrest is in the up position.* This will match the material on the back cushion. Transfer all your marks to the new material. Cut out the body (and sides if this is a whole new assembly). I've used the old curtain, pull strap and side pieces. Remember: I'm doing an insert job.

At the sewing machine sew the hider and pull strap to the body first. If your armrest is made just

Center armrest reminds me of Count Dracula rising from his coffin! Even the seat back looks like vampire bat wings. Nevertheless, it must come out.

This is really easy. They've even given me finger holes to squeeze. One squeeze and the whole armrest unit drops out.

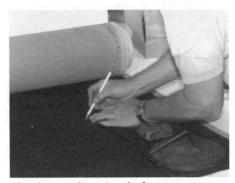

Two Allen-head bolts on each side connect the armrest to mechanism. This is fairly standard. Torx could be used instead of Allen-head screws.

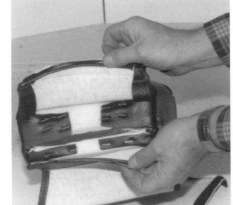

Staples go into the foam and then bend over, just like closing up a carton. Well, watch. We'll get this back together without any fancy tools.

Check nap direction before you start marking. Nap goes down (like the back cushion) when the armrest is in the upright position.

I've sewn the hider and pull strap to the body piece. If you could see the backside you would see I've also sewn the retaining welts to the ends of the fabric.

A little silicon or plastic film and then just slide that sucker on!

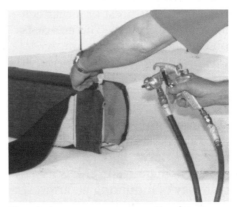

Here's how we overcome the fancy "blind" staple gun. A little cement and the ends are down for keeps.

the opposite of the project (one facing and two body pieces) sew the pull strap or pull tab to the *front* body piece. It's really embarrassing to put everything together and find the pull strap on the back of the armrest totally inaccessible to everyone!

Double-check things and then sew the facings to the body. If there are welt pieces, sew these to the body first.

Installation

Installation is very forthright: spray silicone on all the parts then pull the cover on. It slides on just like a pillowcase. Be sure you have the front of the cover and the front of the frame aligned before sliding the cover on. After all that trouble to make sure the pull strap was on the front, don't let it wind up on the back by turning the cover around.

In the photos you can see the sides of the armrest on the project piece were secured by staples.

This was done with a special staple gun that forces the prongs of the staple out to the sides. You've seen this type of staple on cardboard boxes where the flaps are stapled closed after the box is filled. This requires a special "blind" staple gun which is not a component of our shop. So, I solved the problem by cementing these side flaps in place. After this is done I force the ends of the body piece, with welts attached, into the clamp in the frame and the piece is finished. Assembly is the reverse of disassembly: I bolt the hinge on and snap the mechanism into the back cushion.

Your project may be a bit more involved, especially if it was mounted to the car body. You, of course, made notes, drew diagrams or took Polaroid pictures so things could go back together quickly. There is nothing amateurish about doing whatever makes it possible to reassemble your project. It *is* amateurish to have to take it to a professional to finish it off because you were absolutely sure you could remember which bolt went where! Be kind to yourself: make notes, take pictures or make sketches—or all three!

FINAL THOUGHTS ON REAR SEATS

I'm not going into a lot of detail on the rear seat. Most of the work is identical to making a front bench seat just as you did in Chapters 4 and 5. But there are a couple of things you might make note of.

Dealing with a Curved Back Cushion

The project rear-back cushion is curved. This accommodates the shape of the human body and provides extra comfort for the passenger. It also provides extra headaches for the trimmer.

Remember in Chapter 4 how we worried about lining up the pleats in the seat and back? Well, we must line up the pleats in this

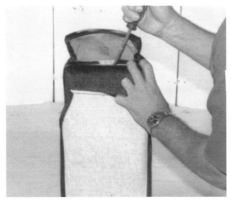

Now, snap the retainers back in (left). Finished armrest (above) smooth as silk.

Fasten the mounting bracket and it's ready to go into the back cushion.

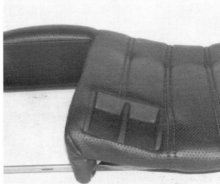

The hard-plastic plackets hold the seat-belt latches so they don't slip down between the seat cushion and back cushion.

seat and back also. Now think a minute about what we have with this curved back. If you put a measuring tape to the back you will find a greater distance across the bottom of the back than across the back of the seat cushion. If you make 3-inch pleats in the back and 3-inch pleats in the seat, working from the center out, the pleats and end cap seams won't line up! Yes, dear reader, you could find yourself up that ol' polluted creek.

To solve the problem you must do some very careful measuring of the pleats in the back, both at the top and bottom. The top (back) edge of the back cushion is straight, not curved like the bottom. The folks at Bavarian Motor Works solved the problem by *molding* the back cushion cover. We can't do that with our fabrics (much less with our tools).

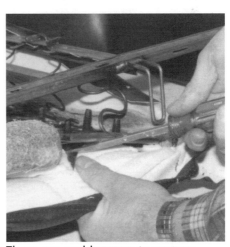

These are real buggers to remove. Plastic caps have serrated shafts that pass through a metal grommet. Serrations prevent the shaft from slipping back. I'm bending the grommets back to let the shafts slide out. I must bend the grommets back into place so they can do their job when I assemble the seat.

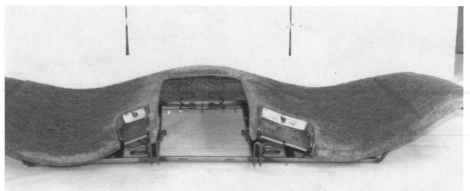

Notice the amount of curve in the back cushion.

Perspective makes the end of the pleat nearest you look larger than the end away from you. Not only is there a perspective illusion, pleats really are narrower at the top than the bottom. This helps accommodate that curve in the back cushion.

SUMMARY

Well, I think this has been the toughest job we've done so far. If not the toughest, at least the most complex. If you've completed a late-model bucket seat, you can be justly proud of yourself.

The most important thing to take away from this chapter is the knowledge that you must make lots of locator marks on the back of the materials to let yourself know where you are and how things go together. Second, although it's a slow way of doing things, make one piece at a time, leaving the other as a guide.

Here are the finished back cushions ready for delivery to the customer.

We, therefore, must make the back cushion pleats larger at the bottom than at the top. This will accommodate the curve.

I might further suggest if you run into this type of a problem, fabricate the back cushion first. Then, mount it in the vehicle. Install the old seat cushion and see if your new pleats line up with the old. If they do, get yourself to the nearest trim shop. They have a job ready and waiting for you! If they don't line up, here's the trick.

With a piece of chalk, mark on the seat cushion exactly where the back-cushion pleat seams meet. Then, remove the seat cushion and make your pleats according to the location marks you just made. Then you know your pleats will line up. Each pleat in the seat cushion will be a little different in width but because they'll line up so nicely with the pleats in the back, the size difference will never be noticed.

8

Making & Installing a Vinyl Top

Here's an opportunity to get out of the inside of the car for a while and work on the exterior. Vinyl roofs are quite popular, so popular in fact, they've bred a revolution in top design. We have full-vinyl tops, half tops, quarter tops and sim-cons (simulated convertibles). All of these—which we cover in the next few chapters—derive their styling from the original vinyl roofs which showed up in the early '60s.

Those '60s vinyl roofs owed *their* styling to the days of the '20s and '30s when the roof of the car was part metal and part asphalt-impregnated cloth. If you're old enough to remember "top dressing"—an asphalt-based paint to reseal the cloth portion of your top—then you're as old as I am!

These cloth-centered tops were what remained of the all cloth tops from the teens which succeeded the buggy. So we've come full circle: from the cloth tops of the horseless carriage to the all-metal roof of today designed to *look like* a horseless-carriage roof!

If you are contemplating installing a vinyl roof on a vehicle

Our project car, direct from the used-car dealership. They would like to dress it up a bit because it's such a plain-Jane.

which never had one, as in our project car, stop and think if this is what you *really* want.

One of the shortcomings of a vinyl top is its uncanny ability to trap and retain water. You know this leads to rust, usually around the backlite (rear-window) area. This means removing the backlite to do the bodywork when it rusts through, not a fun job.

If you're going to replace an existing vinyl roof, be prepared to find rust underneath. When you do, you must remove it. Use a body grinder with a #36 grit disk and get it all out. Use a good body filler to fill the area ground away, level it and then repaint. Note I say repaint, not prime. Primer only makes matters worse. It attracts and holds moisture. How many cars do you see on the street where the owner started to

Just-Rite Auto Upholstering and Restyling Center of Chelsea, MA is where I went to find some of the best work on the east coast. Owner Sidney Levine generously allowed me to follow his crew around for weeks, photographing and asking questions. Thanks, Sid. You and your people were a great help!

Charlie goes right to work. He says if I stay out of his way he can finish in about 5 hours. To start, he must first remove the windshield and backlite seals.

Here's a close-up of the tool you see in the other two photos. Charlie made this from an old screwdriver. With it, he starts the vinyl seal out of its groove.

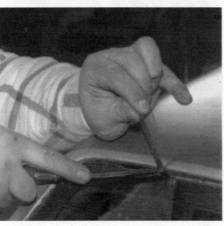

do bodywork, got as far as the primer, quit and now has rust coming through? So grind, fill and paint for that lasting roof line.

GETTING STARTED

Removing the Trim

If you plan on doing the job right, all the trim which will hide the raw edges of the material must be removed. The shops you see which advertise full vinyl roofs for $49.95 don't bother with this step. They just cover over those raw edges with silicone and call it good! We're going to use silicone but not for covering the raw edges. We'll use it to ensure there will be no leaks.

Our trimmer/model/vinyl-roof installer extraordinaire, is Charlie Calanna, who, in the first photo has begun to remove the vinyl seal from around the windshield of this Buick. In his right hand he's holding a tool he made from a screwdriver. It hooks the vinyl seal and starts it out.

Both front and rear have these seals which are held in with serrations on the vinyl and a lot of help from black silicone.

Many vehicles of earlier years used a stainless-steel molding around the front windshield. The local parts house has a tool for removing this trim. This tool lets you reach in between glass and trim to release the retainer holding it. To replace the trim you simply snap it back in place with a sharp blow from the heel of your hand.

After removing any seal, you must also dig out as much of the sealer as possible. In the project car the sealer was silicone. It's very hard to get the seal back in

Left: When a seal is installed around a piece of glass, the installer always uses a sealer. This prevents leaks and helps keep the seal or trim piece in place. All of this old sealer must be removed. Charlie scoops it out with a combination of knife and the tool seen in the previous photo.

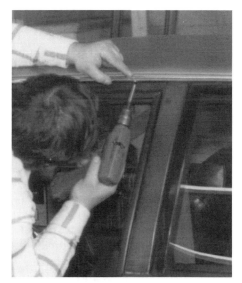

The next step is to remove the weather stripping from the door jambs.

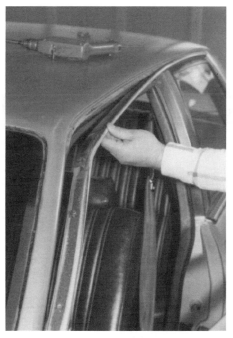

If you haven't a heat gun to help remove the emblem, use a hair dryer or heat lamp. With a heat lamp, be careful not to blister the paint.

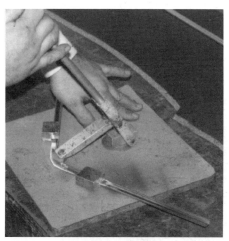

This is a jiffy tool to bend the aluminum trim molding. It's not worth it to make one (or buy one) if you'll only be doing one top. Use a tubing bender or a couple of box wrenches instead.

Charlie checks each bend as he progresses. Notice he works from the center out. This way he doesn't risk coming out short on one end or the other.

correctly (tight) with the old sealer getting in the way.

Next, Charlie removes the weatherstrip retainer from around the doors. On some cars the weatherstrip must be removed first. This may be retained by screws or by the weatherstrip being forced into the channels of the retainer. How it's fastened to the car can usually be seen by poking around a little bit. Look for screws hidden in grooves of the rubber. If you find no screws, you should be able to gently pry the rubber out of its channel.

The channel is then retained by screws, or by pop rivets in some vehicles. The project car had screws through the weatherstrip and stainless-steel trim. It came down as one unit. Because this is a two-door rather than a four-door, the back part of the trim is not as easy to remove. To do so, Charlie would have to remove much of the interior, and then the rear-quarter glass. To save time, and therefore money, he'll force the raw edges of the new top under the weatherstrip in this area. This will be done by prying down the weatherstrip and forcing the vinyl under it with a putty knife or spatula. The last part to be removed is the side

emblem.

These emblems are glued to the rear quarter and come off with heat. This is tricky. You have to heat the emblem hot enough to loosen the glue but not so hot as to blister the paint, a difference of only a few degrees. Work around the emblem with the heat gun for a bit and then try to remove it by prying with your finger nail. Anything else might break the emblem. Continue heating until you can pop the emblem off, then stop. Save the emblem. We'll show you how to put it back on.

Preparing Aluminum Trim
Charlie uses a shop-made tool to put a 90° bend in the aluminum quarter-panel trim. For yours, use a tubing bender compatible with the width of the trim. Other bends which are not perpendicular to the sidewall of the trim may be made with your fingers. Check the fit as you go, working from the 90° bend both ways.

Some body styles will require a two-way bend. If this is beyond the abilities of your fingers, use a wood or leather mallet. When you have the fit just the way you want it, trim the ends to the correct length.

Hold the piece of trim tightly to the car body and trace around both sides with a grease pencil to

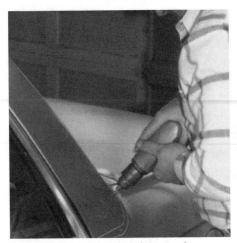

After marking around the trim he drills four or five 1/8-inch holes. Later he'll pop-rivet retainers here.

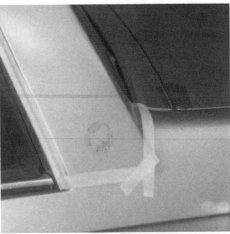

Masking tape keeps cement out of this area. Feel free to mask off any areas on which you might get cement overspray.

make an outline. Set the trim piece aside.

The trim is held in place with plastic snaps. These snaps in turn are fastened to the body with pop rivets. Using an imaginary

centerline through the outline you just drew, drill four or five holes in the body with one about 3/4 inch in from the ends. Use a #30 or a 1/8-inch drill bit. Later you'll pop rivet a snap into each

of these holes. For now, however, cover the outlined area with masking tape.

You don't want any padding in this area. The masking tape will allow you to peel away any glue you get here, keeping the padding from sticking.

PADDING THE ROOF

Padding the roof gives it a nice "feel," softens some of the angularity and hides any flaws in the roof. The padding you'll use is a special closed-cell foam, 1/4-inch thick. Closed-cell foams are much denser than open-cell foams and are less likely to collapse, i.e., flatten out, than their open-cell counterparts. Buy enough of this foam to cover the complete top including the rear roof pillars.

Because of the width of the car, one piece of foam will not do the job. It's necessary to use two pieces as Charlie has done with

REMOVING CEMENT

No matter how careful you are you're probably going to get some cement on your car; especially if this is the first time you've worked with a glue gun. There are two ways to handle this. If you get a real nasty run down the side of the car, don't try to wipe it off. This only makes matters worse. A lacquer-type solvent in the cement tends to melt or soften the finish. Rubbing then, disrupts this softened finish and leaves marks.

Let the run dry undisturbed, then peel it off. Then, after things have settled for a day or so, and the paint has hardened again, go to the local automotive paint shop and buy some ultra-fine rubbing compound. If you're not too embarrassed to tell the clerk what happened, ask him or her to advise you as to the best brand to buy. I like Martin-Senour's BUFF-EEZ®.

Stay away from the amateur brands sold at the parts houses. These are too coarse.

Back at the job, poor a small amount of the buffing compound (about a tablespoon or less) onto a clean, dry, cotton rag which you have formed into a ball. Now, using a circular motion, rub the compound around the area where the cement was removed. Continue this rubbing motion, applying more pressure as you work. In a minute or two the film will begin to dry from the heat you're generating. As the film dries, the gloss in the paint will return, leaving no sign of the run. Make only one application of rubbing compound at a time. Work that application until it's dry, turn to a clean place on the cloth and make a second application if the outline of the drip has not disappeared. A little

paste wax will make everything look brand new.

More often than a big, nasty, drip you'll get little spots of cement on the finish called "overspray." Use a product called grease-and-wax remover to clean these up. This product is also available from your local automotive-paint supply. I like a product called Pre-Kleeno®. Poor a generous amount into a clean rag and wipe off any overspray. Grease and wax removers are made to use over paint and will not harm it.

Use this same product to get old cement off the roof if you're replacing a top. Lacquer thinner gets everything too gummy; the cement, the paint, everything. It even attacks body filler. Stay with the grease-and-wax removers.

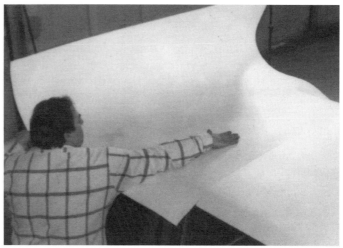

Keep the cement thin and even. Too much cement will eat into the foam or lift the paint. You also run the risk of seeing lumps of cement under the material. Remember to let the cement dry thoroughly *before* bonding.

Wider piece in the rear accommodates the rear roof pillars. Notice how tight Charlie has made the butt joint. Any gaps here would be seen through the vinyl.

Rough out around the top first. Then do the fine trim.

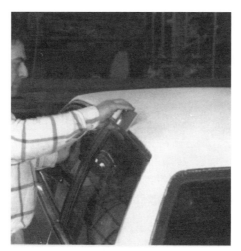

Charlie has found a bubble in the foam. By making a slice in it with a razor blade he lets the air escape and the bubble settles.

After trimming the foam you must sand it smooth and blend in the contours. This is one of the things which will make your job look professional.

Don't omit this step. Very gently sand the top to ensure the vinyl will not lift. Charlie starts in the center and draws the sanding block towards him, making only one pass.

the project top, a narrow piece in front and a much wider one at the rear to include the pillars.

Begin by spraying a full coat of cement onto both top and foam. Let this coat of cement dry thoroughly before applying the foam to the top. To test, apply a piece of paper to the cemented surface. If the paper sticks to the cement, it's too wet; if it comes off without lifting any, it's dry enough. After you've done a few tops you'll be able to touch the cement with your fingers and tell if it's ready.

Testing the cement dryness is important. If the cement is completely dry you can place the foam on the top and then lift it off, if necessary, as long as you don't apply any pressure. This

way you can make adjustments.

If the cement is still tacky the foam will bond immediately (with no pressure). If you then try to lift the foam, it will tear. So give the cement plenty of time to dry before placing the foam.

Installing the Foam

Begin by placing the small piece to the front. It's not necessary to come down over the windshield pillars but it must come a bit beyond the windshield line. *Be very careful to prevent bubbles or wrinkles.* The foam must be perfectly smooth. If it looks as though there is anything going wrong, stop. Figure out the problem, lift the foam and pull out any glitches. Remember *not* to apply any pressure to the foam until you're ready to adhere it to the roof permanently.

Align the rear piece with the front and ensure a good butt joint between the two. Bring the ends down over the rear pillars. When all looks good and you're ready to adhere the foam to the top, wipe it down firmly with your hand.

If any small bubbles should appear, make a slice in its center with a razor blade. This will let the trapped air out and the bubble will collapse.

Use a single-edge razor blade to trim the foam around the windows and doors. Trim exactly along the roof line and perpendicular to it. At the bottom of the rear pillars, trim the foam along the *top edge* of the masking tape.

Then remove the tape. Use good, new, sharp blades. Dull blades tend to tear rather than cut. When everything is trimmed to your satisfaction, you're ready to start sanding.

The sanding operation feathers the foam into the contour of the body line. This is another reason to use closed-cell foam. It can be sanded just like wood while open-cell foam cannot be sanded at all.

Sand the edges of the foam using a sanding block or a simple block of wood with a piece of sandpaper wrapped around it. Any grit from 100 to 180 will work. Round the edges of the foam you just trimmed until they blend into the contour of the roof line. Don't overdo it. This is a real case of "less is more." You just want a nice smooth contour at the edge. When the edges are done, turn your attention to the top of the roof.

The closed-cell foam you're working with has a very thin "skin" formed by the tops of the surface cells. This skin will peel off under some circumstances but you can prevent it. Here's the problem:

When you bond the cover (you're about to make) to the foam (you've just installed) and try to lift it off, it will pull away the "skin." To prevent this, *very gently* draw the sandpaper across the surface of the foam, cutting through this skin. You're not

Lay the block of material you just cut onto the roof of the car. This way you can double-check before you cut the second piece.

Make life a bit easier by blocking it out before returning to the bench. Leave at least 4 inches of selvage all the way around.

After blocking out one side of the top use it as a pattern to block out the other half.

sanding it off, only cutting through it. Now, when you apply the next layer of cement, prior to bonding the cover, it will penetrate through these very thin cuts and seal the skin to the cells below.

Have you ever seen a car with a vinyl top cruising down the highway and the top looks like one giant bubble? The trimmer who installed it omitted the above step. The top lifted, not breaking the glue bond, but pulling the skin off the foam cells. So spend three extra minutes, gently sand the roof and have a long-lasting finished product.

MAKING THE COVER

Cutting & Sewing

For this type of roof, Charlie cuts two pieces and has a seam down the center of the roof. Your project, as often found on Fords, may have two seams, one on each side of the roof. This is a matter of taste for you the trimmer. The one-seam operation is the simplest. If you're concerned about originality and you need two seams, by all means make it that way. Turn to Chapter 9 on sim-cons to see how the three-piece top is fitted.

The two pieces you cut will be a full 54-inches wide and stretch from the base of the windshield pillar, across the top to a few inches past the front edge of the trunk. Provide plenty of material to work with. If you cut it short

Clockwise from above: Charlie prepares the center seam for reinforcement. First he glues down the 1/2-inch selvage from his initial seam. He then uses a roller to strengthen the bond. Another layer of cement is applied to the seam and to a strip of reinforcing vinyl. This is then applied in the same way, using the roller. Finally, he'll sew a top seam on each side of the main seam resulting in a very strong French seam. Without this reinforcement the center seam might pop open over a period of time from the intense ultraviolet radiation of the sun. It also acts as a better seal against rainwater.

you'll only save pennies while wasting dollars of time.

Locate the centers of the windshield and backlite and mark them with a piece of masking

tape. Later you can refine this to an exact center. For now an approximation will do. Lay one piece of the material over the right or left side of the roof. Let the

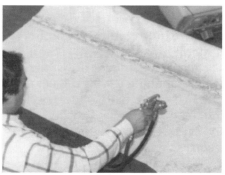

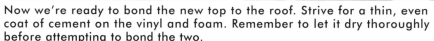
Now we're ready to bond the new top to the roof. Strive for a thin, even coat of cement on the vinyl and foam. Remember to let it dry thoroughly before attempting to bond the two.

Another step to show your professionalism: Keep the cement from the butt joint. By so doing there will be no bond here and the joint won't be seen through the vinyl.

Charlie gets right into his work here. A good strong pull down the seam will make it straight and well-centered. Be sure your center marks are accurate.

Pull your wrinkles out from each of the four corners. This is a bit more successful than working from the center out as we've done before.

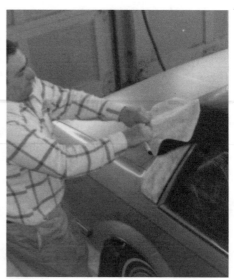

You'll have to do some serious pulling at the backlite pillars to form around the two-way bend at the roofline. Use a little heat if necessary, but be conservative.

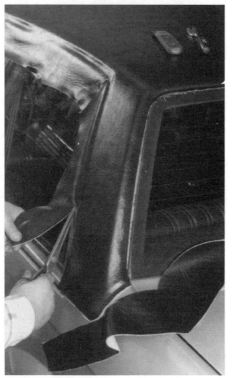

After securing the top, trim the excess. Leave enough to work the raw edges under the various pieces of trim.

edge overlap the previously marked center by 1 or 2 inches. Block out the top by cutting away the material around the windshield, windows and backlite, leaving at least 4 inches of selvage all the way around. This makes the material easier to handle and gives you a shorter seam to sew.

Take this blocked-out piece of material back to the bench and lay it on the other piece of material face-to-face. Match the edges that will be the centerline and cut away the selvage. Now the two pieces are ready to be sewn.

The seam will be a standard, reinforced French seam. After sewing the two pieces together with a 1/2-inch seam allowance, Charlie cements the selvage edges to the body of the material, then cements a reinforcement strip over that. Finally, he top-sews a seam 1/4-inch out on each side of the main seam. This is all the sewing there is. The top can now be cemented to the roof.

Installing the Cover

Return to the car and refine the centers of the windshield and backlite. Measure from the outside of the windshield pillars or from the drip rail and get an exact location for the center. Repeat this for the backlite. The center seam will be located along an imaginary centerline drawn between these two centers.

Spray a thin, even coat of cement over the entire inside of the vinyl top and over the foam on the roof. *Leave a 2-inch strip on each side of the foam butt-joint*

free of cement. If you cement this area, the top will bond here and the butt joint will telegraph through the vinyl. So take particular care not to get cement in this area.

After the cement is thoroughly dry, carry the cover to the car. Place the cover facedown on the hood with the front facing the windshield. Stick the cemented side of the seam onto the centerline mark of the windshield about 4 inches in from the edge.

The top is now lying on the hood faceup with the front edge stuck to the top at the centerline. If you can find a friend to help, gently lay the top back over the roof keeping the seam down the center. Remember not to apply pressure to the vinyl yet. Get up on the trunk as you see Charlie doing in the photo above. Stretch the seam out straight down the center, aligning it with the centerline mark you made on the backlite. Now it's in place. If the seam looks good, press it down *lightly*.

Go now to one of the front corners and pull the top tight, working at about a 45° angle to the centerline. Repeat this at the other front corner. Now move to

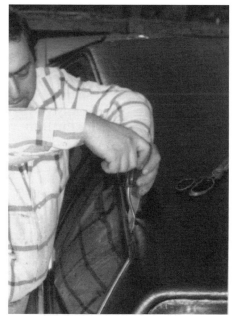

To work around the rear quarter window, Charlie pries back the weatherstrip with a bar and forces the edge of the material underneath with a putty knife.

After filling the gap between the window and roof with sealer, Charlie uses a mallet to force the seal back in place. If you're working with stainless-steel trim you should still use a sealer. It helps prevent leakage around the window and under the edge of your new top. On some older model cars the drip rail is an integral part of the roof line.

Trim your top into the valley of the drip rail, then fill it with silicone sealer. Use your finger to smooth it out. Start at one end and work to the other, leaving a concave surface for the water to run down. Replace all the weatherstrip, being sure it's fastened securely. Use sealer anywhere there might be a chance for water to come in.

Right: Finish off the job by installing the retainers (clips) for the trim molding you made for the bottom of the rear pillars. These are installed with 1/8-inch pop-rivets. For a first-class, long-lasting job, put a dab of sealer on the end of the pop-rivet. This will help prevent water seeping in between the rivet and body panel. In very wet climates this leakage will allow rust to form in the rivet hole. Soon there will be no metal to secure the rivet and the trim will simply drop off. Use the mallet judiciously. Trim is soft and will dent.

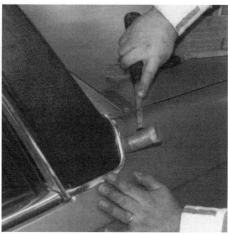

the opposite rear corner and pull out the wrinkles. Finally, pull the wrinkles from the remaining corner.

Don't be afraid to do some serious pulling. The material will neither tear nor pop loose. So get on it and get those wrinkles out. Remember, you're working from the corners this time, not from the centers as you've done before. The last step is to pull the material tightly down over the rear pillars. You may need a little heat to soften the vinyl here as this is a

two-way stretch.

Don't get the vinyl too warm. It overdries the cement, making a weak bond. And, it can cause wrinkling of its own. This is the nature of expanded vinyl. Sometimes in a two-way stretch if the vinyl is too warm it will form unwanted wrinkles. These are very hard to remove, so use care. If you see them starting to form, stop, let the vinyl cool, then go on.

Work the vinyl around the rear pillars then rub the whole top down to ensure a good glue

bond. Now it's taking shape.

Trimming around the Windows

After rubbing the top down and making sure no loose ends are flapping around, you can begin to trim the top to size. Charlie starts by trimming around the windshield and backlite. Be sure there's enough material left after trimming to hide the raw edge under the vinyl bead or stainless-steel trim.

Now go to the bottom of the rear pillars and remove all the

A sharp, new vinyl top. This car will look like a million sitting on the lot.

selvage here but 1-1/2-inches. This will be completely trimmed after you install the aluminum side pieces you made.

As Charlie trims around the quarter window he leaves enough material to work under the seals to hide the raw edges here. He glues the front edges to the tops of the door jambs where the weatherstrip will cover it. When everything is trimmed you can begin putting the weatherstrip and window seals back on.

If your project is like ours, the next step is to finish off around the rear quarter windows. Charlie uses a small pry bar to pull back the rubber and a putty knife to push the vinyl in under it. This seems to work quite well.

PUTTING IT TOGETHER

Installing the Windshield/ Backlite Trim (Seal)

Whatever you removed from around the windshield and backlite must now go back in. Our Buick used a vinyl bead so Charlie will put it back. First, he runs a very generous bead of sealer (silicone) around the edge of the window. Then he puts the bead back in place and taps it down a few times with a plastic mallet. To finish, he wipes away any sealer that squishes out.

If you are replacing stainless, be sure all the clips that hold it in are in good shape. These are fastened to the windshield and backlite frames with screws or pop rivets. Some are mounted on studs welded to the frame. All are removable and replaceable if bent or broken. When all is in order, again, run a bead of sealer around the window. Put the trim in place and hammer it home with the heel of your hand. If this isn't enough force, use a rubber mallet rather than a wood, plastic or leather one. These might dent your trim.

Move to the sides of the car and install the weatherstrip. Some trimmers like to run a bead of sealer between the door jam and weatherstrip. This makes a devil of a job removing the weatherstrip next time. I usually choose not to do it. If you think you need it to stop any water leaks, go ahead. But know that next time you'll be using a knife to get the weatherstrip out of the door jamb!

Installing Rear Pillar Trim

Now you must install the two pieces of aluminum trim you made. Along with the strips of aluminum you should have received a hand full of plastic fasteners and at least four end caps. Pop-rivet these plastic fasteners to the body

of the car. Locate the hole by peeking under the edge of the vinyl. Use a punch or awl to make a hole. You'll never get the pop rivet through otherwise. Finally, use your plastic mallet to snap the trim over the fasteners. Any vinyl sticking out from under the trim should be removed with a razor blade. The last step is to replace the emblem.

The emblem is replaced using hot-melt glue. I'm afraid it's the only thing which will hold it in place. If you haven't got a glue gun you'll have to beg or borrow it. Place a couple of dabs on the backside and pop it on. Use as little as possible so it doesn't squeeze out, looking unsightly. Now you have a new vinyl roof.

SUMMARY

In this chapter you learned to work with closed-cell foam. You'll find a number of uses for this material as you proceed further into the profession. It's used in a lot of areas where a nice "feel" is needed (instrument panels, luggage panels, door panels.) Two things are important to remember: (1) it has a skin which can peel off and (2) when cementing it, let the cement dry thoroughly.

You used a French seam again. This time you cemented everything together first. This made it a little easier to sew but more to our need, it helped keep the top water-tight.

Using the skills you've learned in this chapter we'll get into something a bit more complicated in the next: a simulated convertible top, or as it's called on the street, a sim-con.

ALUMINUM TRIM MOLDING—FINISHING THE ENDS

In some instances you may not be able to find end caps for the trim moldings you make. If this happens, follow these directions to finish the trim ends.

After making all your bends, trim the ends of the molding. Include an extra 1/4 inch at each end. Usually we cut the molding with a hack saw. This leaves a ragged edge which must be filed smooth before installation.

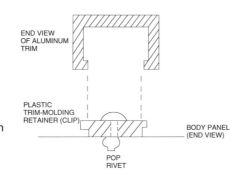

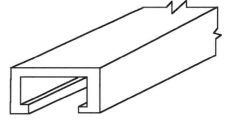

Cutaway view shows how retainer holds trim to body panel.

Using a pair of dikes (diagonal wire cutters) cut a 1/4-inch notch in each end of the trim sidewall.

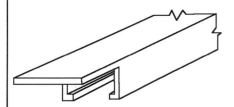

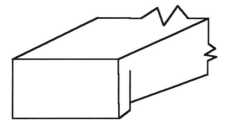

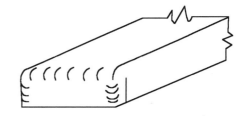

This leaves a 1/4-inch "lip" protruding from the top of the molding.

You should have what looks like a little boxed end. Use a sharp file to bring the lip to the level of the sidewall.

Round off the sharp corners and smooth things up. A little work with fine sandpaper (200 to 400 grit) gets rid of the file marks and leaves a nice burnished finish.

9

Making & Installing a Sim-con Top

Shortly after the last American convertible rolled off the assembly line in the late '70s, people started thinking, "Gee, this body style sure would look swell as a convertible!" Within months vinyl tops were being replaced with convertible-top material. Next, some enterprising trimmer started adding a piece of wire-on across the back as was done on all convertible tops before. Well, faster than you can say "dollar bills" three times in succession, someone developed a fiberglass shell which looked as though it had two convertible-top bows. The simulated convertible top was born and, as they say on Broadway, "the rest is history."

The convertible top has made a resurgence since then but the sim-con remains. This chapter shows you how to recover one.

REMOVING THE TOP

Charlie Calanna is again our guide through "top-land." Having done hundreds of these, he shows us some of his excellent tricks and shortcuts. He begins by removing the reveal molding under the finishing trim at the backlite. This is retained with a half-dozen

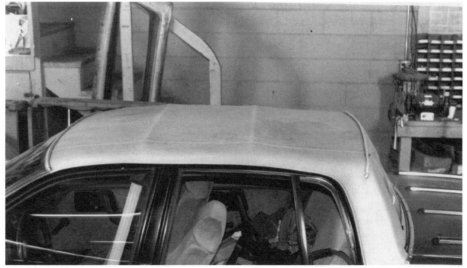

Here's our project car. It certainly doesn't look too bad until you get close and see the stains and wear. When we're through with it, it will look brand-new again.

sheet-metal screws. After removing the reveal molding the retainers can be removed. Finally, the finish trim below the backlite is removed by drilling out the pop rivets. This part must wait, however, until the top is off the car because the rivets are concealed by the edge of the top.

Working around the back of the top, Charlie removes the trim at the rear quarter panel. He then drills out the rivets securing the

When Charlie pulls the reveal molding he finds five clips retaining the bottom of the backlite finishing trim.

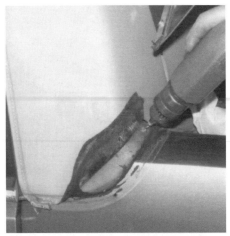

Before finishing trim can be removed, top-shell must come off. To do so, Charlie removes rivets securing rear of the top shell to rear quarter panel of the car body.

Top is also retained in front with rivets which must be removed. These are hidden by a trim piece called *wire-on*. Pry the flap back with your thumb to reveal the rivets on your top.

Edge of top and top itself are sealed to the roof with silicone cement. Charlie uses a kitchen table knife, sharpened to a keen edge, to cut through this seal around the windows.

top to the body. The wire-on across the back of the top does not secure the top to the car. Therefore, this piece is left until after the top is off. Pop rivets in the front wire-on, however, help secure the top to the car.

The wire-on is folded back to expose the rivets. These are removed using a 1/8-inch or #30

drill. These must be completely removed to get the top off. Look for any other fasteners on your project and be sure they're removed before beginning the next step.

Breaking the Bond
All fiberglass top shells are held to the roof with massive amounts of silicone cement. I say "massive"

because there's a big gap between the roof and the top shell and massive to ensure the top doesn't blow off at highway speeds. And yes, in spite of everyone's best effort, they have been known to blow off. It's Murphy's Law at work. Unfortunately for the trimmer, this effort to glue the top onto the roof is quite successful. Getting a secure one off almost requires dynamite.

Charlie has made a tool which does a great job of cutting the silicone bond. He took a common garden hoe and straightened the shank between blade and handle. This changed the blade-to-handle relationship from 90° to 180°. He then added the hand grip from a snow shovel to finish the tool. He uses this with a jabbing motion to cut the bond between the roof and top shell. Of course, he keeps the blade razor-sharp. A dull blade would only bounce off the silicone rather than cut through.

To begin the separation Charlie uses a sharpened table knife to cut through the bond around the side windows. It's unusual, however, to bond around the backlite. There's little danger of the wind lifting the top here. When all the edges are separated, Charlie goes to work with the hoe.

Using sharpened steel bars, a reworked hoe and a lot of muscle power, Charlie cuts through silicone bonding the top to the roof.

I must add a word of caution here: *this operation almost always dents the roof.* This is virtually impossible to prevent. If you put the shell back on there's no problem. If you plan to leave it off you'll have to deal with the dents. In the shop we've never been asked to remove a shell and not put it back. If I were called on to do this I might try using a machete or a butcher knife fastened to the end of 3-foot stick. Then I could slice and not jab. If you come up with a better solution, let us know!

When all the silicone bonds are cut, lift the top from the car and set it on a couple of saw horses. Because Charlie does two or three of these a week, he's built some extensions on his horses so he doesn't work bent over.

After drilling out the pop rivets in the rear wire-on, simply rip the old cover off and throw it away. It will not be used for a pattern. Using one of the wax-and-grease removers described in the last chapter (Pre-Kleeno) wash away all the old cement which held the fabric to the shell.

The old silicone on the underside can be scraped away with a knife or razor blade. Charlie uses a razor blade to clean the silicone from the roof. Finally, using a fine sandpaper (150 to 200 grit), sand the entire top of the shell and around the edges on the underside. If you have a double-action (D.A.) sander or an orbital sander (jitterbug,) use it. We use a D.A. in the shop. A belt sander or body sander will cut grooves in the fiberglass. Stay away from these and do it by hand otherwise.

We do this to remove the wax embedded in the top shell. The wax is a mold-release vehicle used in the manufacture of the top. By removing it, you ensure a better bond between the shell and the top material. This works against Murphy and his law. It keeps the cover tightly cemented to the top shell so no big bubbles appear two weeks after it's finished.

With all the silicone bonds cut through, one man can lift the top from the roof.

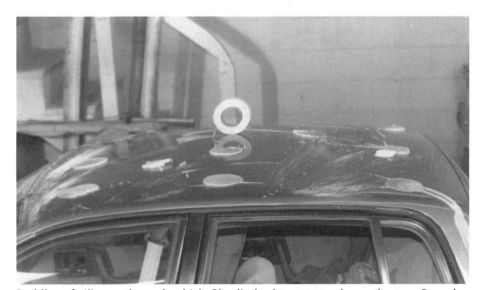

Puddles of silicone through which Charlie had to cut to release the top. Round item in the center of the picture is a roll of masking tape. Someone threw it up there when I wasn't looking!

Right: Top should be "surgically" clean before you begin to cover it. This ensures a tight bond and no lumps. After cleaning with a grease-and-wax remover, Charlie sands the top to remove the wax mold release left over from the manufacture of the top.

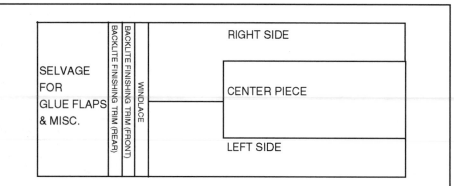

SELVAGE FOR GLUE FLAPS & MISC.

BACKLITE FINISHING TRIM (REAR)

BACKLITE FINISHING TRIM (FRONT)

WINDLACE

RIGHT SIDE

CENTER PIECE

LEFT SIDE

Cutting diagram Charlie uses for almost all sim-con tops: It's a bit unusual but you can see how well it utilizes the material.

Notice what appear to be white cuffs on Charlie's shirt on this and many of the following photos. This is masking tape Charlie has bound around his wrists and shirt. This prevents fiberglass particles from irritating his wrists while he is sanding the top.

FITTING THE MATERIAL

Determining how much material to buy is fairly simple. Measure from the front to the rear with a 3-inch allowance at each end. Add another yard for trim and that's it. If you can't use Charlie's cutting diagram (your center piece is too wide) you'll have to work out your own. Now measure the width of the front, double that and add 10 percent. This is the amount of matching wire-on you'll need. Measure around the window edges and the backlite for the length of binding needed. Buy

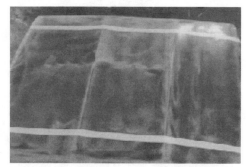

Charlie uses masking tape to lay out his cutting lines. Two 5/8-inch strips, one on each side of the planned seam line will produce a 5/8-inch seam allowance. If you want to have a 1/2-inch seam allowance on your job, use 1/2-inch tape.

about twice this much so you'll have some to practice on before commiting to the project. While you're at the fabric house pick up four stainless-steel finishing tips for the wire-on and 5 feet of rubber windlace core, the 1/2-inch size if they have it. This and a quart of cement will do the job.

The sim-con top shell is made just as the cover for a convertible top: with three pieces. You'll have a center and two side pieces. Before he starts cutting material, Charlie does some preparation on the top shell.

He begins by drawing a pencil line along the center of the radius between the top and back of the shell. This will serve to locate where a number of pieces come together. Then he marks the centers at the front and rear edges.

The center piece of the cover will take up about two thirds of the top. The remaining third will be for the two side pieces. Measure across your top from the centers of the outside radii and determine what two thirds would be. (48-inches divided by 3 equals 16; 2 times 16 equals 32. Therefore, the center section would be about 32-inches wide.) The seam lines would then lie about 16-inches on each side of the center mark.

None of this is carved in stone. You have to use your own judgment. What *looks* good is what's right. You may want to make the center piece larger or smaller. Do what looks balanced to you.

The photo to the left shows Charlie laying down a lot of masking tape on the top shell. Here's what he's doing. These pieces of masking tape locate the seam line and the cutting lines. If the masking tape appears a bit wide for seam allowance, it is. Charlie uses 5/8-inch tape resulting in a 5/8-inch seam allowance. If you choose, use 1/2-inch tape and you'll have your usual 1/2-inch seam allowance.

Charlie lays a strip of masking tape on each side of the previously located seam line. When he fits the center section he'll trim it to the outboard strip of tape. The sides will be fit to the inboard strip of tape. This will leave a 5/8-inch seam allowance on each piece.

Notice the seams at the back edge angle in. This is the way a real convertible top is fitted so Charlie makes his the same way. You could bring the seam straight down without affecting the fit but it wouldn't look right. Angle the seam in about 1 inch from center.

Cutting It Out and Rough Fitting

Measure the top for its three pieces. The sides are measured from the front edge to the bottom of the rear and from the seam line to the bottom edge. The center piece extends from the front to the top edge of the backlite cut-out. Give yourself lots of material to play with. Remember to allow about 3 or 4 inches all around to tuck under.

Begin with the center section. Lay it on the top, anchor it with a few spring clamps and locate the outside cutting lines according to the outboard strips of masking tape. Trim the selvage along the outside piece of masking tape. This will give you the correct seam allowance. Remember, if you use 5/8-inch tape, sew your seam 5/8-inch in from the edge; 1/2-inch tape means you'll need to sew 1/2 inch in.

Don't forget the angle at the top of the backlite cutout. Make a location mark at the radius line you drew between the top and back section. This is an important locating mark. Don't leave it out. This will line up with the corresponding mark on the side pieces. After fitting the center, fit the right or left side.

Again, clamp or tape the material in position so it just covers the inboard piece of masking tape. Be sure it lies straight and flat. Now pull the material smoothly down what would be the rear post if this were the roof of a car. Clamp it at the bottom edge. Next, smooth the material around the back of the shell and clamp it at the backlite cutout. You should now have a big dart of material at the radius line.

Lay this dart forward and pencil a line on the top of the material following your radius line. Lay the dart back and pencil another line, again along the radius. If you open the material you'll see you've drawn a large 30-degree "V." Trim on the inside of your pencil lines leaving about 1/4-inch allowance. Your corner should now look like the photo on page 116.

Trim away the material along the inboard edge of the masking tape for your correct seam allowance. Rough cut around the

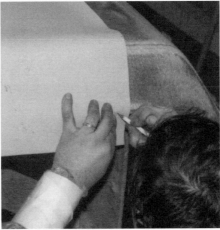

Be sure you buy convertible-top material for your project. The inside must be black; black fabric darkens any voids which might occur between the top and the roof. The outside may be any color vinyl you wish.

Right: Sides are fit next. You'll only need to fit one side, then use it as a pattern for the other.

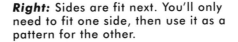

Fit the center piece first. Mark and trim on the outside edge of the masking tape to make your seam allowance.

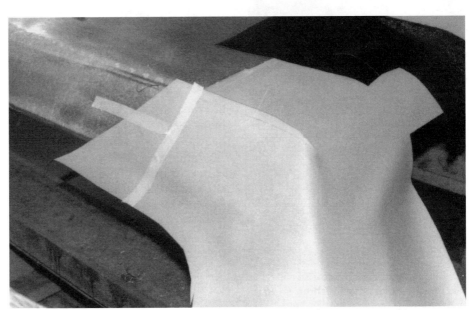

Charlie has smoothed all the wrinkles from the material. He uses masking tape and clamps to hold things in place as he works. Notice all the excess material has been brought together and trimmed away at the radius between the top and back of the shell. He leaves only 1/4-inch selvage here.

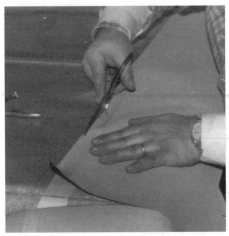

By trimming along the *inboard* edge of the masking tape you can create the correct seam allowance for the side pieces.

Here's the finished side piece being used as a pattern for the opposite side. Note the 30° "V" at what would be the radius if the piece were still on the top.

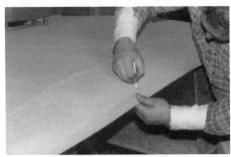

As Charlie makes the finishing fit on the top cover, he's careful to make his seam-line mark directly on the edge of the top shell. If he should err on one side it would be to make his line lower, almost under the edge. A line above the edge would finish the top too tight.

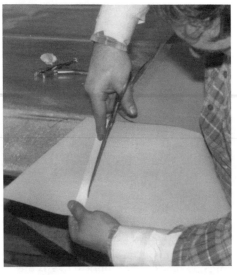

backlite and windows leaving a 1/2- to 2-inch selvage. At the bench, lay this fitted side face-down on the other side piece. Trim the new piece to match and you've finished the rough fit.

SEWING

Fine Fitting

At the machine, sew the center and side pieces together using a flat-fell seam. The selvage faces inboard. Be sure the location mark you made on the center piece at the radius lines up with the "V" you cut at the radius in the side pieces. The "V" need not be sewn. Just bring the two edges together, overlap the 1/4-inch allowance and continue your seam to the end. Later, this "V" will be further refined and trimmed, then cemented closed to the top shell.

Carry the cover back to the top shell, throw it on and clamp it into position. Make it tight and smooth everywhere. Be sure the seams fall along the center of the two pieces of masking tape. Check the "V," assuring yourself it is di-rectly over the pencil line along the back-edge radius. These are all your location areas. If you fit and cut correctly they'll all fall in place. If something is wrong, fix it now, even if it means buying more material. I'm sure it came out tight and true, so let's finish

fitting it.

With chalk, pencil or crayon, mark around the window and backlite edges. Pull the material fairly tight and make your line just a bit *under* the edge, especially around the backlite. When you finish the job, this will help the binding lie close to the body and backlite as it should. Remove the cover and carry it to the bench.

Trim the selvage leaving a 1/4-inch seam allowance. This is important. No 1/2-inch seam allowance here. The seam you sew must be directly on the line you marked. It will then be finished with a binding. First, however, you must cut and fit the inside pieces. These flaps will be cemented to the inside of the top keeping the edges in place.

Cut two strips of top material 3-inches wide and the length of the side piece to the curve around the window. Cut two pieces about 10-inches wide and long enough to finish down the side. You now have enough material to go the entire length of the side piece.

Lay the 10-inch-wide piece of material faceup and under the radius of the side piece as you see Charlie doing in the photo. Mark along the selvage edge and cut directly along that line. Charlie trims the material to look pretty. You can trim it so it's about 3-inches wide. Lay it facedown on the other 10-inch-wide piece of material and cut a piece for the other side. Repeat these steps at the backlite. You'll have one piece across the top edge and a piece along each side edge. The side-edge pieces will carry the radius. Now these pieces must be sewn to the top cover.

Sewing It Together

The easiest way to do this is to staple things together first. Staple the long piece to the long edge of the side.

Be sure the edges are aligned. The face of the long strip must lie against the back side of the top cover. If you turn the assembly

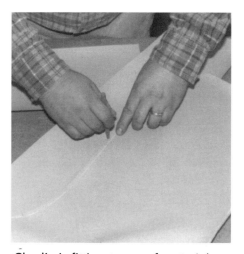

Charlie is fitting scraps of material here to make the flaps that will be glued to the underside of the top, keeping the edges in the correct location. Here he works face-to-back. This keeps the back of the material between the top and the roof black. Any gaps or voids are far less noticeable this way.

Again, you need to fit only one side then use it as a pattern.

Ah, what luxury the professional has. This is a standard Singer® sewing machine set up with a binding attachment. In seconds Charlie can bind the edges of this top. By hand it would take much, much, longer.

over you'll only see the black backs of both pieces of material. Why this instead of front-to-front as before? You want the black back facing out. Any gaps between the shell and roof will only be seen as black voids.

Staple the curved piece to its location. These two pieces should butt together, not overlap. Now the entire edge of the side is reinforced. There are no gaps; all edges match and only the backside of the material shows. Repeat this with the other side and around the backlite then carry the assembly to the sewing machine.

Top stitch right down the pencil line sewing the two layers of material together. Remove the staples when you finish sewing. Trim the selvage now to about 3/16 inch. This will smooth things out. Do both sides and the backlite. Now you can sew the binding. Before you start binding your project, do a little practicing first.

Sew a couple pieces of scrap together with straight runs, inside and outside curves. Trim along the seam line. Wrap the binding around the edge of this assembly

and start sewing. I make the wrap a little unbalanced. Rather than half the binding on top and half on the bottom, I give the bottom just a bit more. This decreases the chance of not catching the bottom with my stitch.

There's a tendency to stretch the binding in the curve. Avoid this by gently pushing into the curve rather than pulling. You'll get the hang of it quickly and can get right on with your project.

The matching binding you bought is about 5/8-inch wide. When folded in half and wrapped around the material, you have just about 1/4-inch coverage. Try wrapping it around the selvage edge. If it doesn't cover the seam, trim away some more material. When it covers the seam completely, wrap it around the edge and sew it on. Sew as close to the edge as possible. Check occasionally to make sure the stitch is catching the other side of the binding. Bind both sides and the backlite cutout. Then you can start cementing the cover to the shell.

PUTTING THE COVER ON

Once again throw the cover over

the shell and pull everything tight. This time pull the newly sewn flaps over the edges so they can be cemented to the inside. Clamp things down so the top is snug and well aligned.

Here's a great trick. Directly at the union of the "V" dart and center panel, over the previously drawn line in the center of the radius, put in a pop rivet. Be sure the seam line is correctly located. Do the same on the other side. Now the cover will stay correctly located while you move it about to spray your cement.

Pull the main body of the cover back over the rear of the top and spray a layer of cement on the center piece and on the center section of the shell. You've removed the masking tape lines but left a mark in the front where you wish the seam to fall. Now let the cement dry thoroughly so it passes the paper test described in the previous chapter. You didn't read Chapter 8? Alright, here it is.

Allow the cement to dry until a piece of paper (brown paper bag) will not adhere when touched to the cemented surface. It should only be pressed lightly. If it sticks to the cement it's still wet. The

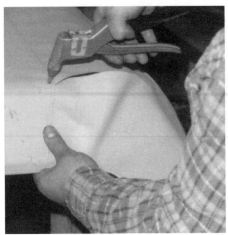

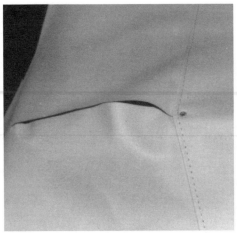

So he can move the cover without disrupting its location, Charlie rivets it to the top at the radius line. This is the also the strongest area of the top and would only pull past the rivets with a lot of excess force.

The cover is cemented to the top shell one section at a time. We begin with the center section and work out. Remember to let the cement dry before attempting a bond.

cement must be dry so the material doesn't adhere to the shell the minute the two touch. You must be able to move the material around a bit.

When you feel the cement is ready, stretch the seam tightly across the top shell and anchor it in the front. Repeat with the other side. If the seams come out straight and true, landing on the marks you made in the front, press the seams down so they adhere to the top. If you don't have a good fit, lift them and adjust accordingly. When everything is right, rub the entire center with the palm of your hand. Make sure the cover is well attached to the shell.

Roll the back and sides up onto the center piece so they and the shell can be sprayed. Again, give the cement time to dry. Begin at the back and pull it down until the bound edge of the cover is in line with the edge of the backlite opening. Smooth this area out, making sure the edge lines up all the way across. Roll the corner over the shell as you see Charlie doing in the photo above (top center, right-hand page). Be sure the "V" cutout remains over the radius. Finish rolling the back down the shell. Keep the edge at the backlite opening in place and the edge around the window area in place. This may require a bit of lateral

stretching. Beware of pulling wrinkles into the material.

Go to the front of the shell and pull the side piece until all the wrinkles are out and the bound edge of the material falls in line with the edge of the shell. When there are no wrinkles and everything is in line, rub the cover down, bonding it tightly to the shell. Now, we'll turn the shell over and glue down the flaps.

This is fairly standard stuff. Spray cement on both surfaces, allow it to dry then bond it together. At the corners, trim the material to

Get on it, Charlie! Make that seam *straight*. No wrinkles here!

Back and sides are cemented next. Be careful not to get overspray on the material. Extra cement can be removed with grease-and-wax remover if you do.

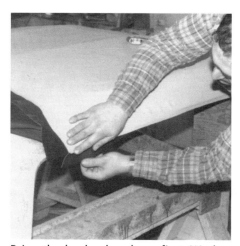

Bring the back edge down first. Work to get the binding around the backlite cutout straight and even.

Roll the corner into position. This is tricky. Notice that Charlie had to peel the back up a little.

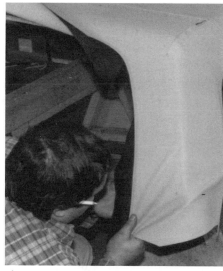

The important thing is to get the edges of the material directly over the edges of the top. Those 45° wrinkles you see on the pillar will pull out easily with a little downward tug.

a 45° angle to cut down the bulk.

On our project Charlie glues only the flaps and the front edge. The bottoms of the "pillars" are not glued. This allows him to pop rivet this area to the body of the car then cover the rivets with the top material.

The most important part of gluing the flaps is to keep the binding straight. If you pull more in one area than another the binding will be wavy. Be careful to prevent this.

The front of the top is finished with what's called a *windlace* or front *weather seal*. This is a round core of rubber about 1/2 inch thick covered with top material. You should have purchased this with the rest of your materials. If not, it's available through your local fabric-supply house. It's sewn up just like a big piece of welt.

Cut a strip of material about 4 inches wide and 4 inches longer than the width of the top. Wrap this around the rubber core, fold the end over about 2 inches and run a tight seam against the core. Finish as you started by folding the remaining end over about 2 inches. Cement this to the inside front of the top shell with the folds

down toward the roof of the car. Be sure the seam does not show and the windlace fits snug along the front edge. With the help of a friend, turn the top over and finish the back edge with wire-on.

Lay the wire-on onto the top with the bead (the part that looks like a welt) facing the rear. Allow about 3 inches of overlap at each end. This will come down the side of the top. Anchor one end with a pop rivet near the pop rivet you installed earlier. The rivet should be close to the bead to allow the hiding part of the wire-on to fold over, covering it.

Pull the wire-on quite tight and anchor the other end. Now place rivets about 6 inches apart along the entire length. Be sure to keep the wire-on straight as you drill and rivet. Fold the large flap over to meet the bead along the full length. Use a plastic mallet, tapping it tightly closed. Finish each end with one of the stainless-steel trim pieces you bought with the wire-on. These should be anchored with a #4 X 3/4-inch countersunk sheetmetal screw. Guess what? The top is finished and ready to mount back on the car!

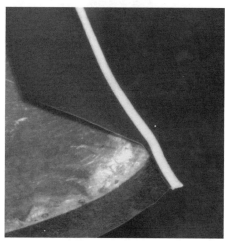

When gluing the flaps on the underside, cut the ends at an angle. This eliminates some of the bulk in the corners.

MOUNTING THE TOP

Everything you do now will be in reverse order of disassembly. Before you can mount the top shell to the roof you must install the finishing trim at the bottom of the backlite. To see Charlie's trick for covering the finishing trim, read the sidebar starting on page 122.

Position the trim under the backlite. Retain it with pop rivets at each end and replace any reveal-molding retainer-clips. Don't put the reveal molding on yet; it goes

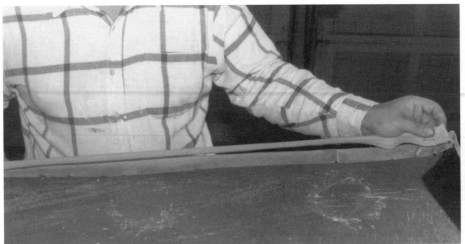

It makes a nice appearance and a good finish to the front of the top. Notice this piece on real convertibles.

Charlie has made his windlace as described in Chapter 11 (page 152). Now he's getting ready to cement it in place.

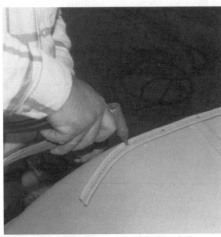

More decorative attachment. The wire-on must be pop-riveted to the shell. On a regular convertible it would be stapled or tacked to the rear bow. Fiberglass will not readily accept staples or tacks. It's not real friendly to screws, either.

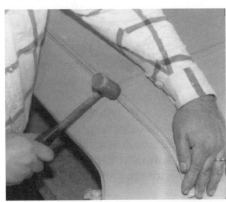

To get a nice tight seal on the wire-on, after folding it over to cover the rivets, Charlie finishes off with a few good taps with a plastic mallet.

on after the top shell is secured. Now prepare the roof of the car for the top.

If you haven't done it yet, clean off all the old silicone. Use a single- edge razor blade for this. Don't worry about making it super-clean. If the silicone is tightly bonded to the roof, the next application will bond tightly to the old. Just get rid of the lumps.

Sealing the Top to the Roof

Buy at least three tubes of silicone for this job. The best price will usually be at your local auto-glass store. Hardware stores carry it, but at a price 30 to 50% higher.

Begin by running a 1/2- to 3/4-inch bead along the front edge of the roof, then one near the rear edge. Keep the front bead back about 3 inches so it doesn't seep out. Make five or six pools around the roof about 4 inches wide and maybe 2 inches high. Make a large bead, about 1 inch, on each of the rear roof pillars close to the window. Not so close, however, as to cause the silicone to squeeze out onto the trim or glass.

If you want to be dead certain your top is secure, place some pools of silicone on the underside of the top shell, corresponding in location to those on the roof. With everything all gooped up, get a friend to help you lift the top onto the roof. Set it down squarely so it

doesn't have to be lifted again to adjust it.

There should be enough silicone under the top to prevent it from setting as you set it down. Therefore, a little pushing and shoving will be necessary. Work it down until the rear pillars align with the rivet holes in the rear quarters and the front edge is seated tightly to the roof line. These are the two areas you'll rivet. If you're aligned here, you're aligned all over.

It may be necessary to clip the selvage around the base of the rear pillar to allow it to slide into place. Clip where necessary, but don't clip past the edge of the shell.

Attaching Top shell to the Roof

You should be able to align the rivet holes in the top shell with the originals in the rear quarter. Lift the top material revealing the shell beneath. Use an awl through a hole in the shell to locate the corresponding one in the body. If you can't do this you're probably not seated well enough. Do some more pushing and shoving until the holes line up. When they do, "pop" in a rivet.

Replace any trim molding around the base of the pillar. Only after replacing the molding should you trim the material. This assures you the top material is

Last piece off, first piece on. Finishing trim at the backlite is installed with a rivet at each end and clips along the bottom.

Right: Charlie called on Marvin, "Convertible-top King," for a little help getting the new sim-con in place.

Make a slash here so the top will sit well on the roof and align over the rivet holes in the rear quarter panel. Try to keep the slash in line with the edge of the fender for the neatest appearance.

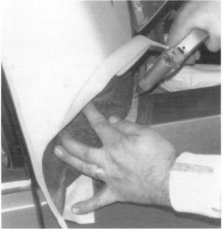

Rivet the top to the quarter panel and install the trim. If you have trouble locating the original rivet holes, use an awl or trim pin. Insert it through a rivet hole in the top and search around till you feel the corresponding hole in the body. Use the awl to push or pull the top into position.

well secured. If you omit this step and trim first, the top material may shrink away from the molding creating an unprofessional appearance.

Now you can snap or screw the reveal molding back on to complete the finishing trim at the base of the backlite. The rear of the top is finished. Turn your attention to the front.

It's unlikely you can align the original rivet holes in the front.

You've covered over the ones in the top with fabric and there are three layers of material between the bottom of the shell and the roof. The solution is to drill new holes.

Start in each corner. Drill a 1/8-inch hole and place a rivet. You'll need a rivet about 1 inch long. You're going through a lot of materials. You'll know you're catching the metal of the roof as you'll feel the top pull down. *Be sure these rivets catch.* Remem-

ber: there's more than one sim-con lying broken beside the highway. Don't let yours be next.

Now, as you did with the rear wire-on, place another in the front. This time the bead faces the *front* and the rivets go all the way through the roof. Try to keep it touching the windlace for the sake of appearance. Finish the ends with another pair of stainless-steel tips and you've got a great looking sim-con!

COVERING THE FINISHING TRIM

If you have a piece of finishing trim at the base of the backlite (and 90% of these tops do) you can get into a sticky mess trying to get the cover on straight. It must be covered on both sides and cemented in place. The bound edge along the top must be arrow-straight. Here's how it's done:

After removing the old cover Charlie lays the metal strip *faceup* on the top material leaving just a little (1/2-inch) selvage at the bottom. He then draws a line along the top of the trim. When he cuts this piece out, the pencil line will be his seam line. Because this cover gets a binding he'll only allow 3/16 to 1/4 inch for seam allowance.

After cutting this piece he uses it as a pattern for the back side. It can be faceup or facedown as it's uniform throughout. He lays it facedown here so you can see it better. Then he sews the two pieces together at the top, with the binding, face-to-back. Therefore, from the backside you see only the back of the material. *Trim the back piece so it's 1/2-inch narrower than the width of the metal strip. This is an important step!*

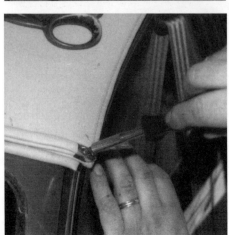

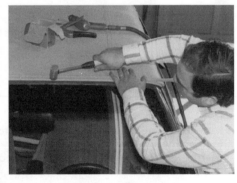

Finish the rear by replacing the reveal molding. Install the wire-on in the front. Be sure the bead faces the front and the rivets are long enough to reach through to the metal in the top. If it's not secure here, you could find your new top on the highway, or worse, someone wearing it!

SUMMARY

Now you've learned a few new procedures. You can sew binding, you've worked with wire-on and made windlace. If you get into restoring old cars you'll make miles of windlace. This was used to seal around the doors between the jamb and headliner areas. In those days it really did help keep the drafts down; hence the name *windlace.*

The demonstration Charlie did for you on this top represents one of several types of designs. If your design was not covered here or in the next chapter on quarter tops, get out the old Polaroid camera and make some shots of anything you feel you might not remember when assembly time rolls around. This can save minutes or even hours of frustration.

t Charlie sprays a thin coat of ent to the *front* of the metal .

Now he opens the newly sewn envelope and sprays a thin coat to the *back* of the front piece of material. He's very careful not to get cement anywhere else. Now he lets the envelope close.

Carefully, Charlie lays the metal strip, *front down* against the back piece of the material, aligning the metal edge with the edge of the binding. Remember that he cut the back piece 1/2 inch narrower than the metal? This now leaves a 1/2-inch surface of exposed cement on the front piece of material to bond to the front of the metal strip. Because there is no cement on the back piece of material, it will not bond here. *Cont. next page*

Here's our finished top. The car, however, is not ready for the road until they replace that broken windshield.

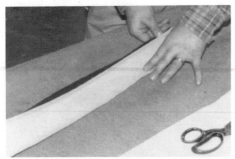

Left: With the bond holding everything in line, Charlie pulls the back material out from under the front of the metal strip allowing these to bond and align correctly with the edge.

Now he needs only to glue the back piece of material to the back of the metal strip.

Right: Charlie finishes by trimming the front selvage along the bottom edge of the metal. If you follow this procedure, the cover will come out smooth and in correct alignment.

The ridges you see running the length of the top is the seam allowance telegraphing through the material. This is perfectly normal and a desired characteristic. The seam allowance must be dead-on or these ridges will look amateurish.

ALTERNATIVE FRONT RETAINERS

Another way to secure the front edge of a sim-con is used where there's a lot of crown at the front edge or when a sunroof is involved. Rather than riveting the front edge of the top to the roof, the top and roof have an interlock device.

A sheet-metal "lip" is riveted to the top and a corresponding lip is riveted to the roof. This design allows the two lips to interlock when the top is slid onto the roof. The accompanying photos and line drawing illustrates this difference.

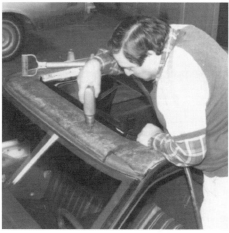

So much silicone sealer was added when the top and roof were joined that the interlock cannot be removed. Charlie must drill out each pop rivet in the interlock device, cut the sealer and then remove the top.

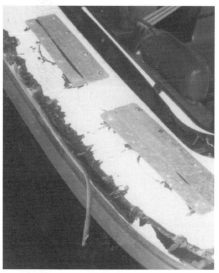

Both sections of the interlock remain together on the roof when the top is removed. The two parts can be separated by cleaning away the silicone around the device.

Top sections of the interlock must be riveted on before applying the cover. As the first trimmer did, Charlie will goop everything with sealer before sliding the top back on.

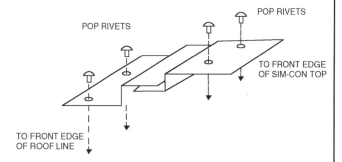

This is a drawing of the the way the interlock connects. The interlock must be slid together as the top is mounted to the roof.

10 Building a Quarter or Landau Top

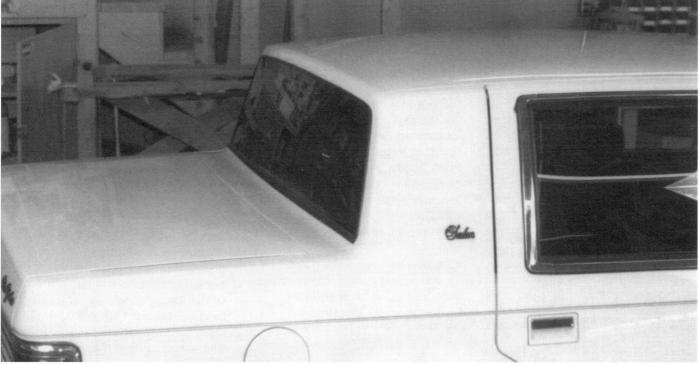

Here's how it comes to the shop: naked. The first step is to use the heat gun to take off the emblem.

This top business is as involved as the interiors. This is our third top project and I've completely skipped half tops, unpadded vinyl-tops, quarter and half vinyl-tops, tops with sunroofs, moon roofs and air vents, plus those designs still on the drawing board! Although there are many of these top designs, the three covered here should equip you to do any of them.

The quarter top is essentially the back 1/4 of a sim-con. There are enough differences, however, to require a new chapter. Rather than fitting the fabric to the top while supported on horses, the quarter top is fit on the car. Some of the backlite must be blocked out. The aluminum trim is different and you'll be adding exterior opera lights. Let's get into it and see how these differences are handled.

PREPARATION

Our project is an after market installation. In other words, the car didn't come with a top from the factory. Our friend Charlie will install it from scratch rather than recover an existing one. The

Charlie test fits the top first. Don't omit this step. Some adjustment is usually necessary. Check carefully for good fit around all the edges.

Because you'll be taking the top on and off a couple of times, use screws rather than pop-rivets to secure it to the roof. Remember to put the screws in the trim molding channels. Indents on side of top are for opera light and emblem.

When mounting door trim, check for alignment. Then be sure the door opens and closes correctly and there's room for the vinyl cover.

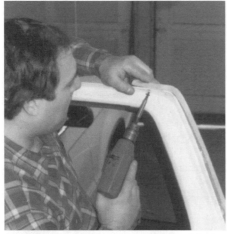

Locate the aluminum tabs embedded in the fiberglass. Mark their location on the door edge and drive your screws into them. Fiberglass will not grip screw threads so be sure you've got the screws in the tabs.

fiberglass shell and aluminum trim are purchased as a kit. The material and opera lights are purchased separately. When Charlie receives the shell the first thing he must do is fit it to the car.

Unfortunately, the shells do not always fit correctly. Try yours on the car. Look for gaps around the edges. Will the doors open and close properly with the top and door posts in place? Is the cutout for the upper stoplight in the right place? Do the shell edges fit tightly around the backlite? You may have to do some filing or

some building up.

Charlie found the door trim did not align with the top shell. To get the thickness he needed he added a layer of 1/4-inch vinyl-top padding to give him the needed extra height. Polyester primers, plastic auto-body fillers, work well also where an area must be built up. These fillers are sold under various names such as *Bondo*® and *Feather Fill*®. They're available at your local auto paint supply house. Check everything before you begin. It will save a lot of headaches down the line.

When everything checks out, fix the shell to the top with sheet-metal screws. Charlie uses #6 and #8 pan-head Phillips in lengths of 1 to 1-1/2 inches. Place the screws in the channels designed for the trim molding. This will allow the molding to cover them. Use this method too, to attach the door trim along the edge closest to the window.

Along the edge of the trim which aligns with the edge of the door, there will be aluminum tabs sealed into the fiberglass. These accept screws driven in from behind the lip of the door as seen in the photo on the left. Should your screw come out through the

fiberglass, file it down or replace it with a shorter one.

After securing the shell to the car, check the fit once more. Can you open and close the doors with no rubbing? Check closely here. Will it clear when material is wrapped around the shell? Check again at the backlite. Does it still seal?

Blocking Out the Backlite

When you're satisfied everything is in order, you must mark out the shell opening on the backlite. All of the area *outside* the line must be blocked out with black vinyl tape. Then, when the driver looks into the rear-view mirror, he or she won't see the shell's ugly edges.

To do this, use a white grease pencil, which should be available at your local trim supply. If not, try your local office-supply store. Mark the backlite around the shell cutout. Don't forget to mark around the area of the stop light. Then remove the shell.

Watch Charlie as he does this job. He begins by carefully edging the *inside* of the line with masking tape. Charlie uses his regular 5/8-inch masking tape. I use 1/4-inch masking tape because it makes the bends easier. Charlie

Trace around the inside of the backlite cutout with a grease pencil or crayon. Don't forget the stoplight cutout.

After removing the top, all the glass that was covered must be blocked out. Charlie outlines his mark on the *inside* with masking tape. Once more, don't forget the stoplight cutout!

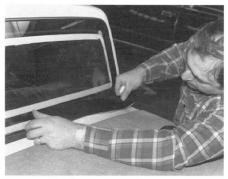

We use block out tape that's a bit lighter than electrician's tape. If you can find it, use it; otherwise use electrician's tape.

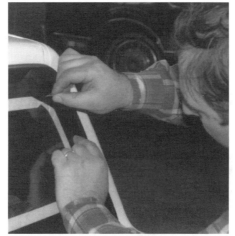

Here's where steady nerves are called for. Trim away the blockout tape along the line made by the masking tape. You can wander about 1/16 inch on each side without affecting the appearance.

Make your location marks on the car *before* you throw the material up there. When you trim, leave plenty of selvage.

says I waste time looking for different-size tapes. You can do whatever you like. Don't forget to edge the cutout for the stoplight. This too, is edged on the inside.

After edging the lines, he layers 2-inch vinyl block out tape over the area to be darkened, allowing the vinyl tape to overlap the masking tape just a bit. This vinyl tape is available also from the local trim supply, or purchase 2-inch black electrician's tape from the hardware store.

After rubbing the vinyl tape down on the glass, the edge of the masking tape will show through as a slight bulge (or line). Charlie uses a single-edge razor blade to trim the vinyl tape along this line. He then removes the masking tape and selvage from the vinyl tape. Now he has a perfectly blocked out backlite. Pretty slick, huh?

CUTTING, FITTING, SEWING

If you did the project in Chapter 9, or read through it, this project cuts, fits and sews much the same. Therefore, I'll skim it lightly and discuss only the differences.

Return the shell to the car, aligning the screw holes you made. Anchor it securely. Measure *across*

from one side to the other, adding about 4 inches to each side. Cut a full width of vinyl the length you just measured. Flip this piece of material up onto the top, center it, leave about 3 inches to overlap in the front, and trim the selvage as you see Charlie doing in the photo above. Leave about 2 inches of selvage around the back edge.

To secure the material to the top, Charlie uses masking tape. Because there's no place to use clamps, this works quite satisfactorily. Keeping the material snug he marks his seam line along the center of the radius. As you do yours,

be sure to make locator marks: at least one in the center and one in each corner.

After marking the top section, Charlie uses the selvage cut from the block of material for the back of the shell. He tapes this material in place and makes his marks. Be sure you make corresponding locator marks on this piece.

At the bench, Charlie trims the material to a 1/2-inch seam allowance then folds the top piece in half, trimming each side to match the other. This should be done with both pieces to ensure

Where would we be without masking tape? We use almost as much as a paint shop!

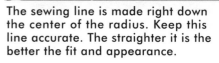

The sewing line is made right down the center of the radius. Keep this line accurate. The straighter it is the better the fit and appearance.

Fold the top piece, face together, directly down the center. Trim each half to match its opposite. This will ensure symmetry on both halves of the top. Repeat this with the back piece.

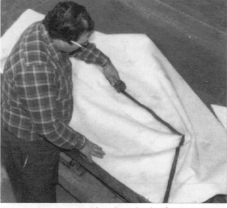

As you've seen Charlie do before, make this joining seam a French seam.

uniformity on all sides. After making a nick at each locator mark he sews the two sections together finishing with a reinforced French seam. Now he's ready to cement the cover to the shell.

COVERING THE SHELL

Again, we repeat the steps learned in Chapter 9. Apply a thin, even coat of cement to the material and to the shell. Allow it to dry until it passes the touch test (no longer sticky). Fold the cover back so you can align the locator marks from the back of the shell. The important part here is to be sure the corners are aligned. When the locator marks are aligned and the corners are in the right position, begin to

stretch the material out over the shell.

Start with the top section working the wrinkles out from the center to the bottom front edge. You can see Charlie doing some serious pulling in this corner. The material must be tight enough to sink into the grooves made for the aluminum trim. Be sure the material lies flat and smooth in these channels.

Cut out a 4- or 5-inch section in the middle of the backlite area. This will allow you to get your hand up into the corners and smooth out those wrinkles. You may want to relieve some of the stress on the material by making some slashes in the corners where the roof pillar meets the rear

quarter panel.

When all the wrinkles are out and everything looks great, remove the screws holding the shell to the roof of the car and set it on the bench.

On the Bench

To finish covering the shell, trim the selvage edge to about 2 inches. Pull the material tightly around the shell edge and cement it in place. Make slashes on outside curves and cut away excess material on inside curves. When all the selvage edges are cemented down you're ready to cover the door trim.

These are covered like the top. A thin coat of cement is applied to both the trim and the material. When it's dry, carefully lay the material over the piece and work it down into the grooves for the aluminum trim. Bring the selvage around tightly to the backside and cement it in place. You may need a little heat at the corners. The material should be stretched tightly here so there are no wrinkles to be seen from the backside when you open the door.

Now you're going to fix the top to the roof as you did with the sim-con, lots of silicone sealer and a few screws instead of pop rivets.

Put large globs of sealer across the inside. Run a heavy bead

Spray an even, light coat of cement over both the cover and top. Allow it to dry thoroughly before bonding. Remember, a piece of paper should not stick to it when pressed gently on the surface.

Be sure the corners are correctly aligned and all the locator marks match up. Work the wrinkles out from the center both ways.

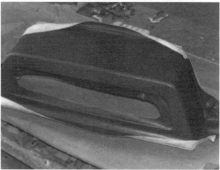

When all the wrinkles are out and everything is smooth, lift the top from car and set it on the bench. The easiest way to get to the corners is through a cutout in the backlite area. Be careful not to cut away too much. Leave enough selvage to wrap around the edges of the backlite cutout.

down each side and a medium bead across the front. The front bead should only be heavy enough to seal. You don't want sealer oozing out from under the front edge.

With the help of a friend, set the top on the car and secure it to the roof with screws. Where possible, use the same screw holes you made for the test fit. Attach the door-trim pieces in the same manner. The top is secured to the roof now and you can begin fitting the aluminum trim pieces.

FORMING & INSTALLING THE ALUMINUM TRIM

Begin with the front trim. This is the wider of the two pieces. *Don't cut anything yet.* You'll need all the length you can get. In a moment you'll see why. Start by fitting the trim to the channel.

Place the trim in the channel

(groove) designed for it on the door-trim piece, checking the fit. If all fits well, chalk a line on each side of the aluminum trim. Pop-rivet a plastic retainer about every 10 inches along an imaginary centerline between the two lines outlining the aluminum trim. If an

imaginary centerline won't work for you, make a real one. Be sure to place a retainer close to the bottom about 1/2 inch up from the end of the trim piece. The last one should be just below the top radius of the door.

Snap the full length of

Finish the cement work by bringing the selvage around and gluing it to the back side. Notice the slashes on the outside curves.

Don't forget the door-trim pieces. The light part of the panel is where Charlie added 1/4 inch of foam to build height. Before the foam, the door-trim pieces were not even with the rest of the top.

Use lots of sealer. Keep the thing on the roof!

aluminum trim onto the retainers making sure the bottom is located at the base of its groove. Hold the trim tightly to the panel with one hand and, with the other, wrap it around the top radius of the door. Charlie is giving a good demonstration of this in the photo on the top right of the next page.

If you'd cut the aluminum trim you wouldn't have been able to get enough leverage to bend the trim. That's why you must leave it long.

Mark the location where you want to cut the trim. Try to locate the cut so there will be as little gap between the trim on the door and the trim on the top as possible. Make allowances for the end caps needed to finish it.

Use a hacksaw to make the cut and finish by filing things smooth. Insert an end cap into the bottom of the trim, snap the trim onto the door-trim panel. Fit the bottom trim in two pieces, one on each side of the car, joining dead center

under the stoplight. Don't forget the little piece on the bottom of the door-trim panel. Insert a finishing end cap into the top. This finishes the first door. Now, repeat the above steps on the opposite door.

The remaining piece of wide aluminum trim goes across the top. Using your hands to bend the material, make a slight arc in the aluminum trim to match the crown of the top. This is not a difficult process. The aluminum is quite soft. When you get a pretty good approximation of the crown in the roof, lay the trim piece in its groove and align each end over the now installed door-trim pieces. Hold it in place and chalk a line on each side. This will neatly line up all three pieces of trim. Again, using an imaginary or real centerline, install your plastic retainer clips every 8 to 10 inches.

After trimming it to the correct size, *slide* the aluminum trim over these retainers. There's so much give in the top that trying to snap the trim over the retainers will

Set the top on the car. Fasten it through the screw holes you made while fitting. Do the same with the door-trim panel.

Well, it looks pretty nice from here. When we add some trim, it will look even nicer.

Charlie checks the fit then draws lines on each side of the trim so he'll know where to locate the plastic snap-on retainers. Notice the bottom one is only about 2 inches up. This keeps the bottom edge tight to the panel.

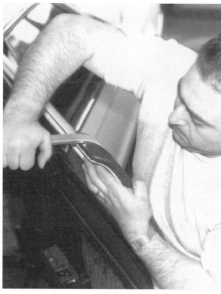

Hang on and wrap the trim right around the door radius; slick as can be.

After marking where you want the cut, cut it off with a hacksaw. File away any burrs so the end caps fit flush.

Fit the top piece of trim and mount the retainers. Be sure the screws go all the way through the sheetmetal of the roof.

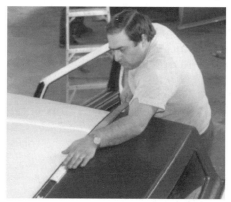

Slide the trim on this time. Don't try to pound it on. You could buckle the roof!

Fit the bottom trim in two pieces, one on each side of the car, joining dead center under the stoplight. Don't forget the little piece on the bottom of the door-trim panel.

Left: Front trim is installed straight as an arrow! That Charlie knows his stuff.

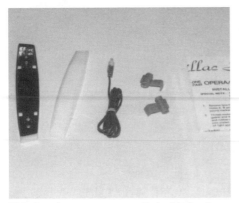

This is what one opera-light kit looks like. Note the light bulb and lead wire are one unit.

When you mount the base to the top, be sure there's a ground into the roof. No ground, no light.

Pull back the trunk-trim panel, get out a coat hanger and fish for the lead wire you just fed into the roof. If you have to hunt for it for more than five minutes, give up and start taking out the interior to get to it.

only result in making the roof jump up and down! File the end of the trim smooth so it doesn't catch and tear the material. Finish off with end caps and the front trim is done.

The rear trim is formed just like the trim for the vinyl top as demonstrated in Chapter 8. Locate the exact center of the top in the trim channel (just below the stop-light cutout) and mark it. Make the trim from two pieces allowing each piece to overlap in the middle where you made your center mark. When everything fits right and the ends of the trim in the front have been made, cut off each piece of trim molding exactly at this mark and let the ends butt together.

Install retainer clips as you did with the front trim. Now snap the trim on and finish with the little cap that goes over the butt joint and you have a new quarter roof! You're not finished, however. You must install the opera lights to give it that "classic" look.

INSTALLING OPERA LIGHTS

Each opera-light kit comes with a base, a light bulb, wire, a lens cover, solderless wire connectors and an instruction sheet. The

tricky part is locating the light wire once it's inside the car between the roof and interior quarter panel. Step-by-step, Charlie will lead us through and even show you his trick for finding the elusive wire.

Begin by mounting the base to the top. Use a #6 or #8 screw long enough to reach through the top and anchor into the roof. This will become the ground. Some bases are grounded with this screw, others with a wire going to the screw. If your kit uses a wire, be sure it gets under one of the two screws you'll use to retain the light base to the top.

Through the hole in which the light bulb mounts, drill a third hole through the roof for the light bulb wire. Test the light bulb to make sure it's working properly. You can spend hours trying to figure out what's wrong with the wiring only to discover the bulb is defective. To test it, use an ohm-meter, a test lamp or the car's battery. Connect the lead wire to the positive terminal and ground the bulb to the negative terminal. If it lights up, the bulb is OK.

To mount the bulb in the base, feed the lead wire through the hole and snap the bulb into its socket. After mounting the bulb you must look for the lead wire. Open the trunk and pull back the

trim panel on the side of the car in which you installed the light.

Get out a coat hanger, straighten it and bend a hook into one end. Now, run it up between the various braces in the body until it's in the vicinity of the wire. Rotate the hook to face the area where you expect the wire to be and withdraw the coat hanger. If the car gods are with you, you'll hook the lead wire and fish it through. If the gods are fickle and after a few minutes of "fishing" you have no luck, you'll have to take some upholstery out to find the wire.

Remove the rear seat cushion and back cushion. This should give you access to the rear, upper quarter panel. Sometimes you can reach the wire from here. If not, remove the rear quarter panel and any other panels necessary to locate the wire.

When the lead wire is found, it must be connected to a hot wire that goes on with the headlights. This is generally the taillight wire. To find this, locate the wiring harness in the trunk of the car. You'll probably have to pull back the trim panels in the trunk on one or both sides. Charlie knew this particular harness was on the left side of the car.

Isolate the wire going to the

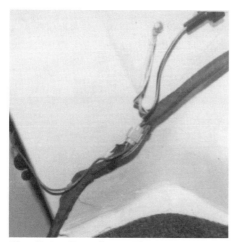

Charlie's all set here. The connector is in place and the lead wire is hooked in. The opera lights come on with the headlights and all is well.

The finished project.

taillight. If you're not sure it's the correct wire, use a test lamp. Pull the connector off the socket at the taillight housing. Turn on the lights, ground your test lamp and touch each prong of the connector until you get a light. If no one has their foot on the brake, the turn signals are off and the car is not in reverse, all that's left is the taillight.

Check the color code of that wire, unwrap the insulation in the area you wish to connect your lead wire and find the correct color combination. Now you can insert a solderless wire connector, according to the enclosed instructions, to connect the lead wire to the taillight wire.

Test the connection. Try it with the lights off, then with the lights on. *Be careful not to connect to the brake light.* If you do, the opera lights will only go on when you apply the brakes!

Usually the lead wire from the other side is not long enough to come across and connect with the wire on the harness side. If this is the case, after locating the second lead wire, you'll need to add a bit more. Use a solderless connector from the auto parts store or solder the wire and wrap it well with electrician's tape.

Don't just twist the wires together and call it good! This is not only dangerous (a short, a spark and a fire) but also makes a poor connection. If you're anywhere but the driest, hottest parts of the southwest, or perhaps the Sahara, you'll get corrosion in this twist and lose the connection. Do it right and be proud of your work.

When the bulb lead wire is long enough to reach the wiring harness from the opposite side of the car, thread it behind the trunk trim panels so it's out of the way. Attach it to the harness with the other lead wire. After you replace the panels in the trunk, the job is done.

INSTALLING A LUGGAGE RACK

There was a time in automotive history when people actually strapped their luggage onto the back of the car. A luggage rack was a necessity then; now it's simply decorative. Decorative it may be but it's certainly popular. Our project car is getting one so let's see how it's done.

Begin by finding the centerline of the trunk lid. Then determine the outside measurement of the completed unit. If this is not given

in the instruction sheet, temporarily assemble the back rail to the two outboard rack bars. Measure this finished distance and divide by three. This gives you the spacing for all the rack bars.

Here's an example: the outboard measurement is 48 inches; 48 inches divided by 3 equals 16. Therefore, the rack bars will be 16 inches apart. From the centerline, measure 8 inches on each side. This is where you'll mount the two inside rack bars.

Measure out 16 inches on each side of the inside rack bars for the location of the two outboards. Now the whole unit is centered on the trunk lid and evenly spaced. Disassemble the back rail and mount the rack bars on the location lines you just drew.

Each bar is composed of three parts: the metal rack, a vinyl base and a vinyl top trim or "bumper." Add to this plastic reinforcements at each screw hole and a decorative tip at each end and you have a completed rack bar.

Assemble each bar as far as a base and screw reinforcements. To the two inboard bars you can add the end caps. For now, leave the end caps off the two outboard pieces.

Center the two outboard bars

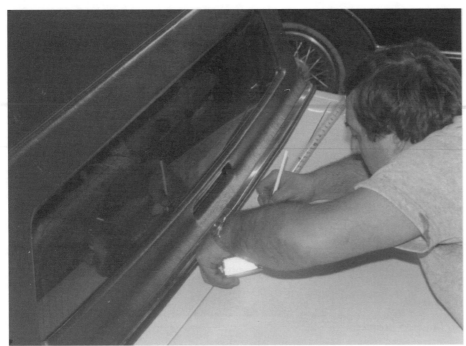

Just about every phase of trim work begins with finding the centerline. Our luggage-rack installation is no exception.

Slide the vinyl base over bottom of rack bar after you install screw-hole reinforcements.

Outboard rack bars are installed first. This may be a temporary installation. If it doesn't "eyeball" well, move it forward or backward.

Don't forget these screw-hole reinforcements. Without them there would be too much stress on the rack bar and on the sheetmetal of the trunk lid.

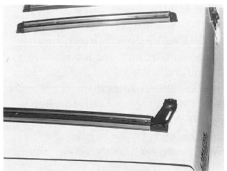

Riser for the rail: Consider its length when centering the rack bar from front to rear.

from front to rear on the trunk lid Measure to be sure they're equidistant and directly over the line you drew. Drill and screw them into place. Temporarily, add the riser for the rail and the front end caps.

The easiest way to get the noses of each bar in proper alignment is to lay a long measuring stick across the trunk lid as you see in the photograph. If you don't have a long measuring stick, use a piece of string. Center the two inboard rails on their respec-

tive lines with the end caps butted up to the stick or string and secure them to the trunk lid with the provided screws.

Remove the risers from the outboard rack bars, assemble rail

End cap can be installed after mounting the rack bar. Don't forget to put a screw in it.

You can see how effective the use of the long measuring stick is here. Just be sure the outboard rack bars are secure when you put the stick up there. If either of them can move, your line may come out sort of cattywampus.

Here's the rail assembled and joined to the rack bar.

Charlie runs a screw into the front and back to hold it firmly to the trunk lid.

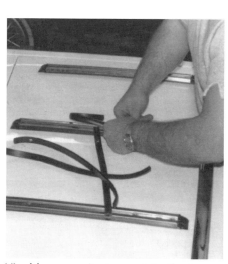

Vinyl bumpers just snap into the tops of the rack bars.

and return it to the racks. Anchor them to the trunk lid with screws. When everything is fastened down, insert the vinyl "bumpers" into the tops of each rack bar.

Your kit should include some little plastic caps. These go over the ends of any screws which might protrude through the trunk lid. Open the trunk and place one of these caps over each screw you can access. This will prevent anyone from getting a nasty scratch from the point of a screw. Double-check everything to be sure it's secure. Then stand back and admire your work.

SUMMARY

The quarter top incorporates many of the skills and techniques you've learned in previous chapters. It also teaches a few new ones. I like the trick of bending the front aluminum trim. I've seen trimmers do all sorts of crazy things to get this bend right *after* cutting the piece to length.

You get the best fit and the easiest work by covering the top while it's fastened to the car. On the full sim-cons this is too much work; we get it down at a more comfortable level by working on a stand.

Finally, you did a little electrical work. The trimmer is often called on to do this. If you're thinking of a career in this field, you'll need to know a bit about automotive electrical wiring. There are a number of good books at the library.

In the next chapter we take on what I feel is the most challenging aspect of automotive trim: the convertible top.

The caps to cover the screw tips really should be installed. Don't get lazy and omit this step. Real danger exists when the bare screw tip protrudes unprotected.

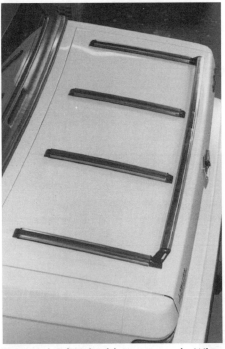

Here's the finished luggage rack. Why is it more decorative than functional? Well, there's a place to strap down *one* side of the suitcase but then...

11 Installing a Convertible Top

In this chapter we unfold the mysteries of convertible-top disassembly, installing new pads and making a new top-well liner. Then you'll discover how the rear curtain (window) is put in with absolutely no wrinkles and finally, how the top cover itself is installed.

This is a long and involved chapter. In practice, however, it goes rapidly. Our guide and mentor through this project, Marvin Carr, has done as many as three tops a day. He's slowing down a bit now and seldom does more than two! So, let's watch and see how he does it.

DISASSEMBLY

Marvin makes it look fast by simply ripping off the top to start. This is quite acceptable but some follow-through is necessary. Let's take it one step at a time.

Right: Here's what a few years of sun, wind and rain can do to a convertible top. Unless you have two side-view mirrors, this type of opaque backlite is against the law in most states. In a few hours this customer is perfectly legit.

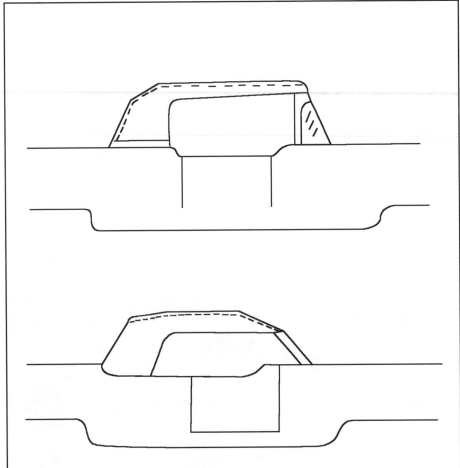

Prior to 1963 (top) most convertible tops were stapled to an exterior rear frame mounted to the outside body. These tops had pads in the rear quarters. After 1963 (bottom) the exterior rear frame was discontinued. The top was then stapled to a tacking strip which was bolted inside the body alongside the rear of the top well. Rear pads were discontinued on most vehicles.

Marvin Carr begins top removal by ripping off the wire-on. This is one of the few places where you can literally rip. To save the tacking-strip beneath, remove the staples carefully.

Name That Part

It helps to learn the names of the parts. The main body of the convertible top is simply called the *top* or *top cover*. The rear window, or backlite, is referred to as the *rear curtain*. This is made of two types of materials: glass or clear vinyl. Please resist the temptation to call it *clear plastic*. Though it is a plastic, it's a vinyl rather than Plexiglas®, Lexan® or any of the many "plastics."

The very first bow over the windshield is called the *header*. Moving to the rear are the *first*, *second* and *rear bows*. Supporting these bows and holding the top assembly together are the *frame-rails*. When the top is in the closed position it is referred to as

top up; in the open position, *top down*. As the top is put down it folds into the *top well*. On some vehicles you may then cover the top with a *boot*.

Beneath the top cover are the *top pads*. These pads form the curve from the flat part of the top to the frame rails. They're on each side, connecting at the header and rear bow. On some older makes of cars you'll find *rear pads* connecting the rear bow to the rear frame-rail.

Also under the top cover at the first and second bows are two strips of material. These form channels, called *listings*, through which a strip of metal is passed. This strip of metal is fastened to the bow (through the listing) with machine screws. This keeps the

top from bubbling up when the car is moving down the road at high speed.

Finally, along each frame-rail and under the header are *rubber weather seals* which, hopefully, prevent water from passing into the interior of the car.

That's enough nomenclature for us to all stay together as we work. Of course, there's more, but we'll name those parts as they come up.

Taking It Off

Marvin begins by removing the wire-on. You see wire-on used on the sim-cons at what would be the rear bow. At each end of the wire-on a stainless-steel cap is usually held with a #4 Phillips sheetmetal screw. Be sure to remove these two caps and save them unless there are replacements for them in the top kit. After ripping off the wire-on, remove the staples which held it in place.

With scissors or a single-edge razor, cut the rear quarters of the top from all of the connecting areas. Move to the front of the top and cut it away at the header.

Just behind the header, connected to the front frame-rail is a wire cable. It passes through a placket sewn in the side of the top cover and connects at the rear

Marvin uses a razor blade to cut the top from the tacking-strip here in the quarters.

After the top cover is off, he removes the weather seals at the back and front frame-rails and across the header.

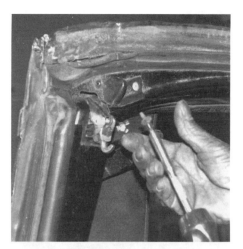

frame-rail. This keeps the side of the top from flapping in the breeze. The cable may be attached with a machine screw or it may fit into a slot in the frame-rail. Unlatch the top, giving the cable some slack and disconnect it. You need only disconnect the front. Leave the rear attached. Now pull the top off the cable, leaving it to hang there.

The top was connected at the back frame-rail (over the rear quarter window) so Marvin removes the weather seal here. It's retained with three sheetmetal screws on this top. Some models employ a "T" bolt through the weather seal and frame-rail retained with a nut. Check this out on your job.

The front weather seal is removed next. Start the car's engine and lift the top into the half-open position. (It's hard on the battery to open and close the top with the engine off.) As with the back-quarter weather seal, remove the front- and side-window weather seals also.

Under the front weather seal remove the windlace (that 1/2-inch rubber core covered with top material). Do this carefully by removing the staples securing it to the *tacking-strip*. Tacking-strip is old terminology left from the days

when tacks, rather than staples, were used. Though we seldom use tacks anymore we still use the term. These tacking-strips won't take much abuse, so don't just rip the windlace off. Save the core to make new windlace.

A strip of top material is stapled beneath the windlace. This was the front of the top. Remove it and expose the now-barren header and tacking-strip.

Under the weather seals you removed will be strips of top material cemented to the frame rails. Remove these too.

Move now to the first and second bow. In the photos, Marvin removes the screws from the underside of the bows. These screws hold the metal bars which retain the top listings. Save the two bars and screws but toss the old listings. New ones are on your top cover.

On the project car, Marvin is down to just the top pads and rear curtain. He'll leave the curtain in place and carefully remove one pad. Again, he's careful with the tacking-strip.

Besides being retained at each end with staples, the pads are also fastened to the second bow with machine screws: one on the outside of the cover at the inboard edge and usually three inside the pad. Remove these.

WORN-OUT TACKING-STRIP?

Often the tacking-strip at the header, or for the front of the pads, is beyond redemption and won't hold staples. The company from whom you ordered your top kit will have a replacement strip. Unlike the factory-original fiberboard, replacement strips are made of vinyl. To install these strips they must be screwed to the metal. Remove all the old tacking-strip, select a few #6 countersunk or pan-head screws from 1/2- to 3/4-inch long and screw the new tacking-strip into the location of the old. Place the screws about 3 or 4 inches apart. Farther apart than this and the tension of the material will "lift" the tacking-strip between the screw anchor points.

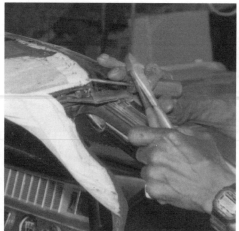

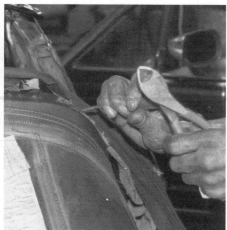

The last thing to be removed before work starts on installation is *one* of the pads. Notice Marvin uses an awl and a pair of dikes to remove the staples.

These screws, passing through the #1 and #2 bows, are retaining a metal bar inside a cloth listing. The cloth listing is heat-sealed to the top cover. This combination prevents the top from lifting away from the bows at 55 mph.

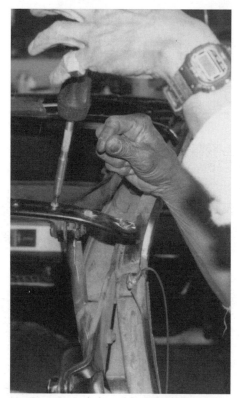

Having ripped the old pad off from around these screws, they must now be removed.

Replace the pads one at a time with the curtain intact to keep the frame in alignment. The rear bow, when released from the curtain and pads, simply flops back and forth. It must be retained in the exact position you found it because this is how the top cover fits it. If you find yourself in the unenviable position of replacing a top when someone else has removed and thrown away all the old materials, you'll have to call your local dealership and beg for help from the parts department. They're often able to give you the correct factory location of the rear bow. They have upholstery parts books just like the parts books for sheet-metal, engine parts, etc. These usually give bow locations in the convertible-top section.

You're ready now to jump in and start making new pads.

PAD INSTALLATION

Pads come presewn with a separate filler. You'll need to buy about 4 yards of 4-inch jute webbing. This reinforcement for the pads is never included in the kit, but it's available through your local supply house.

Look carefully at each of the bows in the location of the pad. You'll see an indent in each. This is where the inboard edge of the pad fits. This provides a smooth transition in the outside appear-

ance. Be careful to keep the edge of the pad aligned with this indent.

If the filler for the pad is folded with the pad cover, remove it and set it aside for now. Place the pad on the car with the flaps up but folded over one another. Center it over the bows with equal amounts of overhang at each end.

Some older-model cars and some European models have a tapered pad. Adjust these pads, with taper to the rear, so they completely cover the tacking-strip at each end.

At the rear bow, remove enough of the curtain to staple the pad in place. On the outside of the pad, at the seam, drive in two or three staples. Be sure the edge of the pad is aligned with the indent in the bow. Move to the front of the car, pull the pad snug along the seam line and staple it in place (the most inboard side of the tacking-strip).

Back to the rear. Pull the material wrinkle-free across the rear bow and staple the *outside* of the other seam in place. At the front, repeat the process.

Open the flaps, exposing what is now the bottom of the pad. Staple this to the rear bow, move to the front, pull it tight and staple it in place. Now you're ready for the webbing.

In years past trimmers used

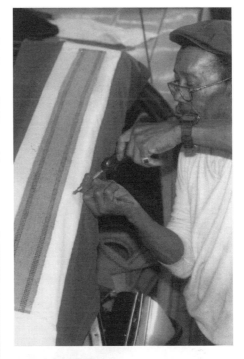

After anchoring the new pad at the front and back, Marvin staples in a jute webbing reinforcement. Before closing things up he replaces the four screws removed from the previous pad. Be sure the bow here is straight up and down.

three pieces of webbing completely covering the inside bottom of the pad. The improvement of materials and the need to save money eliminated all but one piece of webbing for reinforcement.

As you see Marvin doing, staple the strip of webbing right down the center of the pad. Keep it tight. Now, replace the screws in the second bow. This bow flops around a bit (that's why the screws). Just be sure it's in a vertical or upright position. Now it's time to put in the filler.

Spray a thin coat of cement to the bottom inside of the pad. The flaps don't get cemented. Lay the filler in the pad. It doesn't need cement. Trim the excess *inside* the rear bow and header. You don't want to have filler over the bows; it causes lumps in the top cover.

Fold the *inside* flap over, pull it smooth and staple it down at both ends. *Be sure there are no wrinkles.* Any wrinkles at this

stage will be seen through the top cover. Spray a coat of cement on the outboard flap. Fold it over and staple it in place. Not all trimmers finish the pad this way. Many fold the outboard flap over without cement and hold it in place with duct tape. Either way is acceptable.

Trim the ends with a razor blade. At the rear bow, trim *inside* the metal edge of the bow. This, too, will provide a smoother

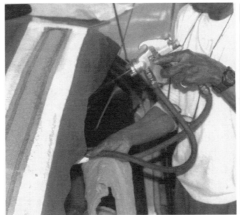

A little cement on the inside . . . and lay in the filler. This particular filler is a paper product. Often you'll find 1/2-inch Polyfoam instead.

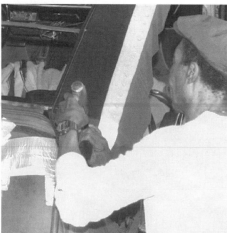
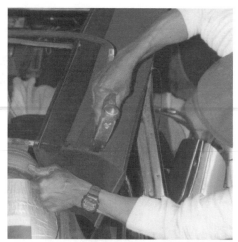

Fold the sides over, inboard first, and staple them down. You may wish to use a little cement on the outboard flap.

Finish the pad by trimming the selvage. Now Marvin will move to the other side and repeat the process.

Tape acts as a padding over these raw ends. I prefer duct tape; Marvin uses masking tape.

appearance under the top cover. That smooth appearance is continued by placing one or two layers of duct tape or masking tape over the front edge of the bow. It's a bit lumpy here and the tape smooths things out. Now you're ready to do the other side.

Measure the location of the rear bow at the finished side, then check to be sure you have the same measurement on the other side. If the rear bow is not perfectly aligned with the body, the top cover will not fit over it correctly. Complete the other pad as you did the first and we'll move to the top-well liner.

FABRICATING & INSTALLING THE TOP-WELL LINER

Removal

If you need to protect the rear deck of your car, place a blanket over the trunk lid, deck and rear quarters before proceeding. Some trimmers even tape blankets or pads along the tops of the doors.

If you need a new top-well liner you may be able to order one from the same company which manufactured your top. Unfortunately, these are not available for every make and model. Marvin demonstrates one way to make them from scratch. Begin by purchasing 2 yards of convertible-

top material or suitable vinyl. This is a judgment call for you. Select what you like. To get started, remove the rear seat, cushion and back.

Now you have some room to work. The front edge of the well liner is glued and screwed to the top edge of the rear seat-back-support panel. The rear of the liner is fastened to the rear tacking-strip beneath the curtain. Remove the screws retaining the front of the well liner. Lift the liner and you will see the tacking-strip bolted to the car body.

Remove these bolts. They're all around the rear of the top, fastening three tacking-strips, a

After establishing the bow-to-deck distance on the first pad, Marvin wants to be sure it's the same on the other side.

Right: Now he can finish the other pad. Note the rear curtain has not been removed in its entirety, only in the area where Marvin is working on the bows. This keeps the back bow in the correct position.

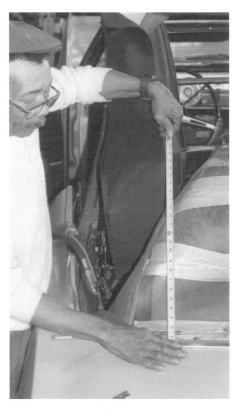

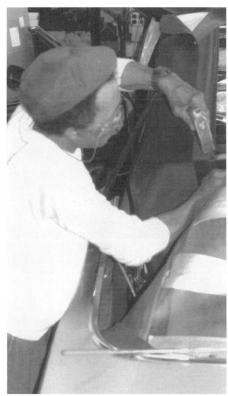

large one in the center and two smaller ones at the quarters. This releases the entire rear section of the top. With a little jiggling you can get everything out and up on the rear deck to begin removing the staples.

Disassembly

Clean everything off the tacking-strip. Try to keep all the materials intact. You're going to need them for patterns and to help you relocate things. Go easy here. When all the staples are removed you should have all three pieces of tacking-strip removed, the well liner out and the rear curtain dangling from the rear bow. Set all this aside except the well liner.

At the bench make location marks on both sides of any seams you have. Then, carefully cut the seams apart with a razor blade or scissors, separating things into their respective pieces. Roll out the new material on the bench faceup. Lay the old well-liner pieces on top, also faceup. Now, mark it off.

Cutting, Fitting, & Sewing

Along the back edge where the

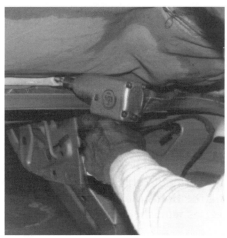

This is what it looks like *under* the top-well liner. Have you noticed yet that Marvin uses either hand with nearly equal dexterity?

Right: Out comes the top-well liner and the rear curtain as a unit.

liner attached to the tacking-strip you'll see where the holes were made for the bolts to pass through. Mark these holes. Next, mark the location of the two smaller tacking-strips.

If you fail to locate all these positions on the new liner, it won't fit for beans. Likewise, it will

throw off the location of the rear curtain and then you'll really have a mess! Therefore, be absolutely sure the tacking-strip is correctly located on the liner. Now, chalk in your own locator marks and cut out the new top-well liner.

At the sewing machine align the locator marks and sew

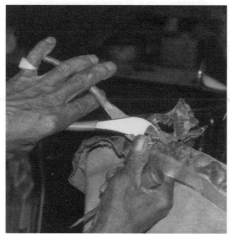

Carefully remove the rear curtain and liner. You'll need both for patterns and to locate things later.

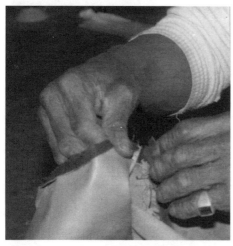

Marvin is cutting the seams in the old top-well liner to use it for a pattern. Be sure to make plenty of locator marks so you get yours back together correctly.

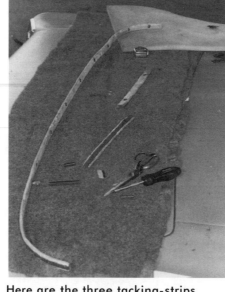

Here are the three tacking-strips ready to be used again. Try to keep them in good shape as you go. After about three years the factory stops making them and they become very hard to replace.

everything together. If there was a hem along the front edge you may leave it off. Sometimes this allows you a little room for "adjustment" should the need arise when you install it. Spend a little time admiring your work, then get it stapled back onto the tacking-strips.

Assembly

In the photos you can see where Marvin made chalk marks indicating the bolt-hole locations. He begins with the center hole,

locates it directly over the center hole in the big tacking-strip and fastens it down with a couple of staples. (Use a 1/4-inch staple. Any longer than this will strike the metal on the tacking-strip's backside. As you build up more materials, use longer staples.)

Next he moves the far side of the tacking-strip, aligns the holes and marks, then anchors again with another staple. The third step is to anchor the other end of the tacking-strip in the correct location, then fill in between these three points with more staples.

In the same way, fasten the two small strips to the liner being sure the marks line up with the bolt holes. Finally, cut the material away around the bolt holes so you can pass a bolt through it. The top-well liner is ready for test fitting to see if you got it all right.

Drop it down in the well, place a couple of bolts finger-tight and see if you like the fit. The important things to look for are: is it deep enough; is it wrinkle-free; does it have a good shape? You don't want the top to tear it when it folds up. If it meets these criteria you're ready to move on to the rear curtain.

INSTALLING THE REAR CURTAIN

Setting It Up

The rear curtain is made of very heavy vinyl. As such, it has a long "memory." If rolled up, as it is in the box, it tends to "remember" its rolled shape and return to it. This is very bothersome and hard to deal with. Therefore, a couple of hours before you're ready to install it, lay it on a dark blanket, cloth or paper in the direct sun. This will soften it and help it lose its memory.

If there's no sun and it's a cold day, use your hair dryer or heat gun to warm it up. In the cold northeast, we have warming cabinets to hang the curtain in. A small heater and fan do the job in just a few minutes.

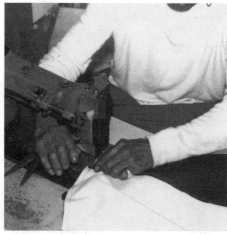

Using convertible-top material, Marvin fits, cuts and sews the new liner.

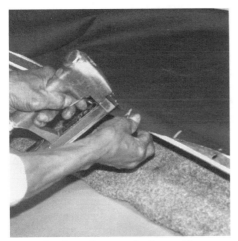

Note the location marks here. These represent the bolt holes from the old liner. They must align with bolt holes in the rear tacking-strip.

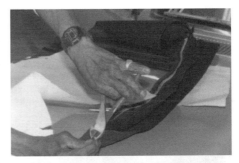

As always, work from the center, out.

Everything must be centered. The top cover is located over the back bow and rear tacking-strip. Anything off-center from here on will throw the whole top off.

When the top is soft and pliable, fold it in half and clip a notch in the top and bottom. Then, find the center of the back bow. Measure the entire length of the bow to locate the center. Don't measure between the pads. You want as accurate a measurement as possible.

Initial Installation

The following instructions apply to glass curtains as well as vinyl ones. The only difference is in the use of heat. Heat won't help with glass.

Carry the rear curtain to the car and drop it down into the top well. Lift the top center, align it with the center mark on the bow and temporarily staple it in place. Place the staple somewhere midway between the zipper and the top edge of the material with the notch and center mark aligned. As you see Marvin doing in the photos, pull one side over, pop in a couple of staples, then do the other side. Don't staple everything down yet; this is all temporary.

Now you have the top of the curtain positioned and you can begin to staple the bottom to the tacking-strip.

In the photos, Marvin is sitting on the rear deck with his feet in the top well. If you're working on a car with a sorry paint job and you weigh less than 110 pounds,

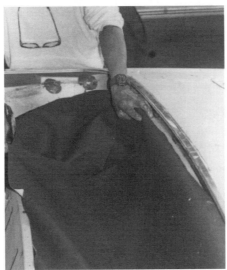

A trial fit shows the liner will work.

then you can do this too. Otherwise, work from a standing position *beside* the car!

Along the bottom of the rear curtain are holes punched in the vinyl. These must align with the holes in the tacking-strip. Usually, this works out. Sometimes it doesn't. I like to lay the old curtain on the new one at this point and make sure the holes in the new correspond to the holes in the old. If they don't, I make adjustments in favor of the old.

Work from the center out. Staple the center, align the holes, then staple the ends. Staple the rear curtain to all three

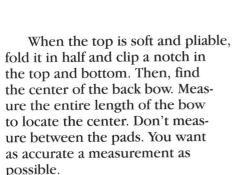

TACKING-STRIP BOLTS

The bolts retaining the rear curtain tacking-strip leave a lot to be desired. For some reason, most manufacturers use fine threads (SAE, NF). After a few trips in and out you generally manage to cross-thread one or two. If you don't want to go to the trouble of taping new threads you can do what we do in the shop: replace the buggers with lag bolts. Yes, dear friends, those big, coarse-thread bolts for holding wood framework together. They're available in every width and length you can use. So, if you're on the west coast, truck on down to the hardware store and help yourself out. What if you're on the east coast? Well, you *shlep* on down. . .

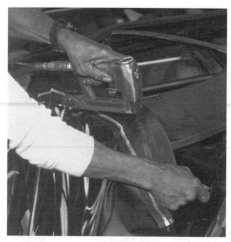

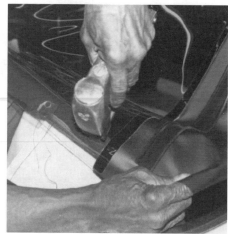

Marvin starts at the top center and temporarily place-tacks (staples) the rear curtain to the back bow.

This holds it in place while he fits the curtain bottom to the tacking-strip. Holes in the clear vinyl are aligning with the holes in the liner and in the tacking-strip.

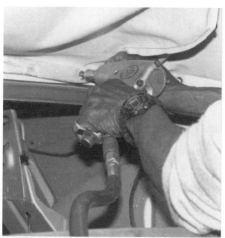

Next, locate and staple the two smaller side tacking-strips. Here, Marvin starts at the front, moves to the back and works forward.

Even the underside of the top-well liner looks better! Marvin bolts the tacking-strip back into the car to check his progress and to continue the installation of the rear curtain.

Two secrets are divulged here: lots of heat and work from the *center* out. It's hard to go wrong.

. . . with a little help from my friend.

Trim the selvage. I've seen this step forgotten. What a mess to do it after the top cover has been installed!

tacking-strips, adjusting the holes to fit as you go. Unlike the top, staple the bottom permanently. Now it goes into the car and under the top-well liner.

Run the bolts back into place securing them tightly. Get out and see what things look like. The curtain should fit fairly smoothly around the body line. There shouldn't be any longitudinal stress. In other words, the top staples shouldn't be tearing out. Nothing should be tearing at all. If all is well, get into the car with your heat gun and begin pulling the curtain tight.

Permanent Installation

Remove the staples holding the top at the center. Leave the ends fastened. Warm the center area of the curtain a bit, stretch it tight and staple it down. Heat and stretch one side tight, pulling out all the wrinkles. Staple as you go. Sometimes it helps to have a friend heat the vinyl while you pull and staple. The finished product should look like a glass window with *absolutely no wrinkles!*

As you heat, pull and staple, you'll know whether the job is coming out right (or wrong). If you don't like the way it's progressing, stop. Locate the problem. Usually, it's at the tacking-strip. If so, get back under the well liner and remove the tacking-strip. Make the necessary adjustments, bolt it down again and return to working along the back bow.

This seems primitive and there ought to be a better way. But for now, there's little else but this trial and error. The rear curtain will take some time to get just right. There's an art to it which only comes with experience. Have patience and stick with it until the job is perfect. Finish by trimming the selvage along the inside of the rear bow. When the rear curtian is finally a "thing of beauty " and a "joy forever," take out all the bolts

One more time. Out comes the rear curtain tacking-strip. Soon the top cover will be attached.

Here's the top thrown over the frame. Note the holes in the bottom of the rear quarters. These are the alignment holes for the tacking-strip.

Marvin uses a straightened coat hanger to pull the side cables through the plackets in the sides of the top. Without these cables, most tops vibrate like the devil along the sides when the car is moving down the highway. New cables are always available if you break or lose one.

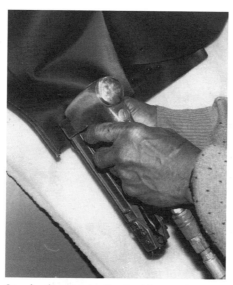

Staple the top to the tacking-strips, aligning the holes as you go.

Bolt it in and test fit it.

That little tuck, perpendicular to the main seam *must* lie directly over the back bow for correct alignment. On some tops it's even cut out at the factory. Therefore, to prevent having a hole in the top, it has to be located over the bow.

Right: Pulling the top tight, Marvin chalks a line indicating the front edge of the header. He temporarily cements the front edge of the top in place, locating it with the chalk line he just drew.

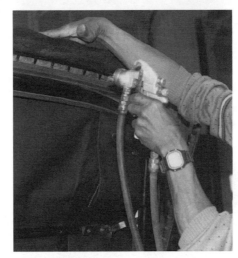

again! It's time to install the top cover.

TOP COVER INSTALLATION

If you're proud of your rear curtain, the top cover will be a snap. Most of the finesse is in the rear curtain. The top cover is pretty straightforward. Instead of talking about your top now, let's watch Marvin put this cover on. Unlike the rear curtain, he makes a mistake with the top but gets himself out of it quite nicely. Let's see how he does it.

Marvin begins by throwing the cover over the frame. Although the top has been folded in the box for who-knows-how-long these wrinkles pull out much more easily than wrinkles in clear vinyl. After placing the top cover on the car, the first thing he does is pull the side cables through their plackets.

Marvin straightens a coat hanger, makes a little hook in the end and passes this through the placket. He catches the cable and draws it through and out the other end. This end is then mounted to the frame. It may be necessary to loosen the top clamps and lift the top a bit to get slack in the cable.

Look back to the photo at the top right of page 149. Just as on the rear curtain, you can see the holes in the top that represent the location of the tacking-strip bolt holes. Marvin will align these holes with the existing ones and staple the top in place. Again, he goes into the car and bolts in the tacking-strip.

Testing the Fit

Outside the car, Marvin begins to pull on the front of the top to remove the wrinkles. There is one place the top must fit perfectly and without wrinkles—directly over the rear bow. Here the top is formed to deal with the two-way

Well, Marvin, you missed it this time good buddy. How will you straighten it out?

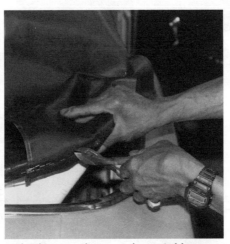

By looking at the way the wrinkles pull, he sees it's too tight at the base of the wrinkle. He pulls up the tacking-strip, removes staples . . .

and gives the top a little slack, (note bolt hole now rides way up on top of tacking-strip) and then staples the top back down.

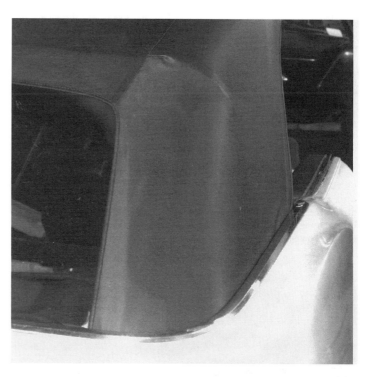

uying a little insurance, Marvin hits the offending quarter
ith a little steam. Now he has the perfect quarter. No wrin-
les, only straight lines and the tuck in the top is right over the
ow!

curve. This form may be nowhere else but over the rear bow.

Unfortunately, there's nowhere to staple the front edge of the top cover on the outside of the header. It's stapled *under* the header. Therefore, Marvin pulls the top as tight as he can and chalks a line on the vinyl at the front edge of the header.

He lowers the top to the half-open position and sprays a little cement along the front edge of the cover and on the inside of the header. Then, aligning the front edge of the header with his chalk marks, he brings the two cemented surfaces together. Now, when he brings the top into the fully-closed position , it should pull everything tight and, hopefully, wrinkle-free. Well, no such luck.

Look at the photos at the bottom of the opposite page. Note the deep wrinkle in the rear quarter and the bow at the edge along the curtain. No good! Again, Marvin removes the bolts holding the tacking-strip in place and lifts the assembly onto the rear deck. In the area of the wrinkle he removes the staples, gives the top a

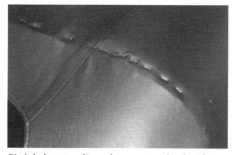

Finish by stapling the top to the back bow all the way across.

Staple the front where it was only cemented before.

Add the new windlace you just made...

little relief and staples it down again in the new position. Then he bolts it back together.

For insurance, he uses a generous shot of steam to eliminate further wrinkles. The results are beautiful, as you can see in the photo.

If your job requires steam and it's unavailable, the next best

thing is a squirt bottle of water followed by the heat gun. Thoroughly saturate the fabric on the *inside*. Then go after it with the heat gun. This generates enough steam to deal with minor wrinkles. Even with an industrial

Get the center retainers back in place by running them through the listings and securing them with the original machine screws. The top must be in the up position to get these metal bars through the listing.

Stretch the wire-on *tight*. This is the secret of the straight wire-on. Staple it at one end, pull at the other . . .

. . . and finish down the middle.

steamer, don't look for the steamer to remove major wrinkles. That's your job.

Feel free to break the glue bond between the top cover and the header and move the cover around. This may be necessary a number of times to get everything tight. When all is wrinkle-free, there are still a number of things to do to finish it off.

Begin at the rear bow. Staple

Glue the rear-quarter side-flaps to the back frame-rail.

the top cover all the way across. Be sure the distance from the edge of the bow to the edge of the top (over the curtain) remains constant and covers the zipper. Move to the front and staple the front edge of the top to the header, even though it's cemented in place. If there are flaps sewn to the top cover at the side front, cement these to the front frame-rail.

Making the Windlace

Remember the big rubber windlace I told you to save? Now it's time to use it. If you haven't done it already, remove the old cover. You'll have to make a new cover. Your top kit includes a piece of material for this job. The windlace cord is covered just like a giant welt cord but with the ends tucked in.

At the machine, lay the rubber in the center of the material about 2 inches back from the front edge. Fold this 2-inch flap over the rubber. Holding it in place, wrap the material around the rubber core as you would around a piece of welt and sew it down. Finish the same way. Cut the material off about 2 inches behind the core, fold it back over and continue sewing to the end. Now you have a windlace finished at both

Replace the weather seal. You'll need an awl to punch the holes for the screws.

ends.

This windlace is attached to the front of the header with staples. The ends should not reach beyond the frame-rails. The seam should not be seen in the closed position.

Finishing

While the top is upright, replace the weatherstrip at the header and front frame-rails. Move inside, pass the metal bars through the listings above the first and second bows. Use an awl to locate the screw holes. Screw the bars to the bows and move outside.

At the rear quarters of the top there are flaps which must be cemented to the rear frame-rail. Do this now. Use an awl to find the screw holes and screw the weather seal in place. Lower the latch and top.

Everything should be snug, well fitting, and there should be no wrinkles. If this is not the case, it must be corrected. You've worked too hard to let a minor glitch destroy the appearance of your finished job. Go back, disconnect, fix it and reconnect. It's worth it.

The top is finished with the installation of the wire-on. Staple one end to the driver's side, over the staples in the rear bow, with the small bead to the rear. Be sure all the staples are covered. Come to the passenger's side, pull the wire-on tight and drop in a couple of staples. Trim the excess so the overlap of the top-cover seams are equal and all staples are covered. Now staple the length of the wire-on, making sure none of the staples below are showing. Fold the large bead over and, with a mallet, frap it down tight right next to the little bead.

Finish the ends with the stainless stell caps you saved or with new ones if they are in your kit. Now the top is finished. One thing remains, however, You must finish the top-well liner.

Inside the car, run a thin bead of cement along the exposed edge of the liner. Fold this edge over on itself forming a 1/2-inch seam (glued, not sewn). Screw this finished edge to the rear seat back support panel. Replace the seat and you're ready!

SUMMARY

Convertible tops can be a snap to put on after you've done a few. Marvin, our guide through this chapter, makes a good living doing only top installations. Check out your local trim shop for installation costs, multiply this by two or three times, and you'll see there really is a career here. Doing the first one, though, may feel more akin to rocket engineering or maybe brain surgery.

I don't mean to turn you off. I want you to do it. That's why I've written this book. The point I want to make is this: You can do it, but there's always going to be some trial and error. We even saw a professional have to go back, remove some staples and get a really sizeable wrinkle out of the cover. But this is true of all upholstery or trim work—much of it is trial. That is why it really is an "art."

Don't walk off and leave the front of the top-well liner flapping in the breeze. Cement a 1/2-inch hem along the front edge, then screw it down to the rear-seat back-support panel.

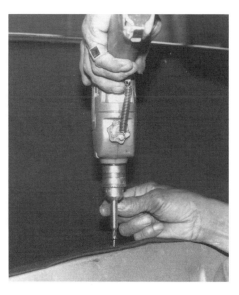

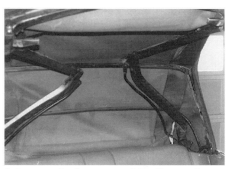
Scissor-style frame used by General Motors through the last 1976 Cadillac Eldorado.

PUTTING YOUR TOP DOWN THE "RIGHT" (INEXPENSIVE) WAY!

While working with the rear curtain you've noticed it has a big brass zipper. According to the instruction manual, each time you put the top down you should open the zipper to remove the rear curtain from the rear bow, then roll it up before lowering the top into the well. Nobody ever does this. Why? Probably because we're basically lazy and it's too much effort.

Here's the "however:" if you put the top down on your *glass* curtain, your chance of breaking it is around 80%. At about $150 (1992 prices) that's a lot of lazy! Drop the top on a vinyl curtain and you put a major wrinkle in it. Drop it on a glass curtain and you buy a new one.

12 Headliners, Door Panels & Carpets

This is the "clean-up chapter" in which we look at the last of the trim pieces. I'll start with the top of the car and work down: headliner first, then the door panels, then the carpet.

HEADLINERS

Sometimes called the *headlining*, *liner* or even *header*, this piece is what you look at when you sit in the car and stare straight *up* (assuming you're in a hardtop and not a convertible with the top down!) It comes in as many styles, colors and fabrics as there are cars.

If you own a late-model car, or even some older models back into the '70s, you probably have a molded, snap-in headliner. Directions for its installation are simple:

1. Order a new unit from the dealership or one of the manufacturers listed in the back of the book.
2. Disconnect any courtesy lights.
3. Remove all trim from around the unit.
4. It drops on your head because it's only held in by the trim.
5. Put the new one in.
6. Connect courtesy lights.

Carpeting gives much more protection than a vinyl heel pad.

7. Install trim and drive away.

That's just about it. Any easier and it would have been a waste of time to even bring it up. There's another style of headliner, though, which requires a bit more skill to install. This is the old-style liner with sewn-in fitted panels and retained to the car roof with bows. This is the one we'll turn our attention to.

This style of headliner has its roots in carriages and was used into the late '60s and early '70s. Because its construction is labor-intensive, it was replaced by the molded headliner.

If you're going to install an old-style headliner, they're readily available in any style or material from one of the manufacturers listed in the back. I would strongly

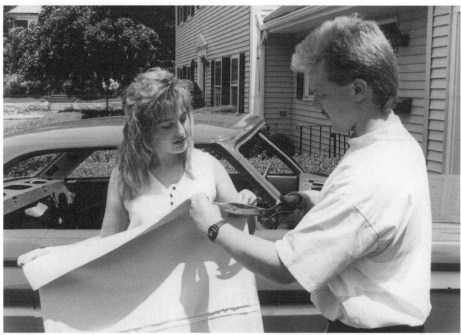

While Kelli holds the folded-in-half headliner, Danny cuts a notch in the front edge. This will let him find the centerline while installing the headliner.

urge you to buy one already cut and sewn rather than trying to attempt this feat yourself. Let's see how one of these ready-mades is installed.

Getting the Old One Out

A headliner can be retained to the top of the car in several ways. In the very old models a listing was sewn wherever a wooden frame member was placed. Listings were tacked to the frame members and the sides of the headliner were tacked around the windows and door frames. Covered panels and garnish moldings hid the tacks.

With the advent of full steel tops, frame members were replaced by removable steel bows. These were formed to fit the curve of the roof with 90-degree bends at each end. The bent ends were cut and trimmed to about 1 inch. These ends were inserted into holes at the tops of the door frames and the base of the rear backlite pillar.

The listings were sewn into loops and the bow passed through. The bow, with headlining attached, was then suspended to the roof of the car as described

above. The edges of the headliner were either glued to the door and window frame or held in place by a serrated panel.

You can tell which-is-which by the windlace around the door frame. If it's a 1/2-inch rubber bead covered in vinyl or fabric, the edges of the liner are held with the serrated panel. If the edge is finished with a U-shape, hard-vinyl trim called *snap-on windlace* (as is our project car) then the liner is glued to the door frame. Now how do you get the rascal out?

No matter how the unit is retained, you start by removing the sun visors. Next, remove the garnish (or reveal) moldings from around the windshield and backlite. If you have quarter windows, remove the moldings here also.

Remove the dome light. If no screws are visible from the outside, the cover snaps off. It should come off with a gentle pull. In some cases you may need to pry out just the dome light lens *carefully*. The trim is retained by screws underneath. The light frame is also retained with screws. Remove these and disconnect the

hot wire.

The safest way to handle a hot wire is to disconnect the battery. If you choose not to handle it this way, place a piece of tape over any exposed metal wire.

Remove any coat hangers, grab rails, rear-view mirrors or other hardware.

If your liner uses snap-on windlace, you can pull it off now. If you have the old-style, covered windlace, you have another step. With scissors, knife or razor blade, cut the headliner close to the windlace around the door frames. Now you can see the serrated panel which holds the edge of the headliner tight to the door frame and windlace.

These panels are held to the door frame with three *wing clips*, so-called because of their butterfly shape. To remove them, squeeze the wings together with pliers. This will release the clip so you can remove it. Often, the clip breaks. If this happens, use a 1/2-inch, #10 pan-head screw in its place. Simply screw the panel back to the door frame through the holes from which you removed the clips.

When all the clips are removed, the panel will come off the door frame. It's best to mark its location so you don't get confused during installation.

Turn the panel over and look at the serrations to see how they hold the headliner in place. Later, I'll tell you how to get the edge of the headliner over these serrations.

Headliners with snap-on windlace can be removed from the door frame and windows by peeling it from the metal after removing the windlace. From here on, both styles are the same.

The ends of the bows are now exposed. *Before removing, mark the hole in which the bow is located.* On most vehicles there are at least two holes in which the bow can go; on some there are three. Don't tell yourself you can remember! Mark it. These holes are there to accommodate other models of the same make. It was cheaper to make a number of holes than a selection of door frames for different models. Mark the bows 1, 2, 3, 4 from front-to-rear. Each is a different length and shape. Get them confused and the least of your problems will be wrinkles in the finished product!

To remove the end of the bow from the door frame, push up on the bow with one hand, just past the radius towards the center of the roof. Hold it in place here and pull the end from the frame. Repeat on the other side and the bow is out. Work from front to rear. On many models a wire at the center of the rear-most bow holds it to the backlite frame. If there is one, remove it.

Your headliner is out. If you find insulation between the headliner and roof and it's secure, leave it. If it's not secure, cement it back in place.

Installation

I have a young friend, Danny Weiner, age 21. He's been doing a ground-up restoration on his 1965 Comet Cyclone since he was 15-years old. Don't sell this young man short. So far, it's one of the nicest jobs I've seen! Danny has helped me a lot on my own car projects and on other book projects. When he asked me if I'd help him install a headliner, I realized what a great project it would be for this chapter. So, together, in his grandmother's driveway, we installed the headliner—with a little help from his friend Kelli Duggan.

If your project car is in this condition, you're a lucky person indeed. To paint his car correctly, Danny removed *everything*. There isn't even an instrument panel in the car! The benefit of no window glass is, we won't have to pull the window weather seals back to cement the headliner behind them. This is especially critical around the backlite. When I want to do a really nice job at the shop, I have the backlite removed before I

If you don't have an attractive helper to hold the headliner for you while you insert the bows, it's best to do it on a bench. It's very easy to push the bow through a listing, or even the headliner, if the material is rumpled while you work.

begin the installation.

After removing the headliner from the box, the first thing Danny does is to check for a centerline. Usually, this is marked on the back side of the material. So it may be seen from the front side, Danny clips a notch in the front and in the back edges.

Although the headliner was removed more than five years before, Danny had the foresight to mark the bows. Now he can install them in the right order. He slides each one in, being careful not to force them. This could lead to a torn headliner!

Insulation

After inserting the bows, he sets the unit aside to turn his attention to matters of insulation. Although the insulation helps control the temperature, its real function is to reduce noise. The more "stuff" you can jam into voids in your car, the quieter your ride will be. Originally, the insulation for the head-

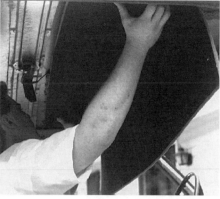

Danny uses a layer of 1/2-inch foam for insulation. Polyfoam, fiberglass pads, jute felt and rebond also work well. See Chapter 1, pages 12-13, for a description of these materials.

This photo demonstrates a number of things: note arrow marking hole from which bow was removed. See how bow passes through listing and sets in its correct location.

liner was fiberglass pads, much like what you find in homes. This is nasty stuff to work with, so we chose to go with Polyfoam instead. This would be far too expensive for factory work but it's only pennies when you're doing a single car.

The foam is held to the roof with cement. Danny used an aerosol can he purchased along with the foam. Notice he's applying the foam *between* the roof frame- members. If he applied the foam over a frame-member, it would create a bulge under the headliner.

Bow Placement

A quick glance at the photo above will show the end of the bow placed in the correct

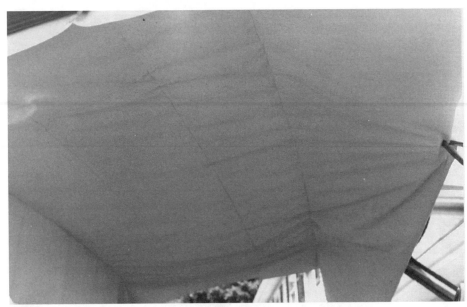

All four bows are located. Note clamp holding the front edge in place. Wrinkles in the liner will be removed by pulling listings tight.

the bow. *Be sure the centerline is in the center before hooking the bow in place.* Adjust the material along the bows so it's not bunched up on one side or the other. Now you're ready to pull the seams tight.

Cutting the Listings

If you try to pull the wrinkles out you'll find they all bunch up at the end of the bows. This is because the listings are longer than the bows. The listings must be trimmed back. Be sure the centerline is still in the center. Starting with the middle bow on either side, cut the listing between the bow and seam about 2 inches. Now pull out a little slack. Go to the other side and repeat the process. From side-to-side, cut a little and pull a little until the seam is wrinkle-free.

This little-bit-at-a-time routine prevents cutting the listing too far. If you cut too far, you'll lose the crown or curve at the bow. The cut must stop when all the slack is out of the material. The listing must be intact to within 1 inch of the end of the bow. It's better not to cut enough than too much. Remember the apprentice carpenter who exclaimed, "I've trimmed this leg back three times and it's still too short!"

Cementing the Headliner in Place

When all of the wrinkles are out and the centerline is in place, you

---

hole. Note the arrow indicating the hole in which the bow returns.

I like to start with the front bow and work back. Scoot the headliner up on each side to expose about 6 inches of bow. Be sure the centerline is in the approximate center of the bow. Place one leg in the hole on either side. Hold the bow in the center with one hand. Keep it below the roof about 1 foot. With the other, lift the opposite leg, insert it in the hole and release your hold in the center. The bow will literally snap into place.

To keep the bow from shifting, use a spring clamp to hold the headliner to the front windshield frame. In the case of Danny's car, this was no problem as there was no windshield. Your project may not have much to grab onto if your windshield is still in the car. In such a case, force a bit of the front under the rubber weather seal. This will hold it enough to keep the bow upright.

Install the remaining bows in their respective holes. If you had a wire securing the back bow, hook it through the listing and around

---

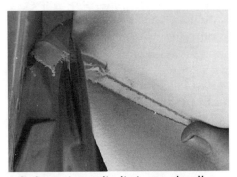

A little at time, clip listing and pull out wrinkles. Clip no further when all wrinkles are gone. Remember to work one side first, then the other.

By brushing on contact cement, Danny avoids getting spray adhesive on his excellent paint job. These little brushes, called *acid swabs,* are available in all plumbing, welding and hardware stores.

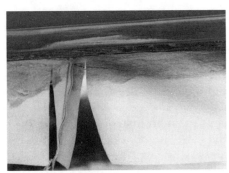

Clip headliner on both sides of the listing seam. Pull firmly to make seam tight.

After anchoring seam, do the headliner sides. Around curved areas, such as the rear quarter window of Danny's Comet, you'll have to make slashes in the material to relieve stress.

Anytime you work a corner, begin with a cut right into the center of the radius.

Backlite pillar (rear quarter pillar): Everything is anchored down, but nothing has been trimmed.

Radius around the windshield corner is greater than the backlite corner. Several cuts will be required to make this corner smooth. If the windshield were in, Danny would have cemented the material *behind* the windshield weather seal.

When all edges are cemented in place, trim the selvage.

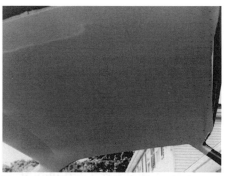

Here is the finished headliner before installing snap-on windlace. No more wrinkles.

can begin to cement the headliner to the door frames. The pattern is: door frames first, quarter windows second, then either around the windshield or backlite.

Danny will use contact cement applied with an acid swab. This keeps any cement off that beautiful paint job. Again, starting with the centermost bow, he pulls the material taut, and applies cement to both the material and the door frame. Now comes the trick. He must cut the headliner material back to the door frame on each side of the seam as shown in the photo. This gives him a "tab" to pull to make the seam straight and tight. If he omits this step, he might get little diagonal wrinkles at the foot of each bow.

On your project, when all the

seams have been pulled tight and cemented in place, go back, pull the sides of the headliner snug, and cement them in place. On any curved surfaces, clip the material to relieve stress. This can be seen around the rear quarter window on the project car.

If yours is the style with the serrated plates, cut the listings to remove the wrinkles, then install the plates as described on the following page. If you wish to replace the windlace, do this first.

You'll note the windlace was tacked, stapled or clamped into place. If stapled or tacked, the strip to which it was fastened is called a *tacking-strip.* By now it has probably turned to dust. It can be replaced with a plastic tacking-strip available at your local auto

trim supply house. The windlace rubber core for you to cover is there also, as is a good selection of ready-made windlace.

When the windlace is replaced and the serrated plates installed, begin installing the sides of the headliner. As above, cut up to the plate on each side of the seam, maybe a 1/2-inch out on each side, giving you a 1-inch tab to work with. Trim this off to about 1/2-inch long.

With a putty knife, push this tab up and under the plate until it catches on the serrations. Pull the seam tight from the other side and repeat the operation. When all the seams are firmly tucked in, trim the edges to about 1 inch. Push them up under the plate with the putty knife just as you did with

Danny pushes windlace into place. He'll finish by giving it a few good raps with a mallet.

the listing tabs. The rounded edge of the serrated plate gives you a nice finished edge, tight against the windlace.

When you finish the door area, turn your attention to the backlite or windshield.

Cementing Around the Window

To get the headliner in tight and wrinkle-free around the backlite, be sure it's first stretched tight top to bottom along the rear pillar. Danny snugs his down and glues it to the frame supporting the rear luggage panel. Then he comes in at a 45-degree angle to the corner with the scissors and makes a

slash right into the corner. Another cut on each side of the first, about 1/2-inch out and the two strips he just made can be cemented into the corner. After repeating this operation in the opposite corner he cements the top and sides in place. Then he moves to the front. If your backlite is still in the car, you'll have to deal with the rubber weather seal.

The operation is just the same. Cut a slash into the corner but just *to the edge of the rubber, where it meets the glass.* Make a couple of more cuts, one on each side, again, only to the edge of the rubber. Apply a dab of cement to each of these tabs. Pull the rubber edge back from the frame and smear a little cement in there. Secure the corner of the headliner in place under the weather seal. When the rubber weather seal snaps back, it will cover over the edge of the headliner, giving a nice finished appearance.

Again, Danny makes a 45-degree cut into the corner of the windshield. The windshield-corner radius, however, is much larger than the corresponding one on the backlite. Therefore, Danny makes several cuts in the corner

to relieve the stress. You can see in the photo how smooth it was when he finished cementing it. As before, if the rubber weather seal is in place you'll have to pull an edge back and cement behind it.

As a final clean-up, trim away the excess material. A razor blade works best for this. I like to leave the trimming until everything is *firmly* in place. This way, if I should make a mistake I can go back, pull the material free and adjust the fit.

Installing Vinyl Snap-on Windlace

Finish off the headlining by installing a new snap-on windlace. This was purchased with your headliner kit to be sure it matched. It's very easy to install, simply push it on! Note Danny doing this in the photo above. The easiest way is to give it a bit of a bend just in front of the area in which you're pushing. This tends to open it a bit, making it go on even easier. After it's in place I usually give it a few raps with a plastic, leather or wood mallet. This ensures its proper seating.

Finish the job by installing the pieces you removed. To locate screw holes beneath the

Here's our project door panel. I can't believe the damage suffered by the poor speaker! Almost all separate arm rests are retained with three screws accessible from the bottom of the unit. These screws can be Phillips, Torx, SAE or metric.

Be very careful with these thin-plastic door-handle moldings. They're very susceptible to cracking.

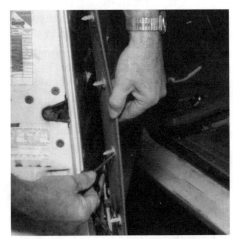

I pry these clips out of the door with a blade screw driver with the tip resting on the clip shoulder.

headliner, search with your finger-tips until you feel the indent. Then more accurately locate the hole with a trim pin. If what you thought was a hole is simply a dimple, the pin will not penetrate the material. This prevents a number of unfilled screw holes in the headliner! A trim pin also acts as an excellent guide to find a screw hole beneath a piece of reveal molding.

I think Danny's headliner is a great success. He did all the work himself with only directions from me. (I was busy with the photography.) If there were any wrinkles, we could have carefully removed them with a heat gun or hair dryer. When Danny installs the windshield and backlite, he may get some, but they can easily be removed with heat.

DOOR PANELS

We're close to seeing the end of upholstered door panels. More and more door panels are being molded as one piece. If you damage something, you must order a whole new panel from the dealer. Inexpensive to make—highly profitable as a replacement part. An interesting side point here: if you built a $20,000 car off the lot from replacement parts, that vehicle would cost somewhere in the neighborhood of $250,000!

Armrests that can be reupholstered are a thing of the past. Molded sun visors too, have taken the place of upholstered ones. Within two or three years of the publication of this book, molded seats will be in almost every new car. These will not be recovered, they'll have to be replaced.

There are still a few door panels which may be recovered such as the ones on my Ford Ranger mini-truck. In the photo you can see a very expensive, though plain-looking speaker down in the corner. I thought this would be a swell location. Wrong! The constant slamming of the door simply destroyed the poor

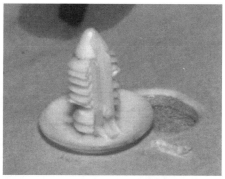

Here's the little fellow. Serrations hold it into the hole. There are as many clips in this business as there are makes and models. One thing is universal, however. Always pry on the clip shoulder, never on the panel fiberboard.

Use old cover to locate pattern designs or hole placements.

little devil. Now I must replace it, and its partner in the other door, with something behind the seat. There's no room in the instrument panel, and I don't want them suspended beneath. This, of course, leaves either an ugly speaker or an even uglier hole in my door panel; so, the panel must be replaced.

Because this is a leased vehicle and the lease is about up, I want the new door panels to look like the old ones when I return it. So, watch over my shoulder as I work my magic.

Door-panel Removal

With auto parts being manufactured in one country and the vehicles assembled in another, there is less and less standardization. You'll find both metric and SAE

Fortunately, the cover peels off easily without pulling up layers of fiberboard. Go slowly here as you start. You can cut deeply into the board if you try to rip off the cover.

Never wrap a heavy layer of padding around an upholstered panel. Take the time to trim it away carefully. The fit to the vehicle will be tighter and more attractive.

fasteners side-by-side in the same vehicle. (My mechanic friends swear to me they make SAE nuts with metric threads!)

This door panel illustrates my point. The window crank was retained with a Torx-head screw. The door-handle cover-plate was fastened in place with a Phillips-head screw. The armrest required a metric nut-driver to remove its fasteners.

A decade ago everything on the door panel would have had a Phillips-head screw. Zip, zip, with an air driver and the job was done. Be prepared, therefore, with enough tools to remove your various trim panels and pieces.

When everything is off, I can remove the panel from the door.

To reduce bulk in the corners, cut tight "Vs" around the radius before cementing corners in place.

Ready-to-install panel. I'll cut my holes *after* the panel is in place. I still have to make a slit for the door handle to squeeze through, plus a tiny hole for the window crank. Padded and sewn, new cover looks much like the old one.

I cut these holes very carefully after the panel was in place.

Completed project. I think it was well worth the effort.

It's held on with serrated plastic clips. These are released by prying them up with a screw driver. The important thing is to be certain the screw driver is *directly under the clip shoulder.* If you pry up on the fiber panel, it will surely break. Be very careful. Pry only the shoulder of the clip.

In the '40s through the mid-'70s these retainer clips were made of spring steel. Although the fiberboard construction of the door panel was heavier, it too, would break under stress. Even on the old cars, get the screw driver under the clip shoulder.

Removing the Old Cover
On this panel, the cover is molded to the fiberboard with a heat press and glued to the backside around the edges. I began the removal by peeling the edge back from the fiberboard. Then I trimmed it off with scissors. Finally, I very carefully peeled the cover from the board.

This is a pretty standard removal. On older models the edges were stapled in place. Some panels will have stainless-steel trim. This is usually retained by tabs pushed through the board and bent over on the backside. Straighten these tabs before removing the trim from the panel.

Making the New Cover
Besides not wanting to damage the fiberboard, I was careful in removing the cover so I could use part of it as a pattern. Note the fancy curved indent around the arm rest and door handle. I want to reproduce this on the new panel so I carefully cut it out. Now it's a pattern.

As before, I bonded a piece of vinyl to 1/2-inch foam. Then, I laid out 1/2-inch pleats. To locate the "fancy curve" accurately, I placed the old cover over the new, aligning the pleats. Now I know right where the curve goes. This was laid in with chalk pencil. Five minutes at the machine and I had top-stitched the pleats and the curve.

This panel is pretty straight-forward. Some you'll run into are a bit more complicated. If there's carpet at the bottom, it's usually made as a separate piece from the cover.

Sewing cover and carpet together creates too much bulk. Carpet on the bottom is usually bound. Instead of binding the entire edge of the carpet, sew one edge of the binding to the top side; leave the other edge loose. Cement the carpet to the bottom of the panel. Wrap the loose edge of the binding *around* the panel and staple or cement it in place. This hides the edge of the fiberboard and gives a neat, trim appearance.

Installing the New Cover

I began installing the cover by carefully centering the board over the back of the cover. This location is critical so the armrest and door handle come out in the right place. When I was sure of the location, I squirted a little cement between the panel and cover to hold things in place.

In the photo you see me trimming the foam to fit the edge of the board. I don't want to wrap the foam around the board because it creates too much bulk. Finally, I trim the edges of the material and cement them to the board. To reduce bulk in the corners I cut a series of "V" notches right up to the edge of the panel. You can see it makes a flat, smooth edge.

All of this talk about bulk behind the panel is professional pride. The panel should fit tightly to the door and look as though it were made at the factory. You, too, must strive to make your work neat and professional. You'll feel great when your friends admire how nice the job looks.

Installing the New Panel

Many of my trimmer friends cut out the holes for the window crank, door handle and other openings, on the bench prior to installation. Usually, this works out just fine. Once, however, I did it on a very important leather job, a Rolls-Royce restoration. The openings did not align. Imagine, for a minute, my dilemma: Connolly leather at $11.50 per square foot, hours of my labor, time lost in shipping out the new piece. And, when the new piece finally arrived it was the wrong dye lot! Well, I don't cut the holes at the bench anymore.

Temporarily mount the panel to the door by pushing two or three of the plastic retainers partway into their holes. Now, feel for,

or observe, where the door handle protrudes or the window-crankshaft pushes against the material. Carefully cut a slot for it. A slot is better than a hole. If the hole is too big, the (escutcheon) cover plate might not cover the hole. Just be careful.

If you're installing a big luxury-car door panel, these truths remain. Cut only the smallest amount possible as you hunt for the stem, post or hole. Also make certain all electrical functions work. It's a real kick-in-the-pants to spend an hour installing a door panel on a big Lincoln only to find the seat won't move or the window roll down. Check it out before closing up the panel.

When all the holes are located, trim carefully. Now you can push in all the retainer clips. I finished my job by installing the window crank, armrest and door-handle cover plate.

I have three options for the armrest: use the old one, order a new one from the dealer, or dye the original.

There are a number of vinyl dyes on the market. The most popular is probably *Colorcoat®* from Sem Products. It comes in aerosol cans in all colors, many of which very accurately match late-model auto trim. It, like the other products discussed, are available through your local trim supply or one of the suppliers listed in the back of the book.

The secret to successful vinyl dying is proper preparation of the piece to be dyed. Begin with the strongest detergent you have and wash the piece thoroughly. Then, clean it two or three times with a good wax-and-dirt remover such as Pre-Kleeno. The dye will have a good bonding surface and won't peel off.

Door-panel Summary

I'm fairly happy with the new door panels. They look nice, match well and give the truck a clean appearance. My criticism might be the thickness of the foam

I used. Although it looks very nice, it's quite a bit puffier than the original. I could have used 1/4-inch foam instead of 1/2-inch. Maybe I'll keep the truck instead of turning it in.

CARPETING

Carpeting, like all parts of the industry, has undergone changes. Up until the '60s all carpeted auto interiors were cut, fitted and sewn to accommodate the assorted humps, bumps and dips in the floor. Now, this is the exception rather than the rule. Today, all factory and aftermarket carpets are molded to fit the floor pan perfectly. Hand-fitted carpets, like horse and pig-hair stuffing, have all but disappeared. What little is done today is done in restoration and custom shops.

Perhaps, though, you're a bit like me and you like the precise, sharp fit of a hand-tailored carpet; or, again, like me, you're cheap. Three yards of carpet at $10 per yard is way below $150 for a fancy molded job. Those of you interested in saving a buck, gather 'round.

Removing the Old Carpet

Most carpet removal is quite simple. Remove the scuff plates from the door frames, pull the carpet out and throw it away! Couldn't be easier. On some models it's a bit more tricky. I had to remove the seat, safety belts and loosen the kick panels.

If you have a center console to deal with, the trim must be removed on many models. On some, the carpet is just forced up under the trim and may be pulled out with no problem. Some older cars were built with steel drive-nails holding the carpet in strategic places, while others used screws. If, in pulling up a carpet, it really sticks in one place, look for a drive-nail or screw.

Some carpet removals require that the boot around the gear shift be removed. On my truck the carpet was forced under the boot.

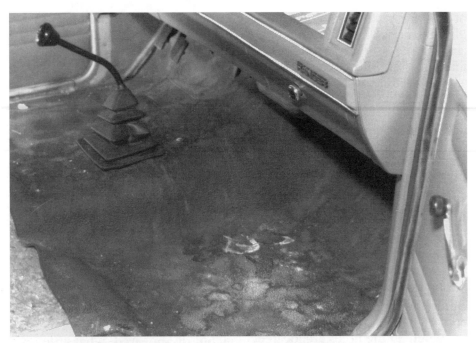

Have you ever seen anything only four-years old look as ugly as this rubber mat? This is the result of salted roads in the winter, thunderstorms in the summer and a half dozen cups of spilled coffee!

Another problem area will be the kick panels, those panels just below and under the instrument panel. Some older cars require removing the accelerator pedal. Wherever it's retained, don't force it; remove what's blocking it.

Padding

All auto carpet should have a pad under it. Factory and aftermarket carpets come with the pad molded right to the back. For our work, we'll make the pad separately and cement it to the floor.

As always, start the project by measuring. With accurate measurements you'll buy the correct amount of material. The carpet padding under my right hand is factory-original rebond (rags).

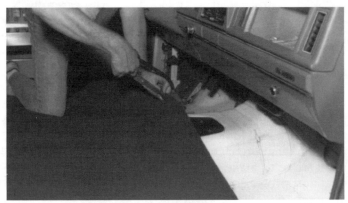

1/2-inch Polyfoam will work well for my carpet-padding use. Here, I'm making the initial cut to go over the shift lever.

Nicely cut and pushed under the boot. I'll have to trim back some of the selvage in the front.

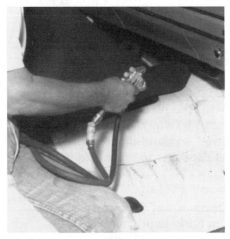

A little cement on the sides and on the floor keeps the padding from bunching up under the carpet. It also provides a secure base on which to cement the carpet.

Padding all snugged down. Notice how easily it forms to two-way curves. This is one of its great advantages.

There are three types of carpet pad. I list them in order of preference: jute felt, Polyfoam and a product called *rebond.* Rebond is an "environmentally sound" product. Rebond felt is made of recycled rags. Rebond Polyfoam is recycled Polyfoam. The majority of household-carpet padding is rebond foam.

Polyfoam sheets (1/2-inch) work like a dream. It will make a tight, two-way bend with no crease. Jute felt has the best insulating qualities. However, it's expensive stuff. Use it on restoration projects.

For my truck carpet I've selected Polyfoam because it has better insulating qualities than rebond and is easy to use. Here's how it works.

I measure the floor pan in both directions and add about 20 percent each way. I cut a sheet this size and push it into the truck. I make sure it's well centered, fold it back at the shift lever and make a cutout. Next, I work this down over the lever, then cut away the excess to fit around the boot. If your boot is removable, just cut a hole large enough for the shift lever to move. Now fold the pad over, spray some cement on the back and on the floor and press down. Repeat on the other side.

If you're working with rebond or jute, you'll have to cut separate pieces: one over the "tranny" hump and one for each side of the floor. On "step-down" floor pans with deep indents, treat each indent as a separate unit, cut and fit your padding into each one. Sometimes, if I feel the padding is too thin, I add a layer over the top of the first. Before cementing the pad to the floor pan *be sure to cut out holes for the seat frame and safety belts.*

When the padding is in smooth and flat and well cemented to the floor pan, you're ready to measure, cut, fit and sew.

Fitting & Installing
The usual process of cutting, fit-

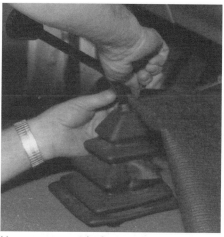
Here we go with the carpet. I made sure the "tranny" piece was correctly located before I began this cut for the shifter.

Trial fit to be sure the boot hole is the correct size. If your boot is removable, you won't have to be quite so meticulous in this operation.

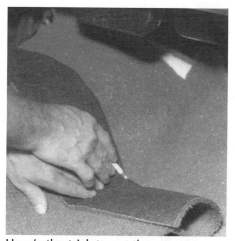
Here's the trick to get the carpet to go up the bellhousing area. Fold it at the bend and mark it from one floor pan side to the other.

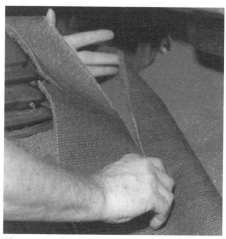
Then cut along your line with a razor blade.

ting and installing begins with the transmission hump and proceeds to the driver's and passenger's sides. This is true, also, for the rear carpet in sedans.

Measure the transmission area from well into the dash panel (firewall) back under the seat, then all the way over from side-to-side. Add about 6 inches to each of these measurements. Measure the floor pan on the driver's and passenger's side, also well up onto the dash and back under the seat.

On most vehicles the seat does not hide the floor all the way out to the door. Therefore, it's necessary to come all the way back with

the carpet to the back of the seat or cut a smaller piece to fill in here. On the truck I came all the way back. Besides a pleasing appearance, it also provides additional insulation.

Cut these three pieces from your bolt of carpet. *Be sure the nap of each piece is going in the same direction.* Carpet, like velvet, has a nap which is woven to lie in one direction. For carpeting, the direction is not too important. However, I like the nap to point toward the dash. The important thing is to have the nap on all three pieces going the same way. To help remember which way the

I'm sewing binding to the edge of this cut closest to the dash. Notice the cutout location for the shifter boot. Location of bound edge is important.

Here's what it looks like installed. Bound edge is on top of the unbound edge, looking like a seam. It's not, however. It's held in place by cementing the sides of the carpet to the padding.

Side pieces are a snap. Just remember to make the deep cut into the corner as you see here.

nap lies, make a line on the top edge, or the edge you want toward the dash. If the lines are in the same location, the nap will be running the same for each piece.

To start the fitting process I lay the "tranny" piece in front of the gear shift. I make certain it's centered equally, side-to-side and there's plenty of material going up the dash. I also have about 3 inches of material spreading out to each side of the hump on the driver and passenger sides. Then I fold it just in front of the gear-shift lever. With a razor blade, I make enough of a slice to allow the carpet to squeeze over the gear-shift knob.

Once over the knob I make radial cuts from the original slice to allow the carpet to pass over the shifter boot. This can be seen in the photo on the top left. Finally, I trim away the excess carpet and hide the bare edges under the boot. If your boot is removable, cut a hole in the carpet large enough to accommodate the shift pattern. The boot is then replaced, covering the raw edges.

On models before the mid '50s there is usually no boot. The carpet must be fit carefully around the gear shift and the raw edge

covered with carpet binding.

If you're working on a vehicle with a center console and all this description is just so much ink to you, take note anyway. You must also start with the tranny area. Do one side first, then the other. Be sure the carpet comes up far enough to allow the raw edges to be covered by the console trim. Now we must fit the part of the "tranny" hump covering the bell housings. This is the part which bends up to the dash panel.

Fold the carpet back on itself right at the crease in the metal where the hump starts up. Mark this crease from the bottom of the passenger's side to the bottom of the driver's side. Then, with a new, sharp razor blade, cut along this line.

Take this whole piece of carpet to the sewing machine and sew a strip of binding to the *back* edge of the cut you just made. Leave the front edge raw (the edge closest to the shift lever).

Return to the car, drape the carpet over the gear shift and spread it out flat. The long cut you made and bound now lets the carpet make a two-way bend. The bound edge covers over the raw edge by about 1 to 1/2 inch and

really looks neat. Take a look at the photo and see if you don't agree.

When I'm satisfied with the fit, I cement it in place. The easiest way is to just do the sides. The top isn't necessary.

The hard stuff is done. The side pieces are easy to fit. Lay them in, chalk line to the front. Make a cut at a 45-degree angle right down to the start of the edge binding on the "tranny" hump. Fold the carpet over on itself and mark a line along the edge of the tranny hump where it bends to make the floor panel.

In a similar fashion, fold over the piece in front of the cut. Draw a line on the back straight up until you reach the front edge of the carpet. Again, take the carpet out of the vehicle, trim along the line you just made and bind the edge. Your finished product should look like the photo.

Before you cement this piece in position, I remind you again to make cutouts for the bolt holes accommodating the seat-frame and seat-belt retainers. These holes are real bearcats to find if you glue the carpet over them. If this happens, before you start tearing out the carpet and pad, look

After trimming along the line and binding the edge, cement new piece in place.

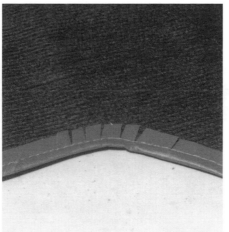

Here's a trick for making the binding fit smoothly through an inside corner. Make a number of slashes on the back side of the binding as you sew it.

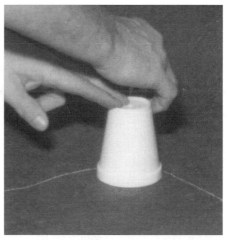

Who says you can't recycle plastic coffee cups? I "recycled" this one into a compass to make nice round corners for my mat!

for the holes *under* the car. If you find them, punch a Phillips screwdriver or a trim pin through so you can see the location from the top side.

Carpeting the Driver's Side

The driver's side is cut, fitted and sewn just as the passenger's side, illustrated herein. There are a few additions and differences.

On some models, especially older cars, the operating pedals (throttle, clutch and brake) were attached to the floor pan or passed through it. You must fit around these. I usually remove the screws holding the throttle pedal to the floor pan, cut a tiny hole for the actuator rod, then bolt the pedal to the floor pan through the carpet.

If the clutch and brake pass through the floor pan, you must make a long slit in front of each of them. These slits are then bound with edging material. Some luxury European models had removable pedals. In this case, small holes could be made and the carpet passed over the push rods. The pedals are then bolted on again.

Where there is a headlight-dimmer switch on the floor, cut just around the push part. This should be the size of a "35-cent piece" (about halfway between a

quarter and a half dollar). Nice plastic grommets are available in a wide selection of colors to cover the bare edges of the hole. Ask for a *dimmer-switch grommet.*

Finally, there's the heel pad. These too, are available in all the colors of the carpet. After fitting the carpet on the driver's side so that it's lying nice and flat in the location you want it, lay the pad where you feel will afford the most protection. With chalk, mark around it in this location. Take it and the carpet to the sewing machine and sew it in place where you marked it.

My personal opinion on heel pads is negative. They wear quickly, look bad after two weeks and cost more than they're worth to be replaced. As an alternative, I make a nice floor mat from carpet. It catches dirt and so can be shaken out daily. it protects a much larger area of the carpet than a heel pad. When it wears out, throw it away and make another. This is much cheaper than replacing the heel pad!

I measure the area of the floor to accommodate the largest mat possible, then transfer these measurements to the backside of a piece of scrap carpet. Using an old styrene coffee cup, I draw the corners. After cutting and binding the

piece, I'm all set to go.

On a customer's car I'll make one of these for each side at no extra charge. It costs me little and makes a very good impression for the shop.

The job is finished by trimming the sides of the carpet, installing the kick panels (if removed) and then the scuff plates. I'll assume you'll remember to install the seat and seat belts!

SUMMARY

Making a fitted carpet is a bit of work and somewhat time-consuming. But, even as a hobbyist, it pays because the cost of the materials are much less than buying a molded carpet. If you're doing custom work, you have to know how to make a carpet. On restoration work, it's a toss-up. There's a large reproduction business across the land turning out original carpets from original factory patterns. But once in a while, someone brings in that Apperson Jackrabbit and we're ready!

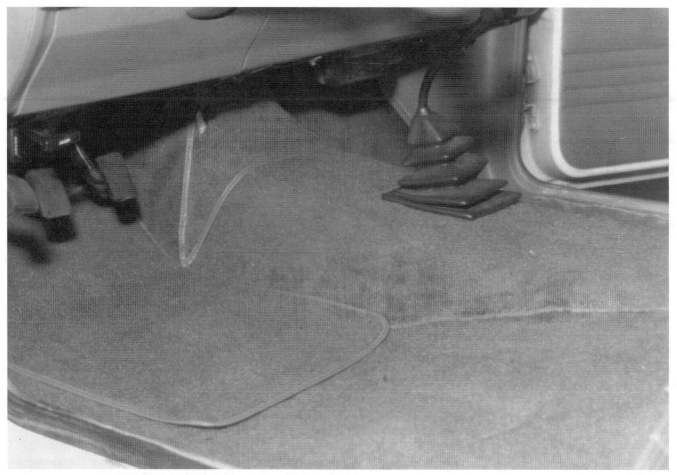

With this nice carpet, me and my passengers will have to kick the mud off of our feet. I'm not about to stop drinking coffee, though!

13 *Building a Boat Seat*

In this chapter we leave the world of automobiles and begin exploring some different areas of upholstery. Our first project will be to build a boat seat from the wood up. Marine upholstery is cut, fit and sewn just as auto trim. Only the materials are different.

Here's our project seat. I can only believe this seat was left out in the weather for years! Rot and plywood ply separation indicate abuse or the wrong materials, or perhaps both.

The ravages of sun and water, both fresh and salt, conspire to destroy in weeks materials that should last for years. Therefore, special materials have been developed for the marine industry. Foremost among these are vinyls with ultraviolet (UV) protection built into the polymers. Without the UV protection, vinyl quickly deteriorates into a gummy mess, attracting grime into its pores. In one season, automotive vinyls exposed to the elements will usually have to be replaced. Although UV protection is more expensive, you can count on marine vinyl to last a number of seasons.

Another product with which you will deal is marine plywood. It is impervious to separation of the plies by water or moisture. It is not, however, totally impervious to rot. Therefore, if it's going to be in

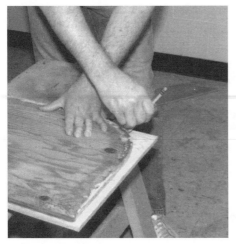

Old seat board is used as a pattern for the new.

Transfer all hole markings at this point. It's the devil trying to locate them later, especially the seat-mounting hardware locations.

If you forget to drill air-escape (breather) holes you'll surely have a whoopee cushion when you're done!

Outside curve for the mold I'm tracing.

After marking, cut with a sabre saw. Use a fresh blade designed for plywood. It makes the smoothest cut.

Here's the first of my four mold pieces: about 24-inches long on each leg with a little extra "beef" in the center for strength.

frequent contact with moisture you'll want to give it a good coat of paint. Don't confuse marine plywood with exterior plywood. The later will not hold up at all in marine applications.

The third important product to consider is fastener material. Only two types of metal are equal to the task: stainless steel and bronze. For my money, stainless steel is superior. Stainless-steel staples seem to last longer than bronze staples when exposed to saltwater. My marine upholstery experience has been primarily with boats that ply the sea lanes

(both coasts) rather than those that see only fresh water. So, I'll moderate that statement even further to say that stainless-steel staples seem to perform better than bronze staples when used in saltwater-marine applications.

So, there are three things to consider as you begin building a boat seat or reupholstering an existing one: buy a marine vinyl that is UV-treated and fasten it to marine plywood using stainless-steel or bronze staples. Anything less and you'll be reading this chapter again next season!

BUILDING THE WOODEN FRAME

How to Bend Plywood Without a $50,000 Press

This seat, like so many of our other projects, cannot be salvaged. The wood has rotted away; the vinyl is gone. The wood appears to be an exterior grade of plywood rather than marine. I don't know the age of this seat, however, so I can't judge it accurately. Separation of the plies, though, indicates an exterior grade.

We'll begin this project by stripping away the old materials—

saving only the Polyfoam and replacing everything else. Having stripped other jobs by this time there's no need to demonstrate. If you're begining with this chapter, go to the front of the book and read through some of the work on stripping, cutting, fitting and sewing.

I'm assuming that by the thirteenth chapter you're proficient in these areas. I will, however, explain a few tricks as we come upon them. Our fitting will be to the new wood so we needn't worry about fitting to the old cover.

The old seat board is used as a pattern. Trace around it carefully. This seat fits into a special location. Any deviation from the original would prevent it from setting in place.

After tracing the outside dimensions, drill whatever screw holes may be necessary. In the illustrations, I'm drilling bolt holes for the mounting blocks which hold the seat back to the cushion. Lastly, drill two or three 1/2-inch "breather holes."

Breather holes let the air escape when you sit down. Remember the stadium cushion? We were concerned with breathers there. Here, too, it's a problem. So let the seat cushion breath with sufficient air-escape holes.

Laying Out the Back

Here is a brief outline of how to bend plywood without a press. First you must make something around which the plywood may be bent and held in position. Next, deep kerfs are cut through all but one ply of the wood. These are cut perpendicular to the curve and across the entire radius at 1/2-inch (or less) intervals. This allows the wood to be "wrapped" around the previously constructed mold without cracking or splintering. It's then held in this position with fiberglass and resin. Slick as can be! Let's do it.

The radius of the bend for our project seat back is the same as

Extra beef also gives us room for a 2-inch hole. This gives another place to clamp.

After laying out the kerf lines, I cut them with the circular saw. Don't try to use a table saw for this operation. It's too easy to lose control.

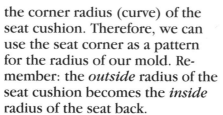

the corner radius (curve) of the seat cushion. Therefore, we can use the seat corner as a pattern for the radius of our mold. Remember: the *outside* radius of the seat cushion becomes the *inside* radius of the seat back.

I begin by laying out the curve (radius) on a piece of 5/8-inch *shop-grade* plywood. Don't use the good stuff for your mold. It becomes firewood after the job is done. This done, I lay out 24 inches to each end of the curve. I then come inside this line about 4 inches and draw a corresponding line. I add a bit in the middle for strength and the result, after cutting, is the piece you see in the photo on the previous page (lower right). For the complete mold I make four of these boomerang-shape pieces and cut 2-inch holes in the center to give a place to insert a C-clamp. The hole may be cut with a sabre saw or 2-inch hole saw. With the molds finished, I can turn my attention to cutting the kerfs in the backboard.

The backboard for the seat back is cut to the overall length of the seat back, plus about 2 or 3 inches more at each end. This gives me a little room for adjustment (or mistakes). The height (or width) should be to the finished measurement. Draw a vertical centerline

on this board.

To determine the location of the kerfs, first find the centers of the radii on the seat cushion. This needn't be too accurate. "Eyeballing" will do. Transfer the center radii from the seat cushion to the backboard. OK, I'll do it step-by-step.

Make a pencil mark in the middle of each curve (radius) of the seat cushion, using your best guess. Now measure from one pencil mark to the other around the back of the seat. Suppose this is 60 inches. Transfer this 60-inch measurement to your backboard by measuring 30 inches out to each side of the centerline. Draw a vertical line here (top to bottom). Now you know where the centers of the radii are on the backboard.

From the radii centers you've located on the backboard, measure out to each side 3 inches more than the full width (circumference) of the curve (radius). Again, draw two more vertical lines.

If the seat-cushion curves are 10 inches along their circumference, your full measurement on the backboard will be 16 inches, or 8 inches on each side of the radii centers. We'll call these lines the *limit of the radius.*

Now, draw vertical lines every 1/2 inch between these limit of the

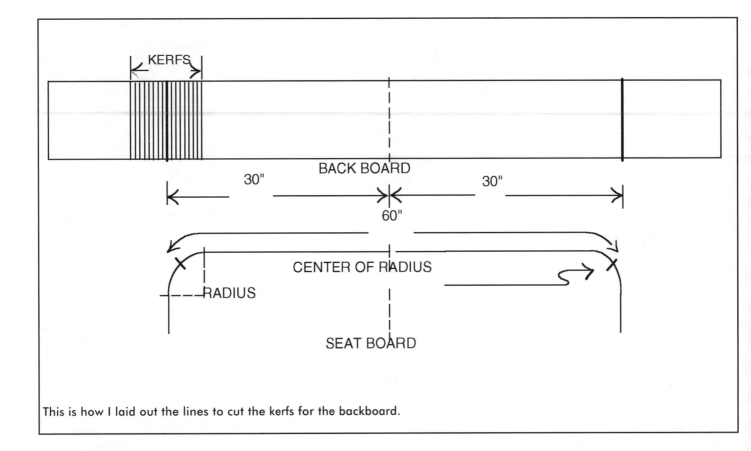

KERFS

BACK BOARD

30" 60" 30"

CENTER OF RADIUS

RADIUS

SEAT BOARD

This is how I laid out the lines to cut the kerfs for the backboard.

radius lines. These are the lines on which you will cut the kerfs.

Cutting the Kerfs

A kerf is a cut, notch or groove in the wood that doesn't go all the way through. We'll do the cutting with a circular saw (often called a *cutoff saw*).

Using a scrap piece of wood, set the blade so it cuts through all of the plies but one. This will take two or three attempts because it must be accurate. If the cut is too shallow the board will crack rather than bend. If the cut is too deep you'll probably go all the way through. So make the depth of the cut as accurately as you can.

It's very important to support the piece you're cutting. Without this support the wood will collapse into or away from the cut. If it collapses into the cut, it will bind the blade causing a kickback. A collapse *away* from the blade will cause a crack or break. So put plenty of support under your board.

Cut a kerf along each of the

vertical lines you've drawn. When this is done, you're ready to bend the board.

Making the Bend

I'm going to bend the back around those forms I cut earlier. I'll place the kerfs on the inside. Your project may go either way: the kerfs on the inside or the outside. I elected to put them on the inside so that the outside would be smooth. The inside will have 2 inches of foam covering the kerfs, the outside only a 1/2 inch foam pad.

Throughout this project I've been talking about the center of the curves or center of the radii. Again, these are important areas. I want the centers of the molds to fall in line with the centers of the seat-back curve. I must be careful to keep these aligned.

After centering the molds in their correct location on the back board, I begin the bend by clamping them to the top and bottom of the back board as seen in the photo on the next page. With plenty of

support under the board, I wrap it *tightly* around the mold pieces, clamping as I go. I've used about every clamp we have in the shop to do both sides.

I was pretty successful with this bend. There are no cracks. If I had heard any cracking as I bent the board, I would have stopped, soaked the cracking area with hot water, then continued. If you're doing this type of bend with a hardwood veneer, it's best to soak the wood before you start. Just let it dry before you start fiberglassing.

FIBERGLASSING

Fiberglass and resin hold the bend in the wood after the clamps are removed. There's not an awful lot to working fiberglass, just a few precautions.

Safety

The thing I fear most about glass or resin is my extreme allergy to the resin. If I get even a drop or two on my hands I break out in a terrible rash. The microscopic shards of glass from sanding operations often cause itching and discomfort to many (me too!). For some, however, it goes beyond discomfort into a rash. Therefore, I wear rubber surgeons' gloves. You should too.

These gloves are available at your local drug store in two qualities: sterile surgical and semi-sterile work gloves. Both are made of latex but should not be confused with the heavy rubber gloves available in the supermarket for washing dishes. These *may* be used but I find they're too clumsy.

My allergy to resins is a result of daily exposure to it during the late '50s and early '60s when I worked in a fiberglass-fabricating business. For most people a little exposure to it is harmless. For others, even a little can be damaging. Don't try to find out which you are. Take full precautions. Wear gloves and a long sleeve shirt. Some folks tape their shirt sleeves to their gloves to prevent contact at the wrist.

Generally, there is no need to sand the cured fiberglass and resin. If for some reason you must, wear a particle mask while you do it. The last thing you need is silicosis of the lungs!

Particle masks are the disposable fiber masks you see at all paint stores and most hardware stores. These masks filter only airborne particles. They do not filter gases. For this type of protection you need a respirator. These are available in major paint-supply houses.

Further precautions should be taken to keep sparks and flames away from any of this work. It's all volatile, especially the acetone used for clean-up. Keep the windows open, a fan going and please, please don't smoke while you work! Make double-sure there are no pilot lights in the area.

Materials
The materials can all be purchased at most auto-parts houses, paint-supply stores, top-quality

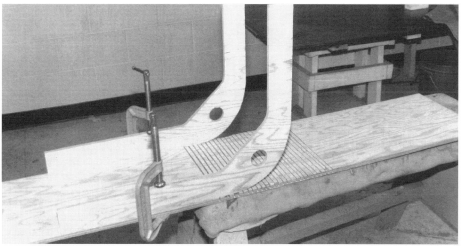

With the molds clamped in place I'm ready to bend. Notice I have full support under the end piece of my board.

Here it is, fully bent. Yes, a lot of clamps are needed to hold it all in place.

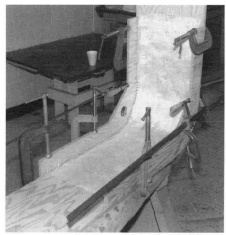

Full layer of fiberglass cloth covers the kerfs. Cut the cloth a bit narrow so it doesn't touch the molds. It's very easy to fiberglass the molds right to the board!

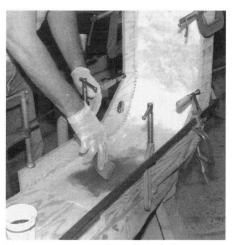

Using a squeegee is optional. Some prefer a paint brush. I have plenty of cardboard around the shop; it's cheap and disposable. Work the resin thoroughly into the cloth—until the cloth turns from opaque to translucent.

Just like this. Although it is hard in an hour or less, let the resin cure for several hours before removing the molds.

Cardboard is indispensable for patterns. The bottom edge of the cardboard is flush with the bottom edge of the seat back. If you trace the pattern from the outside of the old piece, be sure you transfer it to the outside of the new piece. There is, of course, a difference.

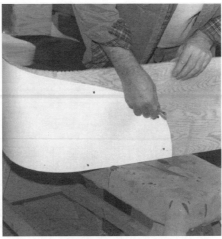

I like to use tacks to hold the pattern in place. You can also use masking tape, staples or cement.

The finished backboard. After cutting through the fiberglass with your sabre saw, throw the blade away. It's useless now.

hardware stores and all boat suppliers. Select a heavyweight glass cloth. You won't need glass mat. It's too heavy for this application. Buy epoxy laminating resin and catalyst (hardener). Polyester and casting resins don't adhere well to wood. Casting resins are also too expensive. A quart of acetone will give you plenty for clean-up; you won't need it for thinning.

Pick up some paper or metal containers to mix in. Don't use any kind of plastic. Resin will eat right through it. Some stirring sticks and two or three disposable paint brushes round out your kit.

The Process

Fiberglass and resin are wonderful stuff, so wonderful they even make Corvettes out of it! It's easy to work, very light and extremely strong *when done right.* Follow the directions here and on the label of the resin container. If you

don't, you'll be starting all over from the beginning.

Temperature and catalyst are the two most important parts of the process. Resin, by itself, will harden in about 3,000 years. Heat it up and it will harden in a few months. Add a little catalyst (hardener) and it will harden in minutes. Add too *much* catalyst and it's hard in seconds. (Try adding too much catalyst on a hot day and it'll harden before you can start stirring it!)

The secret is the right amount of catalyst for the temperature. This information is on the resin-can label. The catalyst comes in a small plastic tube from which it is dispensed in drops. The directions will say, "Use two drops of catalyst per ounce of resin when the ambient temperature is above 70F. Use three drops per ounce between 55 and 70F . . ." These instructions must be adhered to for optimum results.

Humidity also plays a part in the hardening time. The higher the humidity, the slower the action. So, if you're working in a climate where green fungus on the walls is a problem, you may want to add a little more catalyst.

If you must hurry things along, you can add some heat with a hair dryer or very judicious use of the heat gun. *Don't use the heat on the mixture in the container.* Use the heat *after* the resin has been applied to the cloth. Use it carefully. Too much heat will ruin the resin; it crystallizes and cracks.

Finally, limit your stirring of the resin and catalyst to just enough to mix them thoroughly. Too much mixing creates heat which accelerates the hardening process. With glass cloth and resin ready, let's apply them to our project.

Applying the Resin

The glass cloth can be cut with scissors, a razor knife or razor blade. Whatever you use, it'll be dull after the first cut. So be forewarned.

I'm going to cover the bottom of the seat board because it can be seen after the installation.

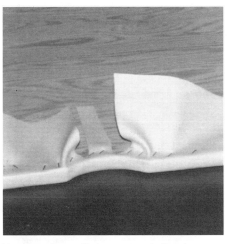

Be sure to pull the material *tight* wherever there's a recess. Note the slashes to relieve the stress.

Front edge of the seat was made of mahogany and well varnished. I'll use it again.

Using steam in the upholstery shop turns a good trimmer into a great trimmer! Using steam on the old Polyfoam relieves the area where it was crushed under the cover. This lets the foam "poof up" just like new. Even the edges become sharp again. If you have no access to steam, take your used polyfoam to a shop and ask to have it steamed.

Gluing the foam to the seat board is optional. I just touch it to hold things in place while I peel the cover over it.

Cut the glass cloth to cover the radius of the curve and 18 to 24 inches beyond. You need this extra for strength. Staple the cloth to the wood *against the kerfs*. It will work on the other side but not nearly as well. Mix enough resin and catalyst to soak and saturate the glass thoroughly over its entire area. Use a brush, roller or, as I show, a piece of stiff cardboard to work the resin through the cloth and into the wood.

Keep the cloth against the wood. It will tend to lift and bubble. Work these back down. Continue to apply the resin until the cloth will hold no more and it just starts to run.

Let this first coat harden. Depending on the temperature and amount of catalyst, it could take from 30 minutes to an hour or more. Check frequently to determine the resin consistency. When it's hard, apply a second coat. When that's hard, a third. The job is done when all of the weave of the glass is full to the top with resin. Usually this takes three coats. For the best bond between the three coats, make the applica-

tions one after the other without a long period between. A long period is several hours, i.e., overnight.

Most resins (other than the laminating resin I advised using) have a wax built into them. After standing for several hours this wax rises to the surface. It then prohibits a good bond with the next coat. You can, however, overcome this by applying the second and third coats as soon as the previous coat hardens.

Should you find yourself in the position of having to wait

Center the cover, work out the wrinkles, peel it down over the cushion and place-tack it. This is standard operating procedure.

I must stress the use of stainless-steel or bronze staples. Regular steel staples will not last the season.

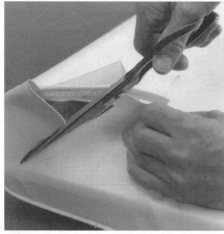

Making this end look neat is a bit of a trick. Cut the material into the corner to relieve the stress.

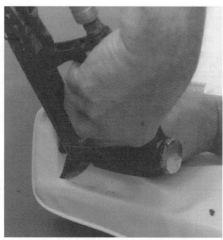

Two flaps created by the step above are stapled to the board and edge.

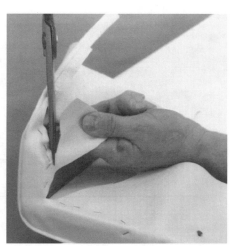

Trim away the selvage.

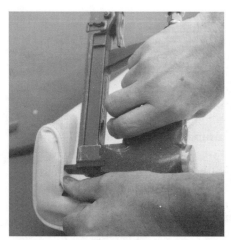

Wrap body of material and welt *tightly* around the edge and retain with staples.

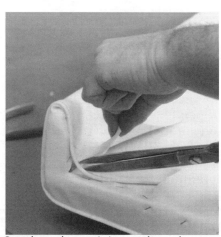

Cut threads retaining welt to the body of the material.

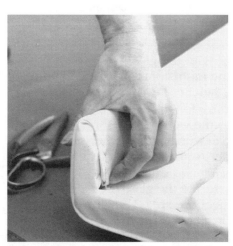

Wrap material *around welt* and staple this folded edge to the edge board. It's not too tricky once you get the idea.

several hours between coats and you're unsure of the resin you're using, simply wash the surface of the previous coat with acetone. Use a coarse-grade sandpaper (60 to 80 grit) to scuff the surface thoroughly. Wash again with acetone and go on with the next application. This will remove any wax formation.

After a good curing period of about 12 hours you may remove the clamps. The newly bent board will stay exactly as it was formed. The process may have taken a number of hours, but it's far better than spending that $50,000 for a press!

SHAPING THE BACK

Now you must transfer any other shaping to your newly bent wood. Our project piece, as seen in the photos, has a slope from the top of the back around sides or "arms." This slope is transferred from the good side of the old back with a cardboard pattern.

Positioning the Pattern

To locate the pattern correctly so it transfers the lines accurately from the old to the new, I'll again work from the centerline. The old back had a centerline. If it didn't, I would measure the entire length of the outside back, divide by 2 and use the results for the centerline location.

I tack a piece of cardboard to the outside of the original back, making a note of the distance from the centerline to the edge of the cardboard. I trace the curve, remove the cardboard and cut along the line I just drew. Now I have a pattern. I locate this pattern on the new back by laying out the previously measured distance from the centerline to the edge of the cardboard, then I tack it in place. After tracing the line on the new back I cut the curve with a sabre saw.

I now have a new back for my customer's seat. It's better (and stronger) than the factory original. With minimal care it should last

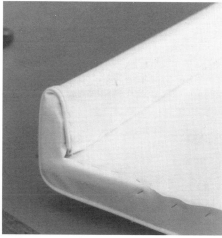

Finished product: from this view you can see all the staples. Turn the seat over, however, and it looks very neat.

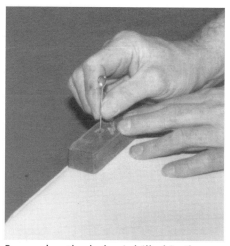

Remember the holes I drilled in the seat board in the first of the chapter? I forgot to locate them before I installed the cover. Now I must find them by searching with a trim pin! You can be in this business a lifetime and still screw up!

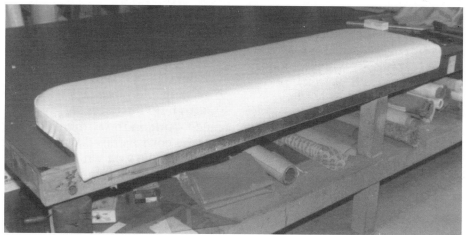

Well, the seat looks pretty good. Don't worry about those wrinkles in the side facings. They'll be covered by the back.

I've cemented a 1/2-inch layer of foam to the outside back of my newly formed backboard. No, it doesn't look like foam; what you see is fabric bonded to the foam. For our 1/2-inch foam we buy factory seconds that would have become molded headliners. This is not only cheap, but gives us a backing to hold thread when we sew pleats, and it saves us from having to buy expensive scrim-back foam. Unfortunately, though, we have to buy in semi-trailer lots!

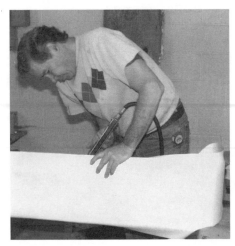

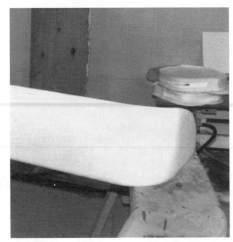

Outside back is a simple wraparound operation.

UPHOLSTERY

Upholstering the Seat Cushion

Upholstery of the project seat starts by covering the bottom side of the seat board. This gives a neat appearance. Then, as in the photos, I remount the front edge board by screwing it to the seat board. The original stainless-steel screws were in good condition so I used them. Next, I cement the Polyfoam pad to the seat board.

The cover is one piece for the top and front with boxing for the sides. The boxing, with welt, fits around the side just past the curve at the back. It is finished like the end facings on the bench seat in Chapter 5. (See how nice this is all coming together!) Mounting the cover, however, gets a bit tricky.

I flip the seat over, pull the cover snug and place-tack a few spots to hold the cover steady while I work on the corners. I want the corner ends finished neatly with the welt wrapped around them and then hidden.

I begin with a diagonal slash

of the boxing right into the corner where the edge board meets the seat board. The two flaps created this way are then stapled to the edge board and seat board. I cut away the selvage right up to the staples.

I wrap the welt and body material tightly around the edge, holding it there with a few more staples. Now, I must bury the welt. To do this, I clip the thread retaining the welt to the body of the material up to the union of the edge board and seat board. I trim away all but about 2 inches of the welt, fold it over and wrap the selvage of the body material around it. Finally, I staple this fold to the edge board. Now we have a neatly finished end of the edge board presenting a nice appearance when turned into the upright position.

Upholstering the Seat Back

The back presents more of a challenge than the cushion. The customer wants the back made of one piece with no exposed seams. We have a two-way curve to deal with in the radii of the back. This will take a lot of heat and pulling!

Almost all boat seats have some kind of curved back. Besides

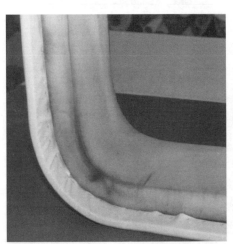

Bottom view of seat back with foam installed. Note 3-inch difference between bottom of foam and wood edge. This is for the seat to fit into.

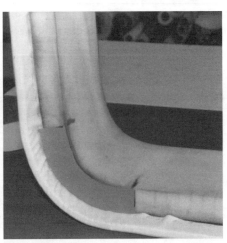

To form an insert in this corner, relieving stress, I begin by making a pattern. All inside edges of the pattern are sewing lines. I must be sure to leave 1/2-inch seam allowance as I trim.

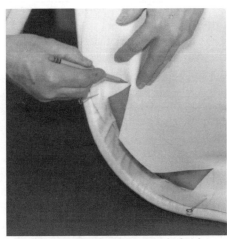

Material for the back is gently laid over foam. I then cut slashes into the corners, right up to pattern lines I drew on foam. I then redraw these same lines on vinyl. I finished by cutting away selvage, leaving a 1/2-inch seam allowance.

the attractive appearance it presents, it helps keep the passenger from sliding about. Therefore, your seat project will probably have a similar two-way curve. The easiest way to deal with this is to fit a boxing around the top (with a welt) just like you did on the project seat in Chapter 6. There you fit the boxing around the front of the seat. Here, the boxing is at the top of the seat.

Another way would be to fit the inside back in three pieces: a center and two ends, with vertical seams at the curve centers. You've seen this style of cover in barrel chairs; and may even be the way your seat back is covered. Watch while I make the two-way curve without *visible* seams.

I begin with a 1/2-inch layer of Polyfoam on the outside back. Then, I wrap a piece of vinyl over this and staple it to the inside of the back. Yes, the staples do penetrate the fiberglass. I'm using about 90 pounds of air pressure. If you're using tacks (be sure they're bronze; I don't know of any stainless-steel tacks) you may want to cement the vinyl to the fiberglass area.

After finishing the outside I cement the Polyfoam to the inside. Now you must follow the

Two inserts to be sewn into the area I just cut away. Three inside edges match the pattern. Outside edge is left long, giving me material to staple to the backboard.

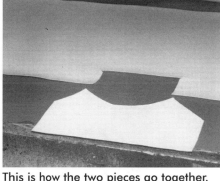

This is how the two pieces go together.

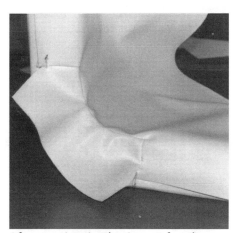

After sewing in the insert for the curve, I pinned it in place to see how it fits. It looks good so I'll proceed.

photos closely to see how I handle this inside corner. Check out the photo (bottom left on opposite page) of the bottom edge of the inside back. My objective is to make an insert in this bottom corner. The seat cushion will cover it so it won't be visible. It will prevent large wrinkles in this area and a possibility of collapsing the foam.

I begin by cutting a cardboard pattern the size and shape of the foam over the entire radius. I also mark the foam to correspond to the pattern. I lay the vinyl into the back and smooth it out in the curve.

Note the trim pins holding it in place. I relieve the strain of the curve with two slashes right up to the edge of the foam, 1/2 inch *inside* the tracing of the pattern.

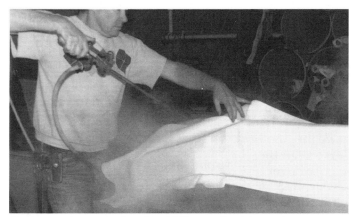

Get some heat on that back! If you do this project, get some help to really keep the heat and the stretching going. I had help doing this. You can't see him because we were too busy with the project to photograph ourselves!

Right: Place-tacks must be neatly aligned. If not, holes may show up after you trim the selvage.

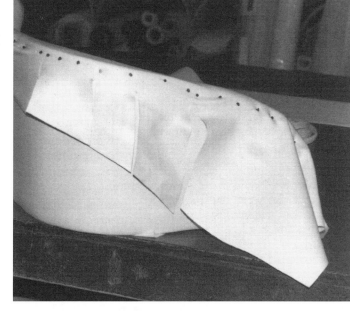

Test-fit the project before you trim anything. You never know.

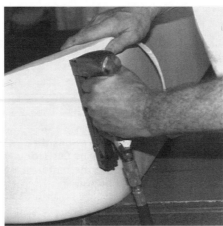

Hidem, the product I'm using here to cover the staples and trimmed edge, has been around since my father was a boy. Now my son, a third-generation trimmer, also uses it.

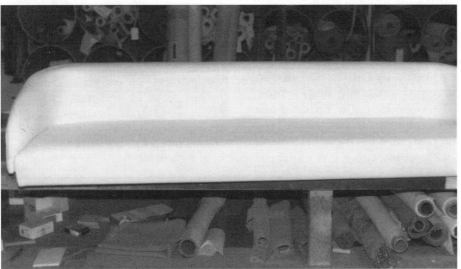

Finished boat seat. The craftsmanship is acceptable, the styling . . . well . . . *plain* would be an understatement!

steam I'd suggest a heat gun or heat lamp. The ol' hair dryer isn't going to do it here! Bring the heat up as high as possible, without melting the vinyl, and begin working it over the back. Work from the center out. Pull a bit and place-tack. Pull some more and tack a bit further. You may want to get some help to keep the vinyl hot while you pull.

I use a product called Hidem (pronounced hide 'em, as in "hide them," meaning the tacks or staples) to cover my staples. I like to use this product on marine jobs because it has no steel wire in it. Remember, wire-on does. You're familiar with wire-on. We used it in the sim-con and convertible top projects.

As I place-tack, I keep my tacks in line and very close to the top of the seat. My final effort will be to staple the material permanently in place, covering the raw edge with Hidem.

When all of the wrinkles are pulled free, replace the tacks with staples. Or, if you're using tacks, drive them in being sure they're all neatly in a line that can be covered by one of the finishing trims mentioned above.

In the first photo above you see the back and cushion together with the seat back vinyl as yet untrimmed. I've done this to check things out before I trim. I want to be sure the inserts I made are covered by the seat cushion. If there is to be any pressure from the seat cushion into the corners of the seat back I want to find out now before I trim anything away. If something is wrong I can still correct it at this stage. Fortunately, nothing is wrong. It fits well and I can finish it off.

FINAL ASSEMBLY

I trim the selvage right up to the staples with my scissors (rather than chancing a razor blade). Then I cover the exposed staples and raw edge with Hidem. Two "beads" form a closed channel in

This gives me my usual 1/2-inch seam allowance.

Then, with a pencil, I mark the *seam* lines (not the cutting lines). The seam lines are the lines traced from the pattern onto the foam. Finally, I remove the vinyl from the back and cut 1/2 inch *inside* the pencil lines. Remember: I'm going to sew on those lines.

Making & Sewing the Insert
I must now cut two inserts to sew into the back. I lay my pattern on a scrap of vinyl and mark around the three inside edges. I leave lots of material on the outside edge as

this is where I'll staple it to the frame. One photo shows the completed insert. Again, I'm going to sew on the pencil line. Therefore, I'll trim 1/2 inch *outside* the line.

To sew in the insert I align the two corners, flip the cover over insert-side-up, and sew around all three sides. The result is the insert you see in the photo on the previous page. It's pinned in place here. Soon I'll staple it down.

The big pull comes now to work it over the top edge without wrinkles. In the photo you see me using a lot of steam. Without

this tape-like product. The two beads are forced apart by the tip of the staple gun. A staple is driven into the tape. The beads then pull themselves back together, closing over and hiding the staple. As with all the trims we use, it is available in a wide selection of colors, but only one style.

SUMMARY

The seat back is now affixed to the cushion and the job is done. It looks a little plain to me. I think it needs some pleats or color to jazz it up. The customer was thrilled, however. He loved it; not only the job but the price: one-third of a new factory replacement!

The important part of this chapter was bending the plywood. This process can be used for seat building of all types: marine, street rod, antique restoration and others. If you don't like the use of resin and fiberglass, there are a number of other ways to bend plywood such as building a full-scale mold from particle board and gluing

successive layers of 1/8-inch plywood around it. Check your library's woodworking section for further information.

Stay alert to the corrosive effect moisture has on the materials you use. Stainless-steel, bronze, brass, lead and chromium are the longest-lasting metals. Upholstery materials should be factory treated to reduce the damage of ultraviolet radiation. Plywood should be bonded with glues that resist moisture. Take further precautions, where applicable, and paint, varnish or fiberglass any exposed wood.

WHY I DON'T USE PLASTIC

There's a process in the boat-seat business with which I disagree. It's using plastic film between the Polyfoam and the vinyl. The plastic film is supposed to act as a moisture barrier to prevent water from coming through the seams and soaking into the foam.

Every seat I take apart, no matter how well wrapped in plastic film, has water-soaked Polyfoam. Regardless of how you try to prevent it, water is going to get into the foam if water gets on the seat. I believe the plastic film does a better job of keeping the water *in* than out! I mention this simply as the reason why those of you with experience do not see me wrapping this seat in plastic film before putting on the cover. If you feel it's worked for you, by all means continue to do it. If you want to try it, it's done daily in shops throughout the nation. I personally feel it's counterproductive.

14 *Reupholstering a Motorcycle Seat*

Because motorcycle riding is one of my favorite pastimes, reupholstering and redesigning motorcycle seats is one of my favorite jobs in the shop. As with each previous chapter, there could be a whole book on this subject. I'll just hit the high points in this one chapter.

If you want to move further into this end of the business, push your mind to think of fresh new ideas and designs using the skills acquired earlier in the book. For example: you can change the basic design of the seat by cementing additional foam to the base seat and then shaping it with the foam saw or a knife.

I've made the back, or passenger's seat, wider to accommodate more ample posteriors. I once cut into the passenger seat to make more leg room for the driver who never carried a passenger. There's no end to the design changes you can do or the fun you can have. Note the design changes I incorporated into the project seat.

TYPES OF SEATS

Fortunately, most motorcycle seats are basically the same. It begins with a frame, usually called a

This is the way the seat arrived at the shop. I'd say it was just about on its last leg! The customer, though, was thinking maybe some black tape . . .

"pan." This may be made of plastic, steel, or a combination of the two. On this pan is a molded-foam pad. More expensive bikes have foam pads with two densities: firm on the inside for support, soft on the outside for comfort.

Over the pan and pad is the cover. Generally, any design work is incorporated into the cover rather than the pad. The cover is attached in one of three ways: cemented, riveted, or stapled to the pan. Sometimes there will be a combi-

nation. Our project seat is so constructed. It's cemented to the pan and reinforced with pop-rivets at various stress points.

There's another way to retain the cover found on some earlier model bikes. Around the bottom edge of the cover a 1/2-inch hem was sewn. Into this hem a piece of soft-steel mechanic's wire was inserted. This assembly was wrapped around the frame which incorporated tabs punched from the metal of the seat pan. As these

After removing the many layers of duct tape I can see the original design of the seat. Sewn-in diamond pleats don't last long even under optimal conditions. Even the back is destroyed. Much of this destruction is a result of environment. This bike was probably left out in the weather year 'round. Garaging is the best; keeping the bike covered is next.

Stress points of the cover are pop-riveted to the seat pan. I'm using an 1/8-inch (or a #30) drill bit to remove them.

Nothing can be saved on the back. It will require all new materials.

tabs were quite sharp and pointed, they pierced the vinyl behind the wire. The installer then bent the tabs down over the vinyl and wire to secure the cover to the seat.

If you go way, way back you can find seats with wooden tacking strips built into them. The cover was tacked to the seat just as in very early auto trim.

SEAT DISASSEMBLY

By the look of this seat you can tell folks wait a long time before they finally break down and bring things in to be repaired. This seat is as much duct tape as it is vinyl! Well, no matter how bad they treat it, we can fix it.

I've carefully removed the duct tape. I wanted to see how the cover was made originally. The

customer wants it shaped as it was, but, without the diamond tufting. He felt this tufting allowed the seat to wear too fast. Besides, the buttons irritated his backside. We can do away with the diamond tufting sewn into the cover but we'll have to do something on the inside curve to prevent wrinkling. A few transverse pleats will do the job fine.

After removing the duct tape I turn the seat over, locate the pop-rivets and drill them out. In the front of the seat are two metal clips. There's a lot of stress at this point. Sometimes gluing isn't enough. So we use clips to prevent the material from pulling loose. I remove these clips and save them. They're very hard to come by. With the retaining hardware removed I can peel off the back. Finally, by breaking the cement bond the cover can be removed. For now, I'll leave the cover on to aid in fitting.

CUTTING, FITTING & SEWING THE SEAT TOP

The great thing about this trade is the basics. Once you learn them, they're repeated everywhere. Cutting, fitting and sewing is the same whether it's a car seat, bike seat, boat seat or any other thing you sit upon. The basics are the same.

Measure the top of the seat from front-to-rear, then side-to-side. Add for seam allowance and a little shrinkage in the pleat area. Write these measurements on a scrap of paper. Measure the seat facing top-to-bottom and all the way around. Note the measurements on your paper. Repeat these steps for the inside back, outside back, and back facing.

When all your measurements are duly noted, cut out the blocks of material.

In the photo on the right you'll count six pieces of material. A quick count of the inventory listed above should indicate five pieces. I elected to use two pieces instead of one to make the seat facing. I'll

You're looking at the seat bottom in this photo. Note two clips which help retain the cover to the pan. These are only available through the dealer. If I lose them, I lose time going to the dealer for new ones. Be very careful to keep all little parts like this under control.

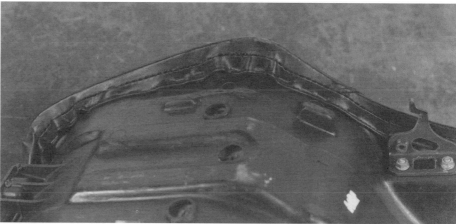

Seat bottom on a Japanese bike. It's retained to the pan by staples in the plastic.

have a French seam in the front-center of the seat.

For the seat top and inside back I'll bond the vinyl to 1/2-inch foam as before. Why? Right. I'm sewing pleats into the seat top and I want that puffed-up appearance for the inside back. Now I'm ready to sew the pleats.

Locating the Pleats

Because I'm making the design decisions here, I decided to use four pleats. These will be divided equally through the inside contour of the seat. There are five seams. If I locate the center seam in the center of the contour it will balance aesthetically and arithmetically (translation: it'll look good and work out). You can see by the photos the plan works.

If I were going to do the diamonds again I would measure them vertically and horizontally. Then, transfer these measurements to the padded vinyl by drawing sewing lines just as I do for the pleats. I would be sure everything was well centered before I committed the material to the sewing machine.

After sewing in the pleats I fit the seat top. Notice these are the same steps we followed in the first project. Sew the pleats, then fit. If you try to save time by fitting first then sewing everything at one time, the cover will never fit right. Make the design, then fit.

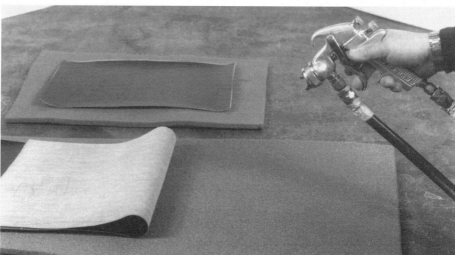

Block out the pieces as we've done before. Cement the seat and back pieces to 1/2-inch, scrim-back foam.

Layout the pleats. If you jump to the last photo in this chapter there's an illustration of a seat with *all* pleats.

The pleats should always be sewn before fitting the panel. This is not always done in production shops, but good custom work requires it.

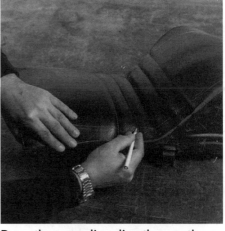

Draw the seam line directly *over* the old welt. If there is any error it should be made to the *inside* of the welt. This will prevent the cover from finishing too large.

We're completely fitted here. Note the following: location marks aligned, seam line with 1/2-inch seam allowance, the piece securely pinned in place. This rechecking will show up any errors *before* the pieces are assembled.

Fitting the Cover

What's the next step? Right, again! Pin the pleated panel to the old cover (or foam, or frame) and mark the sewing line. Note the location of the center seam of the four pleats. This puts two pleats on the upside and two on the down. Be sure to use your locating marks. I've used them at the center-seam location, where the seat meets the inside back and in the front center where the seat-facing French seam will locate.

After sewing 1/2 inch outside the seam line for seam allowance, I trim the selvage right up to my seam. Few production trimmers include this step. It's time-consuming, I'll agree. It does, however, make a neater job. This means a nicer-appearing job. Because you're in no hurry, include this step and realize the nicest-looking product possible.

The facing is fitted just as you have fit facings in the other projects. For this job I sewed the two ends together with a French seam, located it in the center and then brought the sides around pinning them in place. Again, I mark along the sewing line and trim the sel-

vage. To assure myself both sides are exactly the same, I fold the material over on itself and check. If one side is different than the other I'll trim away the difference until each side is a mirror image of the other.

Sewing Facing to Seat Top

At the machine I sew on a length of welt, allowing about 4 inches of overhang at the beginning and end. I also sew on a 4-inch-wide stretcher at the location marks I made where the inside back meets the seat. This will be cemented to the inside-back frame to prevent the seat top from scootching forward. The job is finished after sewing on the facing.

The easiest way to locate the facing is to start at the front. Align the French seam with the location mark in the front center of the seat top. Sew to the end. Turn the job over. Start at the center again, sewing a bit over the first seam to lock it down. Then sew to the end. After you've sewn a few facings you can start at one end, align your marks and sew right around. This takes a bit of skill. You've got to stretch a little here, push a little there to make sure all the marks line up. Too much stretch or push, though, makes

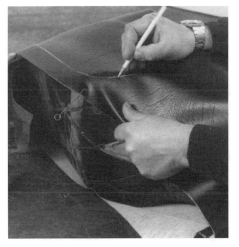

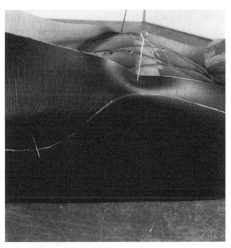

Facing(s) are done next. Be sure there are corresponding location marks on the facing(s).

Both sides of the facing are the same. Omit this step and one side of the seat may not look like the other!

puckers. Starting in the middle and working both ways eliminates the pucker problem!

INSTALLING THE NEW SEAT COVER

Building Up the Seat with Foam
I hope your seat's in better condition than this one. If not, you'll have to build it up with extra foam. For motorcycle seats, especially thin ones like this, I use a high-density (harder) foam. It provides more support. Usually, high-density foam is available from your local auto-trim supply outlet.

Using 1- to 1-1/2-inch foam, cut it about 2 inches larger then the area on which it will be cemented. Spray a thin coat of contact cement to one side of the new foam and the top of the seat. Allow a few seconds for the cement to set then bring the two pieces together. Trim with a foam saw, knife or razor to match the existing foam contours. Now you're ready to mount the cover.

I use a lot of clamps when I install a motorcycle seat cover. Turn the cover right-side-out and lay it over the seat. Pull the front down snug and clamp it in position. Then, stretch it tight at the rear. On my cover I pull on the ends of the welt until the wrinkles are out of the facing, then clamp them

down.

With the cover held tight like this, I can secure it with rivets, cement and clips. Pop-rivets are first. I locate the original holes in the pan, then punch holes through all the layers of selvage just beneath the welt cord. Then I secure this with two 1/8-inch poppers. Now I can discard the two rear clamps. I continue the installation by cementing the bottom edge of the cover to the pan. Of course, I replace the two securing clips I removed from the original cover.

The dark area you see in the front of the seat (top-left photo, page 189) is a piece of black carpet, cut to fit and cemented in. The seat sits at a rakish angle where the underside is visible. This piece of carpet improves that appearance.

The seat-cover installation is finished when I cement the stretcher to the inside back frame. Again, this prevents the cover from "creeping" forward.

MAKING THE BACK COVER

Fitting
There is little to distinguish the fitting of the back from the fitting of the seat. It, too, is clamped into place, the seam line traced over the edges of the frame and location marks made where necessary. Let's talk, then, about how the bot-

Finished cover ready for installation.

tom edge of the inside back is formed.

In the photo on page 189 you can see I've wrapped several inches of vinyl and foam back under itself. Where I made this fold I put a location mark. This is the point where the inside back meets the top of the seat. I want the material folded under this way in the finished job—only not such a large amount.

If I fold 1 inch or more under and then sew the welt over this fold, I'll have a big lump here. If I eliminate the lump by not folding a piece under, I'll have a raw edge to deal with. Solution: cut away the material at the fold, which would be picked up by the stitching of the welt. You can see the shape of this solution by looking at the bottom right photo on page 189. The tab formed this

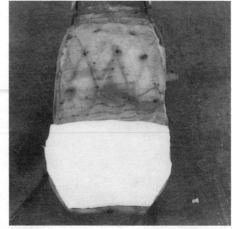

Always cement the foam together. If you don't, it can move around after the cover is installed.

I've got to build this seat up with more foam. I wish I had sold the customer a whole new foam job.

Pop-rivets take the place of the clamps. Here in the northeast I use stainless-steel rivets when they're going to be exposed to the weather.

Lay the cover over the seat . . . and clamp it in place.

way can be folded under to prevent a raw edge. The tab shape prevents bulk at the seam.

Fit the outside back, fit the back facing and get ready to sew.

Sewing It Together

If you stop to think a minute, sewing this back together will be much like sewing the stadium cushion. Compare the two as we move along.

Sew a length of welt to the inside back; side, top, side. Leave 6 to 8 inches of excess. This is to come all the way down the sides of the seat. Repeat this step for the outside back. The front and back can now be joined together by the facing. (On the stadium

cushion the two panels were joined by a boxing.)

Because the back facing is curved, I'll work from the centers out, as I did with the seat facing. I join my location marks at the top of the inside back with the front center of the facing, sewing to the end, turning the work over and repeating. Next, I fold the corners of the facing and make location marks to align with the corners of the outside back. With the faces of the materials together I sew the facing to the outside back, aligning the location marks with the corners. I now have a three-sided cushion-cover. When I turn this cover right-side-out it will pull sweetly down the back frame.

Installing the Back Cover

Remember the condition of the foam when I removed the old cover? Unusable. I replace the inside foam with some more of the 1-1/2-inch high-density foam. Next, I cement a band of 1/2-inch foam around the edge of the frame to protect the cover. Using silicone spray on the foam and on the inside of the cover, I pull it down over the frame and foam, remembering to fold under the tab I made as part of the inside back.

You must use something to prevent the foam from bunching up under the cover. If you don't like the silicone, wrap the back with plastic film, the kind that

Finished underside. Exposed part is covered with black carpet. Note clips.

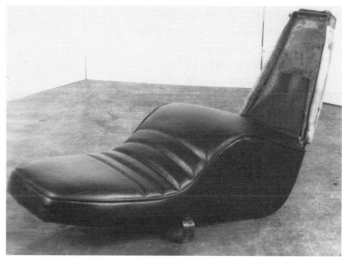

Hey, the top looks even better than the bottom! The stretcher has been cemented to the back frame.

Back fitted to frame. On something this small I fit right to the frame, not giving allowance for the small amount of foam used.

Unless you're short of vinyl, fit the back facing in one piece. A French seam at the top of this back would be too bulky and would receive too much weather abuse.

comes from the cleaners to protect your clothing. Once in, however, it stays there.

Final installation includes clamping the back in place, pop-riveting the welt to the frame and cementing the outside back to the pan.

SUMMARY

Here we have a work-horse seat, the "no-frills special." It will be as comfortable as this style of seat can be and last for many years. Had the customer wanted frills we could have gone all out. This is exactly what he wanted and he's satisfied.

I wish (after the horse has fled

Here are the three back pieces ready to be assembled.

Notice how the inside back is cut and sewn. Angled cut at bottom allows vinyl and foam to be folded under without excessive bulk in corners.

the barn) I had sold the customer on all-new foam. It wouldn't have changed the appearance of the finished product, but I know it would have provided a more comfortable ride for a longer period of time.

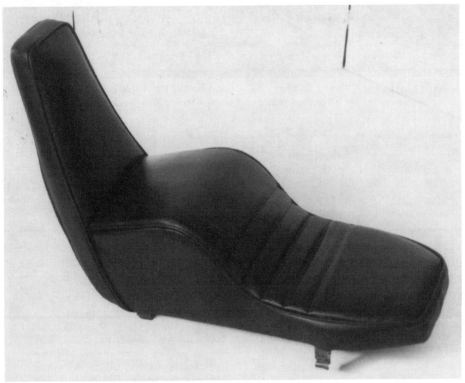

All finished and ready for installation.

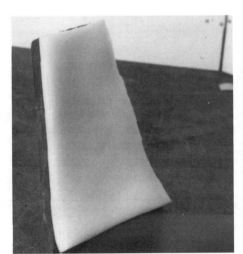

New foam for back. Again, high-density foam works best.

Here is an all-pleat Japanese bike seat. This also makes a nice design.

Pop-rivets and cement hold the cover to the back.

15 *Truck Tonneau Cover*

In the northeast a tonneau cover is not a luxury or dress-up item—it's a necessity! Spring and summer thunderstorms whip up in a matter of minutes. If you're carrying the week's groceries when this happens, it's like tossing everything into the swimming pool! The falling leaves of autumn can build up at the rate of 3 inches per day. Raking wet leaves out of the bed of a truck is even less fun than raking them off the lawn. You may like winter's snow, but I don't think you'd like carrying a ton of it in your 1/2-ton pickup. A tonneau cover helps prevent these little disasters. That's why we feel they're a necessity.

In the great southwest they're used mostly as a dress-up item. However, when I lived there they were great as covers for taking trash to the dump, carrying newspaper to the Boy Scouts' recycling bin and as a hiding place for Christmas and birthday presents. What self-respecting youngster would look in the back of a pickup with the tonneau cover on? Why, there might be work under there!

If you need to protect your cargo or just want to make your "wheels" shine a bit, here's a great project. Jeff Priest made and installed mine using a single piece

The "Lone Ranger" here is badly in need of a tonneau cover. Looks like it needs a couple of tie-downs, too!

of vinyl.

If you want to get a bit fancy, consider making yours out of two or more colors, sewing them into a design. I've seen some great work incorporating graphics on the side of the truck which carry into the tonneau. To do this, the vinyl colors are usually selected first; then the graphics paint is

mixed to match these colors.

If you want to spend a few bucks, take the tonneau to your local silkscreener and have any kind of picture or design screened on. Just be sure the artist uses a paint which will adhere to vinyl. Neglect this and all your hard work will peel off in a week!

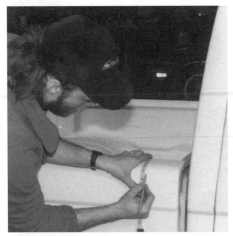

Jeff will place snaps in the center of the bed's top radius. Inside edge of bed becomes the "control point." Measurements, therefore, stay the same on both sides.

After locating his marks along the bed, Jeff draws the line on which he will place the snaps.

Even snap spacing requires careful measurement.

After locating marks for each of the snaps, Jeff drills 1/8-inch holes for the pop rivets. If you use a center punch, be careful not to dimple the body sheetmetal.

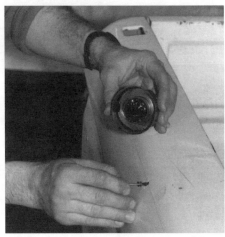

A little body sealer now prevents big rust problems in the future.

Jeff is using his super deluxe manually operated pop-rivet installation device to secure the male portion of the snap to the bed of the truck.

GETTING STARTED

By now you recognize my Ford Ranger, affectionately known to family and friends as "The Lone Ranger." (If you're under 30, you may have to ask your Dad who the Lone Ranger was.) Again, he (the Ford Ranger, not the Lone Ranger) will serve as a "role model" for our project while Jeff whips up a first-class tonneau.

Materials

If you wish to make your tonneau from one piece, be sure to specify this to the salesman at your local supply house. He carries extra-wide vinyl for this purpose. If you'll be using two colors, any 54-inch-wide vinyl specifically treated for outdoor use (ultraviolet protected) can be seamed together to give you the needed width. Measure the length of your bed and order your material accordingly.

Next you'll need a 6-foot length of aluminum-awning rail with a 1/2-inch-diameter retainer. (See photo on the next page.) This is usually available through the upholstery-supply house where you purchased your vinyl. If not, it's always available at awning shops. Lacking either of these resources, you can get it mail order through The Astrup Co. (address in suppliers list).

You'll also need a 6-foot length of 3/8-inch cotton rope (clothesline) and about 40 snap fasteners, both male and female. Again, your supply house will have these or they may be ordered from AuVeCo. This company is also in the suppliers list. You'll need an installation tool to mount the female fastener in the vinyl. At larger supply houses these may be rented by the day. If your supplier doesn't offer this service, you'll have to take the finished tonneau

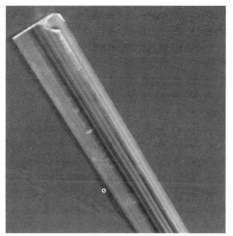

End view of the awning rail. Be sure what you buy looks like this.

Note the lip is installed *down* inside the bed of the truck. Retainer part of the rail faces the front of the vehicle.

and truck to your local auto-trim shop and have them install the snaps for you. This should be quite inexpensive because it takes less than an hour to do.

If you've peeked forward in the chapter, you saw two bows under the cover to give it a crown. These prevent water from puddling in the center. You'll need two 1-3/4-inch by 1/4-inch fiberglass bows and corresponding bow sockets. Some places offer wooden bows. If possible, hold out for fiberglass. The wooden bows are not as satisfactory due to rot, deterioration, breakage and a host of other problems.

Finally, purchase 7 yards of a matching vinyl binding and you have everything needed to build your tonneau cover.

Layout

Starting at the front of the bed, Jeff begins by "eyeballing" the center of the radius on the edge of the truck bed. He then measures from the *inside* edge of the bed to the center of the radius. This measurement is repeated at the rear of the bed and at the front and rear of the other side.

Laying a straight edge between these marks, he draws a line connecting them. At the tailgate, he makes a line across the top edge, down about 1/2 to 1 inch. Now he has a line on two sides and the tailgate. On this line he'll attach

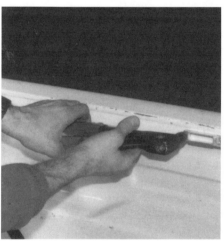

Bow sockets are installed with pop rivets also. A spray can lid holds the pop rivets. In the center of the lid is a dollop of body sealer. Quite handy.

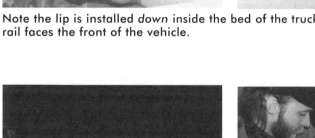

Just "eyeball" about 4 inches of crown. To do this, imagine a straight line from one side of the bed to the other at the top. Now, flex the bow until it's about 4 inches above this imaginary line. Mark it and cut it. Cut the other bow to the same length to ensure a similar height in the crown.

the male portion of the snap fastener. First, though, he must locate even spacing between the snaps.

Starting on the side, he makes a pencil mark at the front of the line just about even with the front edge of the bed; maybe a 1/2 inch or so, back. He makes another mark about 5 inches from the rear of the bed. This will be the placement for the first and last snap. Now, he locates a center between these marks and makes another

line. Again, centers are located between marks. This process continues until there's a locator mark every 7 or 8 inches.

Doing it this way allows Jeff to adjust for the different dimensions of each truck bed while keeping the spacing between the snaps equal. He repeats this process on the other side.

The tailgate is done just a bit differently. A mark is made at each edge of the tailgate. This is the placement for the two outside

Here all the hardware is installed. Now Jeff can begin cutting and fitting the cover.

snaps. Jeff measures the distance between them and divides by 9 (spaces). This gives him 10 evenly spaced snaps across the tailgate. Now he's ready to mount the male portion of the snap.

Mounting the Snaps

To mount the snaps on your vehicle you'll need a drill motor, a 1/8-inch drill bit, sufficient snaps, an equal number of 1/8-inch pop rivets, a pop-rivet gun and body sealer. A simple, mechanical pop-rivet installer purchased for about $10 will do just fine.

In the dry areas of the country, aluminum pop rivets may be used with no ill effects. In areas where they salt the roads, you'll get much longer service from stainless-steel rivets. You'll also note that Jeff uses a little body sealer on each rivet to cover the raw edges of the metal where he drilled the hole.

The corrosive effect of salt is not to be dismissed lightly. Although not as severe, this same corrosive action occurs along all

the saltwater ways of the U.S. (Atlantic, Pacific and Gulf states). Consider these effects as you pursue any project which produces raw edges of metal or allows moisture to remain in contact with unprotected body parts.

At each locator mark (where you wish to fasten a snap) drill a hole with the 1/8-inch or #30 drill bit. Next, place a pop rivet through the hole in the center of the male snap, put a little body sealer or silicone sealer on the tip of the rivet and "pop" it into a hole. This retains the snap to the body. Repeat for all the holes including those along the tailgate. With the male snaps installed you can turn your attention to the awning rail. The awning rail secures the front of the tonneau to the bed.

Installing the Awning Rail

The awning rail is an extruded aluminum bar incorporating a 1/2-inch semicircular retainer and a 1-inch mounting lip. A photo of this piece appears on page 193.

After sewing a 3/8-inch rope

into the front edge of the tonneau cover, you can slide this assembly into the retainer portion of the rail to secure the front of the tonneau to the bed. Although not water-tight it's quite water-resistant.

Cut the rail to fit snugly *inside* the front of the bed. Smooth the cut edges of the aluminum with a file, knife or sandpaper. It's important to remove all burrs to prevent snagging and tearing the vinyl.

Using the same 1/8-inch drill bit and pop rivets, mount the rail to the front of the bed. *The semicircular retainer portion of the rail must face the front of the bed and rest on the top edge.* If you mount it facing the rear of the bed, you'll get severe leakage in bad weather. You'll also be wise to seal the mounting surfaces with silicone. This, too, will help prevent leakage.

Mounting the Bow Sockets

On the preceding page you saw Jeff mounting the bow sockets on the demo project. To get the location, he simply divided the bed into thirds. The Ford Ranger has an overall bed length of about 6 feet. Therefore, he mounted the sockets on 2-foot centers (one at 24 inches from the front, the other at 48 inches from the front). Again, he used 1/8-inch stainless-steel pop rivets.

Fiberglass bows come in 6-foot lengths and must be cut to size. Jeff "eyeballs" about a 4-inch crown; then cuts the bow. You can see the finished preparatory work in the photo above.

This completes the preparation and installation of the hardware. Now, let's look at making the cover.

CUTTING AND FITTING THE VINYL COVER

If, as Jeff is doing with the project truck, you decide to use extra-wide vinyl, just follow along. However, if you're going to do something fancy, now is the time to make your preparations.

A three-piece cover is usually made with the center piece somewhere between 36 and 48 inches wide. Contrasting pieces are sewn on the side to give the full width. If you're using one color of 54-inch wide material, you might want just one center seam.

Usually French seams are used when making these multi-panel covers. Decide what you want, cut and sew to give yourself plenty of overlap, then follow the directions for the single-piece cover.

It's very important for the front edge to be squared with the sides. If this is not the case, the rough fit of the cover will be off at an angle to the bed. This makes it extremely hard to fit. Use a framing square to prepare the front edge.

Sewing in Rope Retainer
Fold the squared front edge back 3 inches. Mark this fold so the dimension remains the same across the length of the front edge. Insert the 3/8-inch rope you previously cut to the same length as the awning rail. (A 48-inch awning rail equals a 48-inch piece of rope.) Center the rope inside the fold.

Now, sew a seam as close to the folded edge as possible until you reach the area of the rope. Come out around the rope as if it were a welt. Sew along until you reach the other end of the rope. Then, return to sewing as close to the edge of the fold as possible.

Remove the cover from the machine, take it to the truck and feed the newly sewn front edge into the awning rail. It goes in one of two ways, vinyl facing out or vinyl facing into the bed. You want the vinyl to face out into the weather.

Fitting the Cover to the Bed
The easiest way to do this is to pull the cover snug, then tape it in place. Jeff uses 2-inch masking tape to do this. I sometimes use duct tape because of its extra "tack." With a grease pencil or crayon make a few location marks directly over the male fasteners.

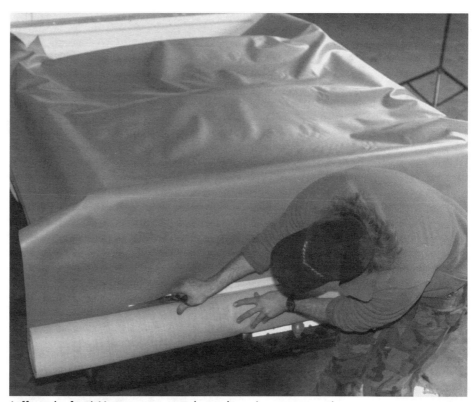
Jeff works fast! He measures and cuts here in one operation.

These are easily seen as small bumps under the vinyl. Jeff makes them at each of the end snaps and one in the middle. Now remove the cover from the truck.

At the bench, lay the cover out flat. You're now going to mark for the trimming edge and the folded edge. To locate these lines, measure out 1 inch and 3-1/2 inches from the location mark. Draw lines connecting these two marks on all three sides of the material. The outboard line (3-1/2 inches) will be the line on which you trim away the selvage. On the 1-inch line you'll make your fold.

Making the Hem
Turn the cover over, cloth side up on the bench. Make a dry fold (no cement) along the fold line and crease it tight. I use the handle of my scissors for this. Some trimmers use a knife handle or the back of a spoon. Just be sure to crease the material well. Remember: you're folding in on the 1-inch line. When the fold is correctly

located and creased you're ready to cement it down.

Jeff uses a glue pot to spray the cement. You can use anything you have at hand, including simply brushing the cement on. When the cement is dry to the touch fold the material over along the previously made crease and rub it down. Jeff uses a heavy roller for this. The back of a soup spoon works great too. Do all four sides at one time.

Dealing with the Corners
The two rear corners must be trimmed away to give a smooth fit over the bed of the truck. Previously you made location marks over the end snaps. From these marks measure towards the corner 1 inch and make a mark at the edge of the material. Connect these two marks with a line using a straight edge. Along this line, cut away the two corners. Now you're ready to sew the hems you just secured.

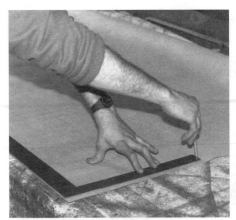

Front edge must be square to the sides. Don't omit this step. You're guaranteed wrinkles if you do.

This makes the demonstration a bit more obvious. Pull the cover tight and tape it in place. Use a wide (2-inch) tape for this process. You need good holding power.

Jeff makes two measurements: 1 inch from the snap mark for the fold line and 3-1/2 inches for the selvage line.

Rope is sewn into the front edge. Leave the flap cementing until the other sides are ready to be cemented. Then, do all four sides at one time.

Male snap is easily seen through the vinyl. Jeff locates each end snap and one or two in the center. From these marks he'll be able locate his trim line and the fold line for the hem.

SEWING THE COVER

Making the Hem

Carry the cover to the sewing machine and lay it *facedown* on the bench with the front edge toward the needle. The front edge is the one with the rope. You're going to make a seam 1/2 inch in from the selvage edge of the material. This will also be 2 inches in from the edge of the rope.

Lock the stitch, sew straight down to the opposite end and lock the stitch again. Remove the material, clip the threads and turn the cover to the next seam. This

Normally a photo like this would end up in the scrap pile, but it's a great representation of the contortions a trimmer must go through. What you *can't* see is that Jeff has pulled the cover tight and is holding the tension on it with his shoulders while using his hands to pull off a length of masking tape to tape the cover to the tailgate!

will be a side.

Repeat the above process along the side of the cover, locking the stitch and making a 2-inch hem. Turn and sew the back side the same way. Finish by sewing the remaining side and the hem is done. You've now hemmed all four sides of the cover.

Binding the Edges

Turn the cover over and radius the four corners a little. If your hand is a bit shaky, draw a line around the bottom of a paper coffee cup. Begin the binding operation at the front of the cover just at the end of the rope. This is illustrated in the lower right photo on page 197. Bind all the way around to the other end of the rope. For a binding demonstration review the carpet section in Chapter 12. You've finished sewing the project now and all that remains to be done is to install the female portion of the snaps.

INSTALLING THE SNAPS

In the photos Jeff has installed the front of the cover and is pulling it tight. He'll again use 2-inch masking tape to hold the corners in place. Let's watch as he installs the snaps.

As I have advised throughout this book, Jeff starts in the center and works out to the ends. His first snap is located at the center of the passenger's side. He pulls the material tight, making sure he has about 1 inch of selvage beyond the male snap beneath the cover. He marks the location with an awl, actually penetrating the material.

He puts the cap in the top jaw of the installation tool and the snap in the bottom. Then he places the whole assembly over his mark, aligning the stem of the cap with the mark. He compresses the handles, which work like a pair of Vise-grip® pliers. This drives the cap and snap together and the unit is installed. He then fastens the male and female snaps together and moves to the other side.

Again, he pulls the material tight over the male center snap, marks the location with an awl and installs a female snap. He moves to the center rear and repeats the process. Now, all three center snaps are installed and fastened.

The next step will be to repeat the process at all four corners. When this is done, Jeff will have most of the wrinkles pulled out. To fill in the remaining snaps, he proceeds from one side to the other until all the snaps are in. You can see by the finished product shown on the next page that he knows what he's doing.

SUMMARY

Making a truck tonneau cover is a lot of fun. It's a quick and easy way to really dress up a vehicle. Even while getting in his way with my photography, Jeff made this cover in less than three hours.

If you're concerned with weather-proofing your truck bed,

Cement and fold the hem before sewing. It makes a smoother, stronger finished product.

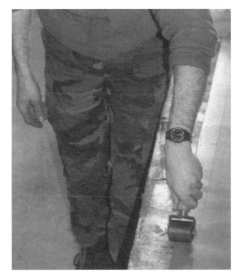

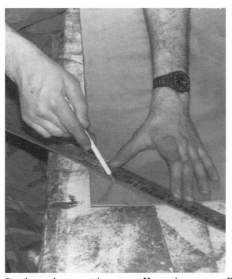

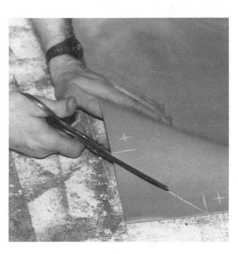

Back ends must be cut off so the cover flows smoothly over the body lines at this location. Notice corners in the finished product. Cut location is determined by measuring 1 inch *in* (toward the end) from the snap mark. These two marks are connected with a line. You'll make your cut on this line as you see Jeff doing.

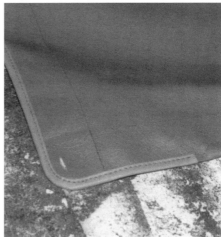

Radius the corners a bit before you bind the edges. Square corners tend to curl up and look unprofessional.

stick with one-piece vinyl. You can do a pretty good job of waterproofing a seam with cement but it's never quite perfect.

Don't try to cut costs by eliminating the bows. The first shower that comes along will leave you with about 200 lbs. of water in the middle of your new tonneau. If you're in luck, the snaps will let go. If your luck runs out, a seam will split. Don't cut corners with materials.

Finally, the last word is on material. Be sure any material you buy is meant for exterior use and is treated to resist the effects of ultraviolet rays.

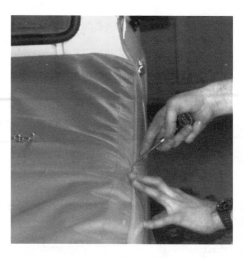

Stretch the cover on tight as you begin to mark for the female snaps.

Right: As always, Jeff works from the center, out.

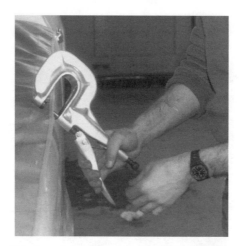

This handy tool is a portable snap-fastener installer. There's also a heavier, bench-mounted tool. For this type of work, though, it would be too slow. You should be able to rent this tool by the day at your local supply house. If you're going to be doing a lot of snaps you might consider buying one. As of this writing you can buy the tool and the dies for the snaps for under $100.

Well, here it is, tight as a drum. My last bit of advice is this: don't make it *too* tight. These covers tend to shrink. If it shrinks too much you won't be able to fasten the snaps.

16

Van Interiors

On this, our next-to-last project, we'll drop in on a van shop and watch them do things you won't find in an auto-trim shop. Among other things, this includes cutting through the body to install windows; a whole new concept of headliners; fabricating side panels; making curtains; building cabinetry; and in general, an overall view of custom van interiors. To prevent repeating myself I won't go into seating. Any van seating you do will be done just like auto seating.

You have all the basics to do most van work. My job now is to point out some of the tricks and perhaps amplify on cabinetry. This is a large part of van work and it's not something we've discussed before.

To help us with the mysteries of van interiors I called on David Lampert of Van-Go, one of New England's largest and finest van-conversion facilities. Van-Go is just outside of Boston in Saugus, Mass. David and his father Mel own and operate this facility which is capable of any type of conversion you might want.

David and Mel are assisted in the showroom by Larry Levine, and in the shop by Barry Vytal. Barry and his crew will show us how all this work is done. After

Finished interior of a standard van. Note headliner and seamless walls. Fashioning these is demonstrated in this chapter.

some discussion of van conversion we'll look in to pick up some pointers.

TYPES OF CONVERSIONS

Generally when you think of van conversions you think of full-size, standard vans. Conversions are also possible on mini-vans. In this chapter we'll stick with the standard, full-size van. However, watch for super tricked-up mini-vans.

Campers and personalized custom vans are probably the

two most-popular conversions. The common thread between the two are interior paneling with sound proofing between the panels and the vehicle body. Also common to both are windows and vents. The customer's requirements and taste dictate what the interior will look like.

Following closely behind these two conversions are business applications ranging from classy trucks for plumbers and painters

Barry Vytal's own van. Roof has been cut out and a fiberglass extension added to give "almost" standup head room. Walls were covered as described in text.

boxes. Wooden overhead consoles for radios and televisions are also popular. Let's see how some of these options are done.

CARPET

Carpeting the floor of your van begins by deciding on a couple of things: whether or not you'll have wall coverings and the thickness of the carpet padding. If you're going to have covered walls you may want the carpet to come up the side of the van a few inches. If there will be no covering, I'll talk about how to finish off the edges of the carpet where it meets the wall. For the demonstration let's assume you'll be doing some wall covering.

My personal preference for padding is a dense, 1-inch Poly-foam. You can use this or the old-style 2-inch. A third option is standard household-carpet padding or jute felt as used in auto carpeting.

Tacking-strips

Begin the project by ripping 15 or 20, 4-foot-long pieces of 1/2- or 5/8-inch particle board or plywood into 2-inch-wide furring strips (tacking-strips). Production shops use particle board because it's cheaper and doesn't splinter. Using 1/8 X 1-1/2-inch screws, fasten the tacking-strips to the floor all around the outside edges, including the wheel wells. Don't forget to go around the edges of the steps also.

Run a strip across the van from about the area of one door jamb to the other. Be sure not to place it in the middle of the seat-base area!

For a bottom-mounting base for the wall covering, fasten more 2-inch strips along the bottom of the wall. Screw these in at each wall brace. The edges of the particle board on the wall and floor should butt against each another. This gives you something to fasten both the carpet and bottom of the wall covering onto. Now you're ready for your carpet padding.

to computerized medical units. In this chapter we'll stick with the first two types: campers and customs.

Let's discuss some generalities about these two categories. Usually a van conversion begins by paneling and carpeting the van interior. In the '60s and '70s this usually consisted of 4 X 8-foot household panels installed "as is" or covered with quilted vinyl or shag carpet. Today the covering of choice is usually a plain, un-adorned fabric or vinyl. Pre-covered panels are used less and less.

Stretching (working) the fabric from one frame-member to the next is the choice of the '90s.

Carpeting is usually reserved for the floor only. Where once a 2-inch layer of foam under the carpet was super-trick, now regular carpet padding suffices.

Lots of solid-oak and mahogany trim is now used where covered panels once predominated. We see this in valances for mini-blinds and curtains, for trim panels covering the bare edges of side panels, and for indirect-lighting

Padding

If you're using anything less than 2-inch padding, fill in any low spots in the floor (areas where ridges have been stamped to strengthen the sheetmetal) with small pieces. Be sure to cement these in place. Usually, 1/2-inch material will do the trick. Over this lay a full sheet of padding. Cement it to the floor and trim it flush with the *inside* edges of the particle board fastened to the floor. Now you're ready to lay the carpet.

Installing the Carpet

Use any good household carpet you like. Auto carpet is too flimsy for the expanse of area to be covered. You need that good, double-back jute for strength.

Begin by cutting, fitting and sewing the area over the rear wheel wells. The easiest way to cut double-back jute carpet is with a razor knife working from the back side.

Make the wheel-well covers of two pieces: one over the top and one across the front. Leave about 2 inches of selvage on the top piece to go up the wall and 2 inches to lap out onto the floor. After sewing the two pieces together, cement the assembly to the wheel well. Although not a "have to" item you might want to first make a French seam; not by sewing, but by cementing the selvage edges against the back of the material. This will often prevent a lump in the seam area.

Next, move to the front and carpet that area as you would any truck or car. Run the carpet back to the tacking-strip you mounted from the area of one door jamb to the other and fasten it there. If you have access to a pneumatic pin gun (a 1/8-inch crown staple) use this to fasten the carpet to the tacking strip. Using a wide-crowned staple will result in it being seen. If you can't find a pin gun, use #10 or #12 tacks.

With the front area and rear wheel wells covered, layout a full

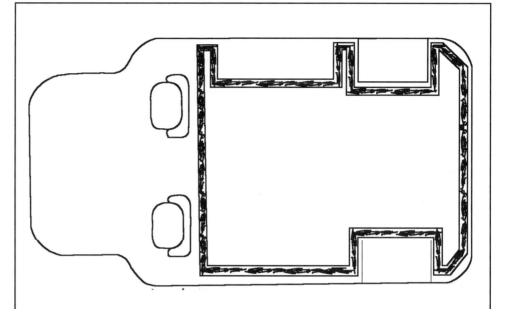

Floor plan view of van bottom, showing layout of particle-board tacking-strips. Mount vertical tacking-strips along sides, flush with those on floor. This gives a mounting surface for the bottom of the wall panels. If walls will not be paneled, omit the vertical tacking-strips. Then, mount the carpet tacking-strips close enough to the existing metal to force the raw edge between the tacking strip and metal to hide it.

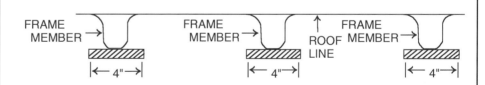

Cutaway cross section of van roof. Note 4-inch-wide tacking-strips mounted to roof frame-members. Front of van is to right in illustrations. Note steps used to mount headliner. The 2-inch strips become both backup and blind-tack strips as you proceed from front-to-rear, one panel at a time.

piece of carpet in the back. Place-tack it in a couple of areas to hold it down. Trim it back leaving about 2 inches or better around the edges for selvage.

Make slashes where necessary to get the carpet to lay flat. Staple or tack it to the strips you screwed to the floor and let the selvage come up the sides. Tack or staple the selvage in place also.

Where the carpet would show a bare edge, such as around the top of the step well, be sure it covers over the front of the particle board and is stapled there. This hides that bare edge. If the carpet is thin enough you can double the edge under, then tack or staple it in place.

Trim the floor carpet around the rear wheel wells flush with the existing carpet. The nap of the carpet on the wheel wells will cover the edges of the carpet on the floor. This completes the carpeting. Let's look next at headliners or roof covering.

HEADLINERS

Preparation
Call them what you like, *overhead, roof panels,* whatever; they're still *headliners.* But, you have to approach making a van headliner a bit differently than an auto headliner. To start with there are no ready-made headliners. You have to make them yourself.

Begin by cutting some more pieces of particle board. Mount these pieces to the roof frame-members. Measure the length (across the van) of each frame-member. Cut enough pieces of 1/2-inch particle board, 4 inches wide by the length you just measured, to cover each frame member. Then, from the same material cut 2 pieces, 2 inches wide, for each frame. Finally, cut enough 2-inch strips to run the full length of the van from the door jambs to the back.

Using 1/8 X 1-1/2-inch screws, fasten the 4-inch pieces to the frame-members matching

centerlines. Now, screw one of the 2-inch-wide pieces to this board, aligning the front edges.

At the ends of these strips run the 2-inch-wide pieces the full length of the van except over the door areas. Keep the strips as high up as possible. The next step is to add insulation.

Most folks use fiberglass insulation which can be purchased from your local hardware or building-supply store. It's the same insulation used in home construction. Select 2-inch batting. Buy enough to fill in between all the frame-members, both on top and on the sides. The more insulation you can crowd in, the quieter and more resistant to climatic changes your van will be. Cement these bats in place between the frame-members. Fill in snug. Keep the roof batting *above* the level of the frame-members so it doesn't poke through the headlining material. Now you're ready to install the vinyl or fabric. Before you start to cut, get a feel for what you're going to do.

Basic Plan
If you have four frame-members supporting the roof, you have five areas to cover. With some judicious shopping you may be able to find 72-inch-wide material for your headliner. If not, you'll have to run the material from side-to-side rather than front-to-rear. When you begin to cut the material you must mark it (usually a chalk line at the top) to keep the nap going in the same direction. Select the driver's side as the side you'll work from. Keep the chalk line at the top of the material on this side.

Cutting Material
Measure Driver/Passenger Area
Measure across the roof from driver's door frame to passenger's door frame. Add 3 or 4 inches to this measurement for selvage. Cut a full width of 54-inch material this length.

To ensure the nap lies in the same direction for all pieces, place

a chalk mark at the top of the piece you cut. This piece and the other four will go into the van with the chalk mark facing to the left side. If all five pieces have the chalk mark on the same side of the van, you'll know the nap of each piece is lying in the same direction.

Measure each of the other four sections, cutting a full width of material for each one. Be sure there's a chalk mark at the top. Now you're ready to install these pieces.

Installing Headliner Pieces
If your van has a garnish (reveal) molding around the windshield, remove it. The molding will hide the bare edge of the material after the headliner is installed. If there's no garnish molding you'll make a covered panel to hide the raw edge.

Notch the edges of the material at the center of each side. With the chalk mark toward the left side, place-tack the center edge of the material onto the 4-inch board on the first frame-member. Place-tack it *behind* the 2-inch board and directly in the center of the 4-inch board.

Pull the material snug toward the windshield and place a dab of cement on the edge of the roof line and material to hold it in place. Be sure the centerline nick in the material is in line with the center of the roof. Now, move to the door areas.

Pull the material snug again and temporarily cement a small area in place over the door. Repeat this process at the other door. Now you have things temporarily fastened at four locations with no wrinkles along the pull lines. This is much like the headliner demonstration in Chapter 12.

To finish the installation, move to the frame-member to which the material is place-tacked, pull it tight, and tack or staple it into place permanently. Remember, you're fastening *behind* the 2-inch piece. Complete this section by cementing and stapling the remaining 3 sides. To hide the raw edges over the door frames and across the front, make panels from 1/8- or 5/16-inch tempered masonite. Cover these with the same material as the headliner and attach them as described in the sidebar on page 212.

The second section is covered as follows: again, work from the center. Blind-tack the edge of the material to the 4-inch piece directly on top of the first piece of fabric. If you've forgotton about blind-tacking, here's a refresher.

Assume a 1/2-inch selvage edge along the length of the material you're working with. Place this edge, face down on the first piece of material, centers aligned. Drive a tack or staple into the material (from the back side). Pull the material snug to the sides and staple again. Then fill in with tacks or staples along the 1/2-inch selvage.

The material is now hanging from the roof, stapled *just behind* the 2-inch-wide piece of particle board. Lay another 2-inch piece of board on the edge of the material you just stapled and press it tight against the other board, clamping the hanging piece of material between the two. Screw this down tight to the 4-inch board, making sure the butted edges of the boards are tight. Now you can see the next step.

Pull the fabric back, stretch it over the 2-inch board on the third frame-member and staple it down to the 4 inch. Staple the ends, then fill in with more staples to the center. Staple the sides to the boards along sides and the second section is done. The remaining sections are completed in the same way. Finish off the rear the same way you finished at the windshield; with a covered panel.

If you want to get super fancy you can screw masonite sheets into the 2-inch batts covering the space between frame members. Then, cement a layer of 1/2-inch Polyfoam over the masonite. Finally, pull the material tight and staple it in place as previously

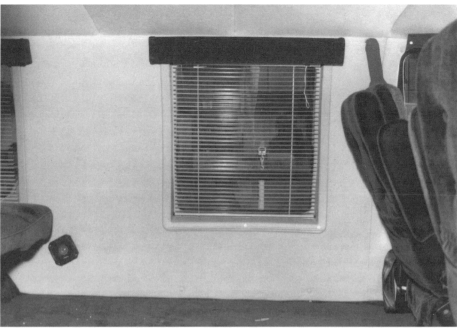

Area in which Barry will install the cabinet. Snap-caps at bottom of wall panel retain panel at bottom. This is discussed later.

described. This will give you a fully-padded headliner with a nice feel.

Making Side Panels
Once again, cut more 2-inch particle-board strips. These will be fastened to the wall frame-members as above. You'll also need 4 X 8-foot or 5 X 10-foot sheets of masonite (enough to cover both sides of the van and make door panels if you so desire). If you use 4 X 8-foot sheets you'll have a gap at the bottom which must be hidden with yet another covered panel.

You'll have to trim the big 5 X 10-foot sheets a bit. The panels must be cut to fit snugly between the headliner and carpet. If you join panels they must butt together along the centerlines of the wall-mounted tacking strips. Don't forget to cut out for the wheel well! You may wish to make a cardboard pattern about the edge of the wheel well and transfer it to the panel. This will ensure a good fit.

Cut the fabric to run the full length of the van. Be sure the nap lies in the same direction on both sides, front-to-rear or rear-to-front. It only matters that both sides are

the same.

Begin installation at the left side. From the backside, staple the panel of fabric to the same board you stapled the ends of the headliner, covering the headliner staples. Stretch the material taut and staple the entire length across the top. Now, insert the masonite panels under the hanging fabric and move them into place so the top edges push the side material snug against the headliner. No headlining staples should be seen above this edge.

Find someone to hold the wall fabric up out of your way or clamp it up. Screw the top of the masonite panel against the board to which you've been stapling. Then, along the wall-frame-member tacking-strips, screw the panels down about halfway to the floor. Be sure each end of a panel falls directly along the centerline of a particle-board tacking-strip. If you wish to pad the panels with 1/2-inch foam, do so at this time. Spray a little contact cement to the Polyfoam and to the panel. Bring the pieces together and trim with a razor blade.

There are a number of ways to

Laying out plywood for cabinet.

Barry cuts cabinet face. Note using a "plunge cut" with a sabre saw. Practice this cut on a piece of scrap first. If you're not proficient with the sabre saw, drill a hole instead and work from there.

shown in the photos; others can be seen in magazines. You should be able to look now at most any upholstered piece and figure out how it was done. Because you're getting so good at this upholstery stuff let's look at something quite a bit different, but very important if you're doing a van: how to make cabinets.

CABINETRY

Barry Vytal and his partner Bill McCarthy are going to take us through the steps they use to fabricate some cabinetry. The cabinets they're going to make will be covered in Formica, a hard-plastic laminate. If you want solid-wood cabinets, couple our demonstration here with some good books on millwork and joinery!

Barry's project will be to fabricate a cabinet to hold an ice chest, Porta-Potty, drinking water and gray water. The counter will have a wash basin and water pump. Additionally, there will be a small overhead storage cabinet.

To start, Barry measures the available space, the components to be stored and arrives at rough measurements. Next, he draws a sketch of the project with these measurements and determines the materials he'll need. For this project it'll be two sheets of 1/2-inch AD exterior plywood. AD means one good side and one rough side. The good side will face the world while the "D" side is hidden away. A pint of Franklin Titebond® Wood Glue (or any good aliphatic-resin glue) and some #6 X 1-1/4-inch wood screws, dry-wall screws or sheet metal screws finish the list of materials.

Barry starts by laying out the front, back and sides. Then, cuts them out. In the photos you'll notice the front incorporates three separate areas and is made from one piece of plywood rather than "framed" with 1 X 3-inch stock. This speeds production and is acceptable because it'll be covered with Formica.

finish off the panel. The easiest way is to lift the bottom edge of the masonite, wrap the material around it and staple from the back side. Of course you can't see what you're doing but it works well nevertheless. Cut a few 2 X 4s 30-inches long to hold the panels, evenly spaced, out from the wall.

If you used 4 X 8-foot sheets, staple the bottom from the outside. You'll then make panels to cover the gap between the edge of the masonite and the floor. This system works well if you want to run electrical or speaker wire in this area.

Cement the raw edge of the

fabric along the door frame then finish it with a covered masonite panel. Fit, cut and cover another panel to close the large gap at the rear between the wall and the frame of the rear door. Fasten the bottom of the panels as described on page 212.

These, then, are some of the tricks of the trade. If you're starting with a van as a first project, carefully read the chapters before this. I've assumed a lot of knowledge on your part for this brief description.

Of course, there are many other ways to cover the tops and walls of your van. Some are

The front and back are assembled to the ends with glue and staples. Barry will, of course, check to be sure this "carcass" is square. The third step is to install stiffeners.

Stiffeners are made of 1/2-inch plywood cut 2-1/2-inches wide and to the length needed. Barry glues and staples them in place around the bottom edge of the cabinet. The stiffeners give the 1/2-inch plywood the strength of 1 inch while keeping the weight down. Now he makes two dividers to separate the interior into three sections. This is done with careful measurement. Patterns would only waste time. After the dividers are in, he can install the top stiffeners. Finally, Barry makes a trial fit to see that everything goes in where it belongs. It does, so now he can concentrate on the countertop.

Glue and staple (or nail/screw) carcass of the cabinet.

Barry uses facia to prevent cabinet from collapsing under side load.

Fabricating the Countertop

The countertop is also made from 1/2-inch plywood. Barry begins by making it 1 inch larger all around. This gives it a little "lip" or reveal edge on all sides.

After cutting the top the desired size he reinforces it with some of those 2-inch-wide strips. Some glue and screws quickly finish the job. Now he must layout the sink and pump openings.

In the photo you see him determining where he'll place things. When you buy these products they come with patterns for cutting the holes. However, Barry has been at this for so long he has a hole cutter all rigged up in a drill motor, set to go. He cuts the opening for the sink with a sabre saw. After cutting door faces, again from 1/2-inch plywood with 2-inch-wide strips around the face, Barry's ready to begin the Formica lamination.

Cabinet with one divider in place.

LAMINATING FORMICA TO WOOD SURFACES

Laminating Formica is a lot of fun. It requires a tool we've not yet discussed. You'll need a router and a "laminate-trimming" bit. If you haven't a router they can be rented. You'll have to buy the bit (about $40.00 at this writing) though. A belt sander is handy, but not essential. Other required tools and materials are contact cement, 1/2-inch X 36-inch hardwood dowels (you can substitute scrap wood, but once you've used dowels you'll be hooked on them) and a mill file. A "mill" file cuts very smoothly but slowly. This is in comparison to a "bastard" file which cuts very coarsely and quickly. A sanding block and some 80-grit paper round out the list. Before we watch Barry work his magic here, let's look at a few areas to be concerned with.

Contact Cement

Formica is retained to the wood substrate with contact cement. A thin coat is applied to the back of the Formica and to the face of the

Barry inserts remaining divider, then trys out location of pieces to be stored therein.

Yes, it also fits in the van.

Now to the countertop. More stiffeners keep it flat and presents a wider appearance than the 1/2-inch plywood indicates.

Check the fit...

Cut the holes...

Voila! Sink and water pump.

wood just as you did with fabric and vinyl. Unlike these two, however, once contacted you'll *never* separate the Formica from the wood! I really mean *never*. (Except in little corner areas

where Murphy must have left his calling card.) So, exercise extreme caution when you're preparing to set the Formica down on the contact surface. Don't let it touch until you're *ready* to let it touch.

The second concern is the pattern of installation. Top pieces and front pieces are the last to go on. Everything must be "edged" first. There are two reasons for this: the first is appearance. The laminate top has the color, in this case white. The interior is a dark brown. If you laminate the top first, then the edges, you'll see a fine brown line all around the perimeter of the top. This is very unsightly. The second reason is:

the top protects the edges. If the edges are exposed it makes them susceptible to being snagged by a foreign object. In this case it'll peel off and break. Here again, our old friend Murphy is at work. So, be careful with the contact and laminate the edges before the top or face.

The Process

In the photos we see Barry and Bill cutting the Formica into the pieces they'll use. On the larger pieces Barry cuts 1 inch larger all around than the piece he'll cover. The smaller pieces he cuts 1/4- to 1/2-inch larger. This gives him a little room for error and ensures a nice trim-out. After the pieces are

Now to cover the ugly plywood. Customer selected a flat-white surface for her Formica laminate. Barry and Bill make the initial cuts with a table saw. It can also be cut with a sabre saw (use a metal-cutting blade) or circular saw.

Spray, brush or roll contact cement on both surfaces.

Allow to dry, then bring them together.

Barry trims laminate with a belt sander. Belt rotation works to pull the laminate toward the wood. Used in the other direction the belt would tend to pull the laminate *away* from the wood.

Sticks (or dowels) allow you to adjust the Formica over counter surface without the two coming together.

When laminate and surface are in correct alignment, Barry removes a center stick, forces the two pieces into contact, and works his way out both ways from center.

cut he begins the lamination procedure.

He sprays contact cement to both the edge of the counter top and to the back of the strips of Formica. The strips are *carefully* fixed to the edges and sealed down by hand. Barry follows this up by placing a block of wood over the laminate and giving it a few whacks with a mallet. This ensures a tighter seal.

In the photos we see him using the belt sander to trim the laminate flush with the wood. This works well if you're very experienced and always use the sander so the belt "pulls" toward the laminate. If the belt "pulls" *away* from the laminate, again, it'll chip and break. Notice also Barry is working at a 45° angle. This helps prevent waves in the work.

If this is your first attempt, use the router and the laminate-trimmer bit. It's fast, efficient and leaves a beautiful edge without any chipping or cracking. Make up a little practice piece to get the hang of how it feels and works. Then go to your project.

Again, referring to the photos, you see the counter laid out with sticks across its surface. The top has been sprayed with cement as has the Formica. Here's the trick: Barry will lay the Formica atop these sticks, adjust the fit and then remove the sticks, one-by-one.

A quick zip around the parameter with a laminate-trimming bit in the router and Barry has the job trimmed up in a snap. He'll finish by filing the sharp edge just enough to prevent injury.

Finally, Barry mounts the sink and pump permanently.

Barry turns his attention to the cabinet. He laminates the ends first, then the front.

Laminate bit leaves a tiny curved radius in the corner. This must be removed with a file.

Customer also wants a small, overhead storage cabinet. Barry begins by making a pattern to get the correct curved relationship between the wall of the van and the headliner. He's doing this by "eyeball trial-and-error!"

When pattern is correct it's transferred to plywood side-pieces.

Just as he did with the bottom cabinet, he cuts the face from a single piece of plywood.

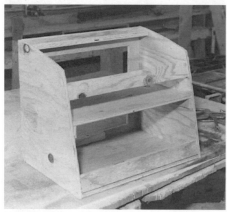

Here's the cabinet backside. Note stiffeners, primarily on back. These also serve as anchor points for mounting.

Barry makes certain the mounting screws go into a roof frame-member at the top and a wall frame-member in the back.

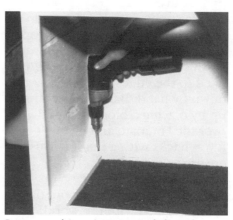

Bottom cabinet is mounted directly to the floor pan.

This ensures a perfect fit. Note he starts in the middle and works out toward the ends. This reduces the chance for capturing any bubbles between the wood and laminate.

If you recall, I mentioned the use of 1/2-inch hardwood dowels. These work in two ways. You can roll the laminate back and forth to make adjustments. This is very difficult to do with the boards. Second, if the board is wide, say over 1 inch, it can get trapped by being pinched between the wood and laminate. A dowel won't do this. It presents a much smaller "footprint" and tends to roll in front of the pressure rather than being caught by it. Small problems, really, but easy

to happen; especially to the novice and this writer.

After Barry assures himself good bonding has taken place, especially around the edges, he uses the laminate trimmer to finish the job, including cutting out for the sink and water pump. He drills a 5/8-inch hole in the middle, inserts the bit and cuts away.

In the remaining photos Barry covers the ends and then the front. The insides will be painted. The final step in the process is to use the mill file to file down all the edges carefully and gently. These are sharp as glass and will quickly put a nasty gash into any available flesh. Remember to file into the bond, not away from it.

MOUNTING THE CABINET

As yet Barry has not fastened the counter to the cabinet. He'll do this *after* he fastens the cabinet into the van. Mounting the cabinet into the van is pretty forthright. Barry screws it to the floor pan through the stiffeners in the bottom. I suggest you make sure there are no fuel lines, brake lines or electrical wires in the area where you drill!

When the cabinet is secure to the floor, Barry runs a couple of screws into a frame member of the wall. This baby's not going anywhere! The final step is to screw the countertop to the cabinet. Again, Barry screws through the stiffeners and into the countertop. The finishing touch will be to install the clean-water and gray-water containers and mount the doors.

Barry and Bill have done a great job on these cabinets. Had the customer wanted wood cabinets Barry would have used a veneered plywood for the all but the front face of the cabinet and the countertop edge. These would be made of solid wood to hide the edges of the plywood.

SUMMARY

Custom van work is terrific fun. Part of the fun is that you sort of make things up as you go along. If one process doesn't meet your needs, try another. Who's to say whether it's right or wrong—it's your van!

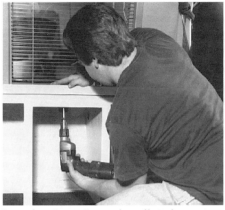

It makes it easier to handle when you wait until the cabinet is in the van to mount the countertop.

All plumbed up.

Finished product. After the customer saw the completed job she decided she wanted doors added to the cooler and potty cubby holes.

Right: While I was waiting for Barry to get to another process I shot a picture of the curtains. Plastic rails and tabs (with stiffeners) are available through most van-supply stores. If you can't locate them in your hometown, refer to the suppliers list. Curtains are easily made. Use a 2-inch hem at the top and bottom and 1/2-inch hems on the side. Then sew the little slider tabs on after the job is completed. Curtain-wrap ends are retained with Velcro.

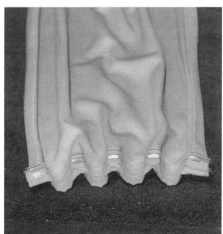

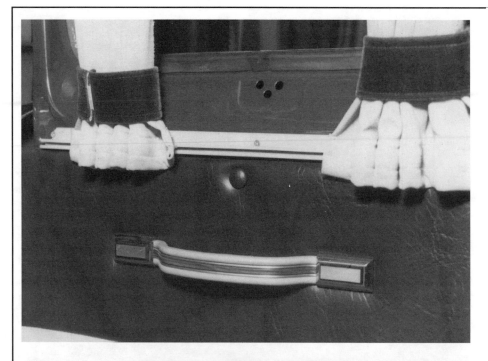

Close up shots of the snap-cap. Notice it's a two-part application. Male portion of snap retains panel to mounting surface with a #6 screw. Male part of snap is covered by a female "cap" trimmed with the same material as the panel. Most van shops will be happy to make these for you for a small labor charge.

SNAP-CAP FASTENERS

Throughout this chapter you see evidence of what appear to be buttons holding panels in place. These are not buttons as you knew them in seat upholstery, but rather, a clever snap fastener. Basically, these are the same snap fasteners we used on the truck tonneau cover. The male portion of the snap, rather than being pop-riveted to the surface is screwed to the substrate through the panel. A #6 sheet-metal screw with a narrow Phillips, countersunk head is used. You, of course, determine the length of the screw you need. If you have trouble locating these narrow-head screws in your area, they're available from AuVeCo (suppliers list).

The head, or female portion of the snap, is covered as you would any button, using a Handy Jr. button machine. By covering the head with the same material as the panel, then snapping it onto the male portion, it gives the appearance of a #30 button.

As before, if you elect not to invest in this rather expensive button machine, you can get the tops (or caps) made at most any trim shop doing van or boat work.

WINDOW INSTALLATION

Window installation is a technique unto itself and has little to do with upholstery. However, it's an important component of van work. Whether or not you elect to do your own, I thought it would be helpful to show Barry doing an installation.

Window kits come with an inside and outside cutting pattern. Because Barry does several of these a week, he's made his own patterns from corrugated cardboard. The patterns included with the window kits are of paper and must be taped in place. With the cardboard pattern Barry needs only to hold it in place with one hand and mark around it with the other.

Installation begins by determining the location of the window inside the van. If at all possible, locate the windows *between* frame-members. If not, and you'll be working with one of the large bay windows, cut no more than *one* frame-member. If you would need to cut more than one to fit the window, either select a smaller window or move interior furniture to accommodate the window rather than the other way around. Because of the location of the project window, Barry will have to cut one frame-member.

The inside pattern that usually comes with window kits is larger than the outside pattern to accommodate the reveal molding. But Barry uses his *outside* pattern to locate the window *inside* the van because the inside location is so critical. Then he'll transfer the location to the outside.

To do this, Barry drills a hole from the inside of the van all the way through to

 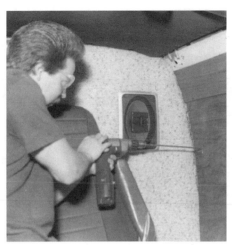

Barry's going to install a window in this plumber's van. Notice he has very little room to maneuver. Unfortunately, there is a frame-member he won't be able to avoid cutting through. The process begins by laying out on the inside, the pattern for the outside. The long bit lets Barry mark the outside from the inside of the van.

Here's the mark. The end of the drill bit.

Barry gets second location mark by measuring down from the drip rail.

With two location marks Barry can locate his pattern exactly where he wants it. It must line up inside the small space you saw in the first photo.

2-inch masking tape protects paint from cutting tool.

Electric nibblers work like a charm.
There's no distortion of the metal
with this tool. If you don't have
access to a nibbler you can do a
good job with a sabre saw.

Barry uses a hacksaw blade to cut
cement bond between body panel
and frame-member.

Finished opening showing exposed
frame-member.

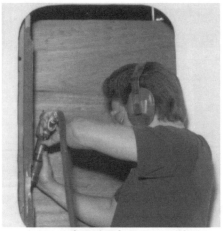

Barry goes after the frame-member
with a pneumatic chisel. Without this
tool, prepare for a lot of work.

Don't forget the weather seal.

Left: Trial fit shows hole has been
accurately cut.

the outside. Then, on the outside, he can measure how far down he wants the window to be. Now he has two locations for the pattern: the top and one side. He lines up the outside pattern with his two locations and pencils in the cutting line.

In the photos we see him laying strips of 2-inch masking tape around the outside of the line. This is to protect the paint as he makes his cut.

Barry uses a pair of electric sheet-metal snips, often referred to as *nibblers*, to cut the hole. You can use a sabre saw if you use a good metal-cutting blade. "Good" is the important word here. Your standard drugstore hardware section of four blades for a dollar will not do. I use Rockwell® blades at about a buck a piece. Any commercial blade, however, will do the job.

Referring to the photos again, Barry has run into the frame-member. These members are spot-welded at the top and bottom but cemented to the wall area. To break this bond, he uses an unmounted hacksaw blade. A little duct tape around one end will protect your hand. Finally, using a pneumatic chisel, he cuts the frame-member away, flush with the opening.

This is a hard job without this tool. Some large rental services rent them (if you have a compressor which can keep up). Otherwise, plan on spending some serious time with the hacksaw, cold chisel, nibblers, snips and small charges of dynamite. These frame-members were designed to protect you in a rollover situation and they don't give up easily!

Barry makes an inital fit

test of the window. Sometimes you'll have to make an adjustment in the opening to get just the right fit.

When everything looks good, he applies weather seal to the lip of the window. Don't forget this step if you want to keep a dry van.

Back inside the van, Barry cuts the interior panel to accept the window-reveal molding. The kit contains a pattern for this but Barry has the larger dimensions etched on the sole plate of his sabre saw. This saves the time of going back and laying out the pattern.

To do the installation Barry gets a little help from Bill who will hold the window square with the drip rail and door frame while Barry screws in the inner retainer.

Because of the tight location of this window, the reveal molding didn't fit. Rather than cut or grind the edges to make it fit, Dave, up in the front office, ordered a narrower model from the factory.

So I could wrap up this project, Barry removed the reveal molding from a window in his own van to show how it looked. That Barry, he's a heck of a guy!

Final trimming on inside for reveal molding.

Where would we be without Bill's extra pair of hands. Here he makes sure the window stays "square" while Barry screws it in place.

Snugged in, the window looks as though it was factory-installed.

Outside view.

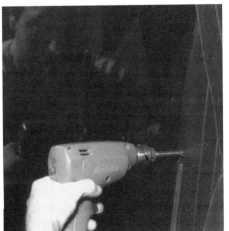

Barry removes reveal molding from his van to show how it's installed. Note also the snap-cap retainers, the covered panels that hide raw edges of wall panels and trim over door.

Another interior book for your automotive book shelf:

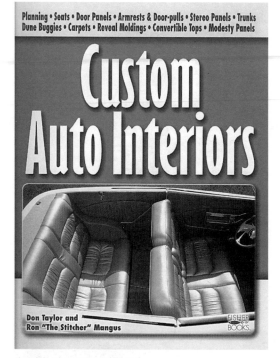

Planning • Seats • Door Panels • Armrests & Door-pulls • Stereo Panels • Trunks
Dune Buggies • Carpets • Reveal Moldings • Convertible Tops • Modesty Panels

Custom Auto Interiors

Don Taylor and
Ron "The Stitcher" Mangus

FISHER BOOKS

ISBN 1-55561-140-0
$19.95 U.S.
$27.95 Canada

Author Don Taylor has teamed with Ron Mangus to write and illustrate this great book on Custom Auto Interiors. You've become acquainted with Don's thoughtful guidance in this book that you are now reading. He's covered the basics of automotive upholstery very thoroughly, but Custom Auto Interiors are so special and enough different that another book was needed.

Ron Mangus is another trimmer who has spent his working lifetime intensely focused on auto interiors. Interiors from his shop, Custom Auto Interiors in Bloomington, California, have been regularly featured in street rod and other automotive magazines in the 1990s. How-to articles showing Mangus' techniques have appeared in *Hot Rod, Rod & Custom, Street Rodder, Truckin',* and *American Rodder.*

Ron has become famous as the stitcher to create fabulous interiors. A roadster with his interior won America's Most Beautiful Roadster at the 1992 Oakland Roadster Show. His work has received numerous Best Interior Awards at a variety of car shows. He has created interiors for Boyd's Hot Rods, Tim Allen, Billy Gibbons of ZZ Top, Pete Chapouris Of PC$_3$G, Linda Vaughan (Miss Hurst), Thom Taylor, Bruce Meyers, Kenny Bernstein, Robby Gordon, Sammy Hagar, Michael Anthony, Cory McClenathan and James Brubaker of Universal Studios.

Learn how to create your own designs, in the style you want for your nostalgia rod, luxo-cruiser or techno rod. Helpful directions and tips from these two professionals are easy to understand. Clear photos and drawings—over 800 illustrations in all—guide you every step of the way. Explains materials, special fasteners and tools need so your job will turn out looking completely professional.

Available where you purchased this book, or order direct from Fisher Books with your VISA or MasterCard.

Ron Mangus

17

Street Rod Interiors—
A Guided Tour of the annual Father's Day L. A. Roadster Show

"Yeah, it's pretty nice, but on mine . . ."

Fabricating street rod interiors is the brain surgery of auto upholstery. There's no one more demanding of perfection than the owner of a show rod. Owners of classics, antiques and special interest cars run a close second, but at least they have rules to go by. Street rods. . . well, you make it up as you go along. Mr. Rod Owner knows exactly what he wants; it's right there in his mind. All you have to do is drag it out of his imagination, build it, install it

and be darn sure it's a show winner!

Every skill we've discussed so far—plus some we've missed—is brought to use when you begin to build a rod interior. And a lot is just seat-of-the-pants craftsmanship. The rule for successful street rod upholstery is novel application of standard techniques of the trade.

To demonstrate this, I've changed the chapter format. Instead of following along while "Tom Trimmer" does the interior

of a street rod, I'm going to take you on a guided tour of some of the cars at the annual Father's Day Los Angeles Roadster Show. Bill Fisher kindly whizzed out from Tucson to take these pictures for me while I dug out from a long, New England winter. Thanks, Bill, you did a terrific job!

Let's take a walk around the show and I'll point out some of the techniques used.

Photo #2. A few feet inside the gate and millions, yes millions

2

3

of dollars of street rods overwhelm our senses. This guy's curious as to why his picture is being taken!

SEATS

Photo #3. These are standard Recaro® seats recovered to match the rest of the interior. These seats are very popular in all aftermarket applications.

Each section of the seat is a separate covering. What look like large pleats are actually individual covers with end facings. The covers are sewn together with listings and listing wires. These are then ringed to the seat frame.

Photo #4. The interesting feature of this seat is the concave figure of the seat's back. This is achieved by sculpting the polyfoam beneath the pleats. The pleats are then cemented to the foam to hold the shape.

Although it looks like a simple cement job, closer observation indicates a listing on each side of the big center pleat. Do you remember the center section of the Studebaker seat in Chapter 6? This is quite similar but for one difference: the listing must be shaped to accommodate the curve. Getting a bit tricky, huh? I think there's also a listing on the outboard side of each pleated section.

Because the pleats are so full and rounded, I suspect they're individually filled. This was a common technique of the '50s and gave us that old familiar handle, *tuck and roll*. I'm a product of the '50s Southern California hot-rod (they weren't street rods then) and custom car-building era. Back then we called it *pleat and roll*. I think the use of the word "tuck" for "pleat" was the gift of our brothers from Dixie who grew to dominate hot-rod racing. They call it stock car racing now. But I digress . . .

Individually filled pleats are made just like blind-stitched pleats (Chapter 6) only without the foam between the facing material and backing. Also, the facing is made 1 inch (or more) larger than the backing. Cotton is used to fill the pleats.

Your local furniture upholstery supply shop should carry pleat stuffers. These are inexpensive, two-piece, aluminum half-rounds about 36-inches long. They come in widths to match the width of the pleat. A piece of cotton batting (usually 85/15) is rolled up to make about three layers, 8 to 10 inches longer than the pleat. This roll is inserted into one of the half rounds and covered with the other. The user must make sure *all* the cotton is covered by the pleat stuffer.

The loaded unit is pushed into the pleat until the cotton protrudes evenly from both ends. Then, each of the stuffer sections is removed, one at a time. This leaves the pleat filled with the roll of cotton.

I can't give you more specific dimensions because it's all a matter of taste—hard pleats, lots of cotton; soft pleats, less cotton. I usually make up a sample of about three pleats, making adjustments until I get what I want.

There are a couple of shop-rigged devices that trimmers make to stuff pleats. In the hands of an expert they work well. As a novice, stick to the pleat stuffer, you'll be a lot happier with your results.

Photo #5. This rumble seat demonstrates another use for the woodcraft technique demonstrated in Chapter 13. There we built a curved, boat-seat back. Can you see how the same technique was used to form the foundation for this back?

First, a cardboard pattern was made to get the correct curve. This was transferred to wood and shaped accordingly. Then, a ply-wood panel, cut to size, was kerfed to accommodate the bend. In our boat project, the kerfs were on the inside of the curve. Here, I'd make the kerfs on the *outside*. This would make it a lot easier to staple into the wood where the listings must go.

Again, sculpted foam makes

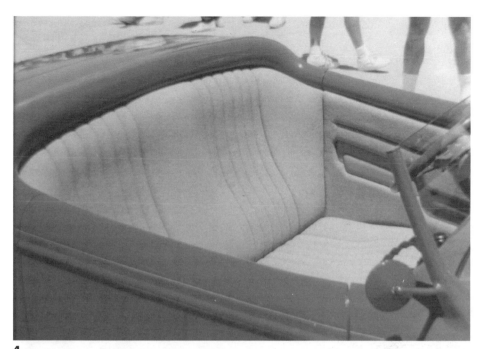
4

5

6

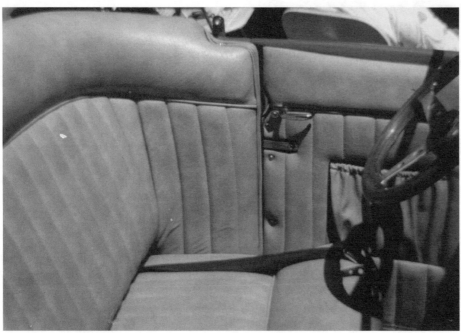

7

up the filling in the black areas. Another way to do the seat centers would be to make individual cushions (as in the stadium cushion in Chapter 3), then cement them to the plywood back.

Photo #6. This seat cushion is a bit unusual but fairly easy in execution. You would begin by sewing *one* complete panel of pleats about 2 or 3 inches wider than the cushion (front-to-rear). Here, they're blind sewn but they could just as easily be top-sewn. After the pleats are sewn, sew a seam along the line where the cover will be divided. Fold the cover back on itself at this seam line. Then, using about a 3/8-inch seam, sew a listing to the back. The listings would then be used to pull these "rolls" you see in the photo into position.

The second way would be to make three, pleated panels and sew them together. This is a bit easier to handle in the sewing machine but a real bugger to make all the pleat seams line up.

As a bit of a side issue, note the covered door handle. It appears to be covered with one piece. After cementing the material to the handle, I would hand stitch it together on the backside. This would prevent the edges from lifting due to use. You could also cover a thin piece of cardboard with material and cement it to the backside, covering the raw, hand-sewn edges.

Photo #7. This is my favorite type of interior: used. This car shows signs of being driven frequently. It's a car that gets shown. To me, this is the essence of the hobby. (But I keep injecting my asides here. I'll try to stick closer to the point.) I included this photo to point out the wide, two-way curve in the roll above the pleats. This is exactly like the boat seat. The important thing to remember here is to get the stretch of the material going along the *length*. You might also lay it out on the diagonal of the material and fit the curve *before* sewing. I would experiment a little here before I went for the gold. Notice they used Hidem along the door jam to cover the raw edges of the material. This is the way we finished the boat seat.

CENTER ARMRESTS, DIVIDERS & CONSOLES

Photo #8. This is an elegant, high-tech interior. I like the seat design. I think they used a Recaro (or perhaps a Cerullo) seat but removed the inboard wings and replaced them with this nice divider and armrest. These are probably built from plywood padded with foam. I hope they retained the ability of the seat backs to lie forward. This would give cab access to the trunk area.

I like to sculpt dividers from styrofoam if they're not going to take a lot of abuse. You can get *any* shape you want. It's cheap, fast and easy to work with, and if you miss, chuck it out and start over. I buy my styrofoam at hobby and craft shops. It works better than the styrofoam panels used in home insulation.

Styrofoam presents only one serious drawback: contact cement eats into it like a lion into a gazelle! However, after years of "research," I've found a way to bond styrofoam. The trick is worth the price of this book. Use plaster of Paris. It dries hard in about five minutes and is virtually bomb-proof. It can be sanded, filed and worked just like the styrofoam.

Interestingly, I didn't learn this in the business or discover it through trial and error. I learned it in a night-school art class. Education is everything.

We'll talk about the door and quarter panel a bit later in the chapter. They too, are excellent.

Photo #9. The three inside sections of this seat are built much like the Recaro seat in photo #3. The point of interest, however, is the center divider.

If I were building this, I'd sculpt it from styrofoam as above, on a plywood base to get all those

8

9

10

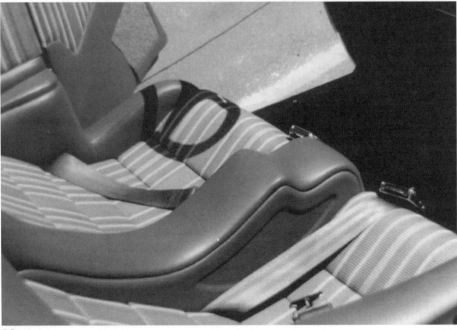

11

compound curves, then cover it with Polyfoam. It could also be built-up from high density Polyfoam covered in a layer of soft Polyfoam. Notice the trimmer made the cover from two pieces with a seam down the center. This is the only way to get a wrinkle-free cover. The ends were probably built the same way as the center divider.

Photo #10. The vinyl (or leather) roll was built into the car first along with the center divider and console. Then the quarter panels were added. Finally, the seats were made to fit into the remaining area. I'll bet there's a plywood panel under all of this to which everything is fastened.

Note the padded, velvet-covered piece over the center armrest/console. I think this is a hinged cover allowing access to a hollow storage-console.

This interior is an excellent application of all custom-built parts. The designer (and trimmer) can be justly proud of this job.

Photo #11. We're far enough along now to know how this center armrest was built but what about the fancy design stuff on the side? Easy, this is a separate piece from the body of the armrest. It begins with a masonite panel cut to the contours of the armrest. It's probably 5/32-inch as opposed to 1/8-inch. Most trimmers prefer the extra bulk of 5/32-inch masonite.

Over this panel is cemented 1/4-inch closed-cell foam. This is the same foam Charlie used under the vinyl top in Chapter 8. Using an X-Acto® knife or razor blade, the trimmer cut out and removed the center section. Then he sprayed a coat of cement over the assembly and one on the back of the vinyl. Then "plop," he brought the two pieces together carefully forcing the center down into the void left by the removal of the foam. Finally the edges were cemented to the back.

This is a standard method now of "sculpting" door panels, quarter panels and other trim pieces.

I'll point this out in other photos as we progress.

"OK, Don, how did they fasten the finished panel to the armrest?" What, you haven't figured it out? Well, I left out a step in the above explanation. Here it is. Use blind nuts (teenuts) under the foam. Holes are cut in the masonite panel to accept teenuts (available at most hardware stores). The location of these holes are transferred to the armrest and bolt holes drilled therein. Then, when the panel is finished it's bolted to the armrest from the inside. Slick, huh?

Some trimmers use a bit different application. They epoxy a countersunk machine screw into the panel. Again, with corresponding holes in the armrest the panel is bolted thereto. This works out fine until you have to remove the panel. Sometimes the epoxy fails and the machine screw spins in its hole. Use teenuts where possible.

DOOR, QUARTER & KICK PANELS

Photo #12. Panels are where everyone goes crazy. Anything is fair game, mild or wild. Let's start with this "mild" application.

There are two approaches here: the detail may be sewn to thin cardboard and then cemented to or sewn directly into the panel. You saw the latter in Chapter 12 when I did the door panels on my Ranger.

The former is to cement the foam and vinyl to a piece of chipboard then sew in the design. This assembly is then cemented to the moisture proof cardboard panel. This is a nice trick if you're using your wife's commercial machine.

If you want a heavy saddle stitch, take the panel, with the foam and vinyl cemented in place and the design sketched in with grease pencil, to the local shoe repairman. He can do a beautiful job. Be sure you arrange this in advance. Don't go walking in with

12

13

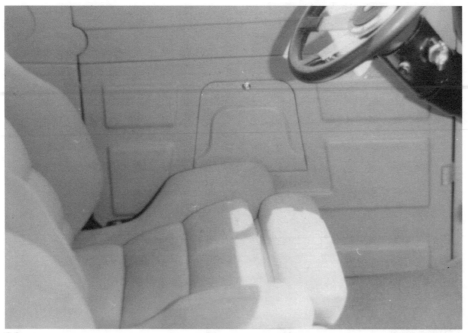

14

15

parts in hand expecting the poor guy to drop everything and take care of you!

Note the windlace between the door panel and rear quarter panel. This is made as demonstrated in the sim-con chapter (9) and is fastened to the door jamb, not the door panel.

Photo #13. Wow! This has it all. The project begins with the large, "C"-shaped exterior panel. This is probably 1/4- or 3/8-inch plywood with 3/4- to 1-inch Poly-foam. Beneath this is a masonite panel covered in the same material. It's probably fastened to the big plywood panel with #6 X 3/4-inch countersunk screws. Finally, the graphics are applied.

These are pieces of masonite with 1/2-inch padding covered with a contrasting material. They, too, are probably fastened from the back side with screws. They look too delicate for T-nuts.

I think the material used in this project is a hard mohair. Mohair is 100-percent wool, extremely expensive, and one of the nicest fabrics in the world to work with. If you can afford it (close to $100 per yard retail at this writing) use it. It's absolutely beautiful.

Photo #14. Here's extensive use of 1/4-inch closed cell foam under leather (vinyl?) for that sculpted look. Refer back to photo #11 for the process. The bell-shaped gizmo in the center is probably an access panel to a storage compartment.

Photo #15. This puppy has it all. By now you can probably figure it out on your own. However, if you skipped everything else in the book up to this point, here it is again. The top panel is the main body and is a medium thickness plywood with heavy Polyfoam padding. Within the cutouts, the material is wrapped around and stapled to the back. This includes the very thin channel seen at the top.

Backing these recesses is a covered masonite panel. In this application, as before, it's covered in

16

17

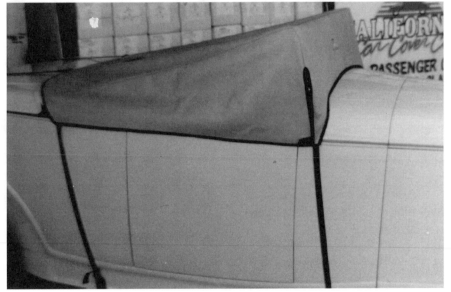

18

the same material as the main panel. If it's your design, it could be covered in anything you like.

Finally, there are two panels covered in leather or vinyl that set off the two elevations of the body and backing panel, creating a third elevation. This is excellent design and execution. I'm impressed.

Photo #16. This "suicide" door incorporates everything we've talked about and then some. Let's look at the curved line at the bottom. As before, there's a top panel over a thinner base panel, both in the same light-gray material. The base panel is the full size of the door with the top panel added after the base panel was covered.

Put the base panel in your mind without the top panel or the "finger graphics" at the top rear. Working from the carpet up, the trimmer created the curved line that's the top of the carpet. This was done as a pencil line on the panel. Next, he or she cut a piece of carpet the same shape as the bottom of the panel and the curved line but with a 1/2-inch seam allowance along the curved line at the top. Then, our trimmer

sewed a welt along the top of the
carpet just as they would if this
were a seat facing. The fourth step
would be to blind sew a 1-1/2-inch
strip of fabric along the bottom of
the carpet. Finally, a top piece was
fitted to match the curve, laid face
down over the welt and sewn on.

This carpet/fabric assembly
was cemented to the base panel
with edges aligned. The fabric
strip at the bottom of the carpet
was wrapped around bottom edge
of the panel and stapled to the
back. The base assembly was then
screwed to the top panel. The
loose edges of the top panel were
wrapped around the base panel
and stapled. I give the designer
and trimmer a lot of points for
ingenuity on this job.

OTHER INTERESTING ITEMS

Photo #17. Remember the
sim-con? That's what we have
here, a simulated convertible top.
I suggest this is a fiberglass top covered in Cambria. Review Chapter 9
to see how this was trimmed. However, It probably has a layer of
Polyfoam between the shell and
cover.

Photo #18. I just thought this
was a neat idea. Make a box, bind
the edges, add four straps with
buckles and nobody throws their
trash in your interior when you're
away from your car. For a source
for buckles and straps see Astrup
Co. under "Awnings & Accesso-
ries," in the suppliers list.

Suppliers

ADHESIVES
3M Industrial Specialties Div.
3M Center Bldg. 220-7E-01
St. Paul, MN 55144-1000
(612) 733-1106

Alpha, Inc.
21680 Protecta Dr.
Elkhart, IN 46516
(219) 295-5206

Astrup Co.
2937 W. 25th St.
Cleveland, OH 44113
(216) 696-2820

Consolidated Admiral
PO Box 382
Woodbury, NY 11797
(516) 921-2131

Custom Auto Interiors
18127 Marygold
Bloomington, CA 92316
(909) 877-9342

Maume Fabrics Co.
PO Box 431
Toledo, OH 43692
(419) 243-2191

Multi-Fastening Systems
4629 Clyde Park SW
Wyoming, MI 49509
(616) 534-0702

Russell Products, Inc.
21419 Protecta Dr.
Elkhart, IN 46516
(800) 545-5620

BUTTON-MAKING EQUIPMENT
Fasnap Corp.
PO Box 1613A
Elkhart, IN 46514
(800) 624-2058

Handy Button Machine Co.
1750 N. 25th Ave.
Melrose Park, IL 60160
(708) 450-9000

Maume Fabrics Co.
PO Box 431
Toledo, OH 43692
(419) 243-2191

CARPET, AUTO
Auto Custom Carpet
PO Box 1167
Anniston, AL 36202
(205) 236-1118

Blacksmith Distributing
PO Box 4405
Elkhart, IN 46514
(219) 262-3558

Consolidated Admiral
PO Box 382
Woodbury, NY 11797
(516) 921-2131

Custom Auto Interiors
18127 Marygold
Bloomington, CA 92316
(909) 877-9342

Maume Fabrics Co.
PO Box 431
Toledo, OH 43692
(419) 243-2191

SDI Corp.
5882 E. Berry St.
Ft. Worth, TX 76119
(817) 429-3278

CONSOLES
The Accessory House
5156 Holt Blvd.
Montclair, CA 91763
(714) 621-5953

CONSOLES, OVERHEAD
A & S Fiberglass
479 Heckscher Dr.
Jackonsville, FL 32226
(904) 751-1661

The Accessory House
5156 Holt Blvd.
Montclair, CA 91763
(714) 621-5953

Custom Auto Interiors
18127 Marygold
Bloomington, CA 92316
(909) 877-9342

OEM Supply, Inc.
53112 Faith Ave.
Elkhart, IN 46514
(219) 262-2600

CONVERTIBLE TOPS
Acme Auto Headlining Co.
550 W. 16th St.
Long Beach, CA 90813
(310) 437-0061

Bill Hirsch
396 Littleton Ave.
Newark, NJ 07103
(800) 828-2061

Just-Rite Auto Restyling
200 Everette Ave.
Chelsea, MA 02150
(617) 889-0600

Robbins Auto Tops
711 Olympics Blvd.
Santa Monica, CA 90401
(310) 450-3444

FABRICS
Astrup Co.
2937 W. 25th St.
Cleveland, OH 44113
(216) 696-2820

Auto Trimmers Supply
2958 E. 22nd St.
Tucson, AZ 85713
(602) 325-3319

B & M Foam & Fabrics
3383 Durahart St.
Riverside, CA 92507
(714) 787-0221

Bill Hirsch
396 Littleton Ave.
Newark, NJ 07103
(800) 828-2061

Consolidated Admiral
PO Box 382
Woodbury, NY 11797
(516) 921-2131

Custom Auto Interiors
18127 Marygold
Bloomington, CA 92316
(909) 877-9342

Fabric Services
PO Box 36
Elkhart, IN 46515
(219) 262-3900

G & T Industries
1726 Henry G. Lane
Maryville, TN 37801
(800) 247-9901

J & J Auto Fabrics
247 S. Riverside Ave.
Rialto, CA 92376
(909) 847-3040

Keystone Bros.
(nationwide)
9669 Aero Dr.
San Diego, CA 92123
(619) 277-7770

Maume Fabrics Co.
PO Box 431
Toledo, OH 43692
(419) 243-2191

Three Rivers Supply
477 W. 7th Ave.
West Homestead, PA
15120
(412) 462-3900

Velcro Laminates Inc.
54835 CR 19
Bristol, IN 46507-9466
(800) 235-1776

FASTENERS
Astrup Co.
2937 W. 25th St.
Cleveland, OH 44113
(216) 696-2820

Atlas Supply of Texas
700 E. Parker St.
Houston, TX 77078
(713) 699-0276

Auto-Vehicle Parts Co.
7 Speati Dr.
Covington, KY 41017
(606) 341-6450

Consolidated Admiral
PO Box 382
Woodbury, NY 11797
(516) 921-2131

Eastwood Company
580 Lancaster Ave.
Malvern, PA 19355
(800) 345-1178

Fasnap Corp.
PO Box 1613A
Elkhart, IN 46514
(800) 624-2058

G & T Industries
1726 Henry G. Lane
Maryville, TN 37801
(800) 247-9901

Maume Fabrics Co.
PO Box 431
Toledo, OH 43692
(419) 243-2191

Velcro Laminates Inc.
54835 CR 19
Bristol, IN 46507-9466
(800) 235-1776

HEADLINERS

Acme Auto Headlining Co.
550 W. 16th St.
Long Beach, CA 90813
(310) 437-0061

Bill Hirsch
396 Littleton Ave.
Newark, NJ 07103
(800) 828-2061

Consolidated Admiral
PO Box 382
Woodbury, NY 11797
(516) 921-2131

Fabric Services
PO Box 36
Elkhart, IN 46515
(219) 262-3900

G & T Industries
1726 Henry G. Lane
Maryville, TN 37801
(800) 247-9901

Maume Fabrics Co.
PO Box 431
Toledo, OH 43692
(419) 243-2191

INSULATION

Quality Heat Shield
3873 Carter Ave.,
Suite 202
Riverside, CA 92501
(909) 276-1040

LEATHER

Bill Hirsch
396 Littleton Ave.
Newark, NJ 07103
(800) 828-2061

Consolidated Admiral
PO Box 382
Woodbury, NY 11797
(516) 921-2131

Custom Auto Interiors
18127 Marygold
Bloomington, CA 92316
(909) 877-9342

Garrett Leather
1865 Kenmore Ave.
Kenmore, NY 14217
(800) 342-7738

ROD DOORS

R.W. and ABLE, Inc.
636 Nord Avenue, #B
Chico, CA 95927
(916) 896-1513

SEAT FRAMES

American Metal
Fabricators
55515 Franklin St.
Three Rivers, MI 49093
(616) 279-5108

Better Products
57912 Charlotte Ave.
Elkhart, IN 46517
(219) 522-7891

C & L Upholstery
12913 S. Marquardt Ave.
Santa Fe Springs, CA
90670
(310) 921-6545

Glide Engineering
10662 Pullman Court
Rancho Cucamonga, CA
71730
(909) 944-9556

SEATS

Cerullo Automotive
828 Towne Center Dr.
Pomona, CA 91767
(909) 625-3611

Custom Auto Interiors
18127 Marygold
Bloomington, CA 92316
(909) 877-9342

Recaro
905 W. Maple Rd.
Clawson, MI 48017
(800) 873-2276

Tea's Design
2038 15th St. N.W.
Rochester, MN 55901
(507) 289-0494

SEWING MACHINES

Consolidated Sewing
Machine
56-65 Rust St.
Maspeth, NY 11378
(718) 894-7777

Keystone Sewing Machine
833 N. 2nd St.
Philadelphia, PA 19123
(215) 922-6900

Quality Sewing Machines
224 West 3rd
Grand Island, NE 68801
(308) 382-7310

UPHOLSTERY
SUPPLIES

American Upholstery
Supply
1355 N. Marion St.
Tulsa, OK 74115
(918) 834-6691
(800) 331-3913

Astrup Co.
2937 W. 25th St.
Cleveland, OH 44113
(216) 696-2820

Auto Trimmers Supply
2958 E. 22nd St.
Tucson, AZ 85713
(520) 325-3319

Custom Auto Interiors
18127 Marygold
Bloomington, CA 92316
(909) 877-9342

Eastwood Company
580 Lancaster Ave.
Malvern, PA 193555
(800) 345-1178

G & T Industries
1726 Henry G. Lane
Maryville, TN 37801
(800) 247-9901

Keystone Bros.
(nationwide)
9669 Aero Dr.
San Diego, CA 92123
(619) 277-7770

Maume Fabrics Co.
PO Box 431
Toledo, OH 43692
(419) 243-2191

Peachtree Fabrics, Inc.
1400 English St.
Atlanta, GA 30318
(404) 351-5400

UPHOLSTERY
TOOLS

Auto Trimmers Supply
2958 E. 22nd St.
Tucson, AZ 85713
(520) 325-3319

Eastwood Company
580 Lancaster Ave.
Malvern, PA 19355
(800) 345-1178

Index